Rs. 500/-

INDIA AT THE POLLS

India at the Polls

PARLIAMENTARY ELECTIONS IN THE FEDERAL PHASE

M.P. SINGH

REKHA SAXENA

Orient Longman

ORIENT LONGMAN PRIVATE LIMITED

Registered Office
3-6-272 Himayatnagar, Hyderabad 500 029 (A.P.), India

Other Offices
Bangalore, Bhopal, Bhubaneshwar, Chandigarh, Chennai, Ernakulam, Guwahati, Hyderabad, Jaipur, Kolkata, Lucknow, Mumbai, New Delhi, Patna

First Published 2003

ISBN 81-250-2328-3

Typeset by
Scribe Consultants
New Delhi

Printed in India at
Baba Barkha Nath Printers
New Delhi

Published by
Orient Longman Private Limited
1/24 Asaf Ali Road
New Delhi 110 002

Contents

Contents

List of Tables

List of Abbreviations

ABJS	Akhil Bharatiya Jana Sangh
ABLTC	Akhil Bharatiya Loktantrik Congress
AC	Arunachal Congress
AGP	Asom Gana Parishad
AIADMK	All India Anna Dravida Munnetra Kazhagam
AIIC(S)	All India Indira Congress (Secular)
AIIC(T)	All India Indira Congress (Tiwari)
AITC	All India Trinamool Congress
ASDC	Autonomous State Demand Committee
BBM	Bharipa Bahujan Mahasangha
BJD	Biju Janata Dal
BSP	Bahujan Samaj Party
CPI	Communist Party of India
CPI(M)	Communist Party of India (Marxist)
CPI(M-L)	Communist Party of India (Marxist-Leninist)
DMK	Dravida Munnetra Kazhagam
FB	All India Forward Bloc
GGP	Gondvana Ganatantra Party
HVC	Himachal Vikas Congress
HVP	Haryana Vikas Party
INC	Indian National Congress
INLD	Indian National Lok Dal
IUML	Indian Union Muslim League
JD	Janata Dal
JD(S)	Janata Dal (Secular)
JD(U)	Janata Dal (United)

JKNC	Jammu & Kashmir National Conference
JMM	Jharkhand Mukti Morcha
JP	Janata Party
KC	Kerala Congress
KC(M)	Kerala Congess (Mani)
LDF	Left Democratic Front
LF	Left Front
LS	Lok Shakti
MADMK	MGR Anna Dravida Munnetra Kazhagam
MDMK	Marumalarchi Dravida Munnetra Kazhagam
MGP	Maharashtravadi Gomantak Party
MNF	Mizo National Front
MPP	Manipur People's Party
MSCP	Manipur State Congress Party
MUL	Muslim League Kerala State Committee
NC	National Conference or J&K National Conference
NC (Soz)	National Conference (Shaifuddin Soz)
NCP	Nationalist Congress Party
NF	National Front
NTRTDP(LP)	NTR Telugu Desam Party (Lakshmi Parvathi)
PDF	Progressive Democratic Front
PMK	Pattali Makkal Katchi
PT	Puthia Tamilagam
PWPI	Peasants and Workers Party of India
RJD	Rashtriya Janata Dal
RJP	Rashtriya Janata Party
RLD	Rashtriya Lok Dal
RLM	Rashtriya Loktantrik Morcha
RPI	Republican Party of India
RSP	Revolutionary Socialist Party
SAD	Shiromani Akali Dal
SAD(M)	Shiromani Akali Dal (Simranjit Singh Mann)
SAP	Samata Party
SDF	Sikkim Democratic Front

SJP	Samajwadi Janata Party
SP	Samajwadi Party
SS/SHS	Shiv Sena
SSP	Sikkim Sangram Parishad
TDP	Telugu Desam Party or TDP (Naidu)
TMC(M)	Tamil Maanila Congress (Moopanar)
TRC	Tamizhaga Rajiv Congress
TUJS	Tripura Upjati Juba Samity
UDF	United Democratic Front
UDP	United Democratic Party
UF	United Front
UGDP	United Goans Democratic Party
UMFA	United Minorities Front Assam
WBTMC	West Bengal Trinamool Congress

Preface

Electoral and party political processes following the Congress-dominance phase, during which the parliamentary tenor of politics in India came to be considerably federalised, have evoked ambivalent and contradictory responses from competent political observers and analysts. Whereas some have seen in the transition from a one-party dominance to a multi-party system, a gateway to political instability and chaos, others have welcomed the first real and sustained opening to forces of territoriality and proportionality (regional, ideological and sociological minorities) to find electoral representation and a breakthrough into the threshold of federal coalitional power-sharing. While some have become disillusioned with the dysfunctionalities and corruption of electoral and party political processes in general and turned to alternatives like on-party political processes and new social movements, others have proceeded to seize the opportunity to offer panaceas such as Hindu nationalism, Mandal social justice, regional pride and power and neo-liberal policy packages of economic liberalisation and restructuring. With parties being fragmented along regional and ethnic and personalised followings, India is having the effect of proportional representation even under the first-past-the-post electoral system in single-member parliamentary constituencies with one balloting!

This book seeks to explore and analyse the contours of parliamentary elections and party political processes in India, at a time when owing to the transition to a multi-party system India's parliamentary federal system has become markedly federalised, especially in contrast to the period of one-party dominance, or what Kothari (1970) called the 'Congress system'.

We call this new moment in Indian politics the federal phase for reasons mentioned below. The prime concern of this study is with India's electoral experience examined through the prisms of three Lok Sabha polls in rather quick succession in 1996, 1998 and 1999. Various aspects of the electoral process have been closely examined and the roots of electoral patterns and voters' alignments in relation to parties and social cleavages portrayed. In the backdrop of the growing menace of defectional and criminalised politics in legislatures, our brush with electoral behaviour in this study was more encouraging. Although India is counted among 'stable postcolonial democracies' as contrasted with 'postauthoritarian democracies' and 'former democracies' in the developing areas, (Myron Weiner, 1987: 7–8), elections in India have become relatively more institutionalised than the party system. After analysing the three parliamentary elections, we devote a full chapter at the end to the party system and electoral reforms of India.

Treating elections as the focal point of a decisive and redefining moment in the political system, we provide what the anthropologists call a 'thick description' of the background to the polls, candidate selection by major parties, issues highlighted in party manifestos and campaigns, the factors that influenced the electoral outcomes and the emergent coalitional parliamentary-federal frameworks of governance thrown up by these two elections that continued the new pattern and trend heralded since the 1989 Lok Sabha elections and only partly modified by the 1999 mid-term polls. The modification refers to the slight change in the electoral and legislative matrices such that the National Democratic Alliance government is the first since 1989, that is not dogged by the status of a minority government subject to the president's directive to prove its parliamentary majority before it proceeds to govern.

Another change of some magnitude is also apparent after the 1999 mid-term polls. Capitalising on the nationalist fervour in the wake of the ambiguous legacies of Pokharan-II and Kargil, the BJP-led National Democratic Alliance won a coalitional victory of sorts and formed a government with a greater degree of confidence and manoeuvrability with its regional allies than in the past. The continuance of coalitional governance based on an intricate network of regional alliances suggests that the federal features and forces of the Indian political system could be expected to grow to maturity. This augurs well for India's unique parliamentary-federal governance premised on a parliament with pretensions of supremacy countervailed by autonomy-conscious state governments within the matrix of a balanced supremacy of the Constitution as finally interpreted by the federal Supreme Court. In the new constitutional ambience of an increasingly federalising parliamentary system, the whole range of constitutional offices of the president, governors, the Election Commission of India and a whole set of inter-governmental agencies like the National Development Council, Inter-State Council, etc, are acquiring a new salience and unprecedented autonomy from both the Government of India and the state governments. To give just two examples, it is now difficult to understand and authoritatively interpret Article 356 relating to president's rule in a state without reference to the Bommai judgment of the Supreme Court (1994) that makes it subject to judicial review. And, the same applies to the politics of constitutional amendment; here again, we cannot do without alluding to the apex court's verdicts in the Keshavananda Bharati and Minerva Mills judgments in 1973 and 1980 that propounded and amplified the doctrine of unamendability of the 'basic structure' of the Constitution. These new developments are beyond the scope of this study, yet it bears pointing out that they are, by and large, the products of the new patterns of elections and party systems in the recent decades and the crystallisation of a new trend of judicial behaviour and activism (M.P. Singh, 2000). Moreover, in the last two decades, there have appeared on the scene, new stirrings from the civil society by way of a more vigorous kind of new social movements organised around the issues of quality of life, hitherto neglected groups and regions, failure of political institutions, etc. A new breed of non-governmetal organisations funded nationally and internationally has also begun to alter the previous predominantly bureaucratic mode of ensuring development, empowerment of the weak and providing services to the groups and communities.

In retrospect, new patterns of electoral and mass movement politics reached their culminations by the end of the 1980s, the processes in some states having started in the early 1980s itself. As against the patterns in the 1970s—mobilisation of massive majorities by Indira Gandhi in electoral and parliamentary arenas counterbalanced by a mass movement of formidable proportions led by Morarji Desai and Jayaprakash Narayan on the issues of corruption and authoritarianism—the new electoral pattern came to be marked by fragmentation of the party system with an accent on regionalisation of old parties and mushrooming of new, regional political formations exacerbating religious, caste, tribal and linguistic cleavages. Though a number of new social movements brought in a whiff of fresh air, they did not qualitatively change the political scenario. They avoided direct party affiliations and massive political confrontations and tended to be organised around single issues pertaining to quality of life, basic human needs and rights, ecological protection, gender justice, etc, rather than the overarching issues of economic production and distribution and fundamental groups and classes. In some states, rural violence centring on the caste-class nexus whipped up by self-styled, anti-systemic Naxalite organisations continued.

Our basic argument for reform in the existing state of affairs centres around the crucial role of political parties in elections, governance and opposition. Wherever in the world, democratic politics and stability of parliamentary governments have become institutionalised, it is mainly through the mechanism of a democratically disciplined party system and free and fair elections. For this reason, we have devoted a full concluding chapter on the party system and electoral reforms. Our analysis is mainly foregrounded on the Indian political experience. However, we also go into the Canadian political experience in this regard. For Canada, endowed with a great deal of cultural and regional differences and disparities, constructed the first parliamentary-federal system in modern times in 1867, as India later did in 1950. Also of particular interest to Indians is the Royal Commission Report on Electoral Reform and Party Financing submitted to the Government of Canada in a set of four volumes in 1993. It is with some degree of dismay and disappointment that we note that though the Government of India had appointed the Commission to Review the Working of the Constitution chaired by Justice M.N. Venkatachaliah in February 2000, party and electoral reforms are not within its purview. Two parliamentary committees headed successively by Dinesh Goswami and Indrajit Gupta had submitted two packages of party and electoral reforms in 1990 and 1999, respectively, but they remain largely unimplemented. The Law Commission had also submitted a report on the same problem and covered some new ground. We have discussed these reports at some length in this book.

Acknowledgements

This study forms part of a larger, major UGC research project on federalism and political parties in India directed by Professor M.P. Singh since the Fall Semester of 1995. We acknowledge our thanks to the University Grants Commission, University of Delhi, Election Commission of India, leaders of various political parties in New Delhi and some states, and our students for their institutional and individual support to this project.

This work was originally planned as a study of the 1996 Lok Sabha election. The work was practically completed the same year except for the detailed analysis of the electoral outcome which was held up for the non-availability of constituency-wise election results. By the time we completed the manuscript, the United Front government had fallen and the 1998 mid-term polls had been called for. We, therefore, decided to expand this work into a comparative study of the two elections. This work over, the publication was stalled by the fall of the Vajpayee government and the announcement of the 1999 mid-term polls. We could not have gone to the press with another election on our hands. Meanwhile, our work was also delayed by personal tragedies in our families. Also, Rekha Saxena got a doctoral fellowship from the Indo-Canadian Shastri Institute for a session-long study in Canada. For these fortunes and misfortunes, the volume is going to the press much later than intended. Our only consolation is that our book is considerably enriched by a more comprehensive analysis of the intervening developments. In any case, understandably, we were as apprehensive of the new mid-term poll as the political class in the parliament of 1999.

Our thanks are also due to Professor Douglas V. Verney (York

University, Toronto, Canada) and Professor Francine R. Frankel (Center for the Advanced Study of India, University of Pennsylvania, Philadelphia, the USA) and Professor James Manor (Institute of Development Studies, University of Sussex, the UK) for their interest and intellectual support in the course of carrying this project out.

We are grateful to Hemalata K. Shankar, Publisher, Orient Longman for patiently bearing with us for its completion, and to Annu Kurien for her competent editorial care of the manuscript. We also gratefully acknowledge Mr. Sayan Chatterjee, Deputy Election Commissioner, Mr. V.K. Ohri, Advocate in the Supreme Court of India and Mr. Nilanjan Mukhopadhyay for providing us with relevant documents, reports and judgments.

M.P. SINGH
REKHA SAXENA

CHAPTER ONE

Electoral and Party Politics in India

There would appear to be more departures than continuities in politics in India since her independence. The early dominance of the Indian National Congress suffered gradual erosion in several ways and in multiple directions. The first erosion was internal. The pluralist and federal aggregation of social and political forces by the party of Indian independence worked reasonably well until around 1967–69.[1] Thereafter, this process came under the concomitant pressures of centralisation under Indira Gandhi and the splitting up of dissenting elements. Second, feeding on the growing pace of downward political mobilisation of caste, religious and tribal hierarchies of the society, the processes of competition and accommodation among the political elites became more strained. As a result of this, elite accommodation in the larger framework of the dominant Congress party became increasingly difficult, opening spaces for opposition parties, old and new. Third, articulation of regional identities, diversities, and disparities in politics put additional strains on the accommodating and reconciliatory capability of the overarching Congress party when, at the same time, its internal pluralist and federal organisational structures and processes were undermined by centralising trends under a prime ministerial system that appeared to be more 'presidential' (in the American sense) than a cabinet system (in the Canadian and the British senses).[2]

The four directions from which the decline in the electoral strength of the Congress Party started can be seen as follows. The first diminution came from the centre of the ideological spectrum of the party system itself when the newly emergent regional party bosses in the last days of the Nehru years acquired a decisive say in determining the successor to Jawaharlal Nehru, and shortly thereafter to Lal Bahadur Shastri, between 1964 and 1966. But, Indira Gandhi, who was given the nod by this power bloc in the party in preference to Morarji Desai, turned the tables against the old guard of the party, mostly rightist in orientation, thus compelling them to join forces with Desai, the most devout right-winger in the party. Making an issue of progressive economic reforms in favour of the poor and the downtrodden, Indira Gandhi finally forced the right-wing Congress leaders, popularly called the Syndicate by journalists, to split by the end of 1969 and form a separate party, the Congress (Organisation), the first large enough opposition party to qualify for the status of official opposition in the Lok Sabha.

The vicissitudes of the Gujarat and Bihar movements against corruption and authoritarianism in the governments in the 1970s, culminated in the internal Emergency declared by the prime minister, Indira Gandhi, in 1975. The 1977 Lok Sabha elections that followed, unseated the Congress governments in New Delhi and most states of north India. This was the most severe electoral debacle suffered by the Congress party. It had managed to recover from the previous reverses in the late 1960s and dominated the electoral and legislative arenas of politics under Mrs Gandhi since the 1971 Lok Sabha elections.

The Janata Party that took the reins of power from the Congress in 1977, was also a centrist political formation like the Congress. But it was more comparable to the Congress of yore in its pluralist and regionally composite character than to the highly centralised and personalised Congress under Indira Gandhi in the 1970s. The Janata Party also had some features of a mass movement bequeathed to it by the 'JP Movement', so called after Jayaprakash Narayan who was drafted from virtual political retirement to offer an overarching leadership to the Gujarat and Bihar movements that gradually spread like a prairie fire throughout north India. The major non-Congress and non-communist opposition parties that had participated in the movement sparked by students' protests in urban areas and who had suffered Emergency authoritarianism in jails, hurriedly merged into a single, new Janata Party once the elections were abruptly announced in early 1977. But the parties that so merged—Congress(O), Lok Dal, Jan Sangh, Socialists, and Congress for Democracy—never carried the process of integration to its logical conclusion.. Hence, the party remained, for all intents and purposes, a de facto coalition. Thus, in contrast to the pluralist organisational texture of the Congress under Nehru and a centralised, personality-oriented Congress under Indira Gandhi—both by and large parliamentary-federal in structure—the Janata Party turned out to be a horizontally segmental and vertically confederal party with minimal overarching organisational coordination by the prime minister and the party president.

The organisational base of the Congress was comprehensively pan-national. It was held together by a parliamentary-federal party structure under Nehru and a centralised one with a parliamentary bias under Indira Gandhi. Within each linguistic region, in almost every state, it was, in terms of its social base, a multi-ethnic and multi-class political formation. The Janata Party, too, was more or less similar. There was, though, one basic difference between the two major centralist parties: whereas the Congress had a broadly middle-class, upper-caste urban orientation almost throughout the country, the Janata Party was dominated by middle-class, middle-caste elements with a rural and other backward classes (OBCs) bias as its centre of political gravity in the Hindi-speaking states along with Gujarat, Orissa and Karnataka. However, the confederal organisation of the party could not hold these diverse elements together, and its government fell prematurely in July 1979, in a confidence vote. Factional feuds among pre-merger party constituents and personality clashes among Desai, Charan Singh and Jagjivan Ram culminated in a terminal conflict over the 'double-membership' of former Jan Sanghis in the Janata Party as well as in the Rashtriya Swayamsevak Sangh (RSS). This double affiliation was objected to by former Lok Dal/socialist elements. The party was split, with the constituents' leaving to revive their earlier organisations. Among the parties so revived, the Bharatiya Janata Party (BJP) turned out to be more durable and expansive.

Besides the erosion from the centre in the form of the Janata Party, the Congress also encountered challenges from the Left, Right and the regional sectors of the party system. The parties of the left wing had earlier been supportive of the progressive policies of the Nehru and Indira Gandhi governments. From the mid-1970s on, strains developed in their relationship with the Congress. The Communist Party of India (Marxist) [CPI(M)], moved out of the Congress orbit during the Emergency and so did the Communist Party of India (CPI) after the Emergency and the 1977 elections. The CPI(M) had also by this time established strongholds in three states—West Bengal, Kerala and Tripura—where it headed and dominated Left Front coalition governments. The CPI(M) and CPI, especially the former, gradually adapted their Leninist principles of centralised party organisation to the Indian political situation where political power eluded them at the national level until the late 1990s, when they came to share power as smaller parties in federal coalitions. On the other hand, their state units have enjoyed political power for decades. This has tended to confederalise their party structures such that their state units in West Bengal and Kerala carry greater weight than the overarching central party organisations. This tendency has also been typical of their major ally at the national level—the Janata Dal. Regional or state parties in the National or United Front were/are, of course, by definition state-based.

The Left Front has continuously ruled in West Bengal since 1977. The Left Democratic Front and the Congress-led United Democratic Front in Kerala have held power alternately for decades. Congress and CPI(M)-led coalition governments in

Tripura have similarly held power in rotation for some time now. The ideological challenge from the Left which developed a strong identification with regional, linguistic culture, especially in Bengal, explains the unbroken ascendancy of the CPI(M) in West Bengal for a quarter of a century. Only since the late 1990s has a *mahajot* (great alliance against the Left) been sought to be forged by the Trinamool Congress (a West Bengal splinter of the Indian National Congress founded by the ebullient Mamata Banerjee), first in liaison with the Bhartiya Janata Party and now with the Congress.

The right-wing challenge to Congress dominance was originally weak in the electoral arena but rather strong though somewhat dormant in the society. After a spurt in the electoral presence of right-wing parties—Bharatiya Jan Sangh (BJS) and the newly formed Swatantra Party (1959)—in the 1960s, they apparently declined or disappeared through the 1970s and early 1980s. This came about through two interrelated processes: (1) an assault from the left-leaning centrist Congress Party led by Indira Gandhi; and (2) the merger of the Swatantra Party with the Bharatiya Lok Dal (BLD) led by the Jat peasant leader, Charan Singh in 1974, and the merger of both BLD and BJS with the newly formed Janata Party in 1977. This merger had a liberalising influence to some degree on the BJS elements in the same way as the Congress merger under Nehru and Indira Gandhi had on the socialists and communists. The Hindu, traditionalist BJP was revived by the former BJS elements in 1980, after the collapse of the Janata Party government in 1979. The BJP electorally resurfaced in 1984, though it was largely smothered by the Congress riding high on the crest of an electoral wave stirred up by Mrs Gandhi's assassination and the Hindu backlash to Sikh fundamentalism. In 1989, the BJP actively angled for the Hindu revivalist vote in the wake of the abortive, growing liaison between the Congress and RSS during the last days of Indira Gandhi and early days of Rajiv Gandhi, her successor as prime minister. The Hindu fundamentalist cards revived the electoral fortunes of the BJP which became the third-largest party, being preceded by the Congress and Janata Dal in

1989. In 1991, the BJP made it to the position of its being the second-largest party, and in 1996, the largest, though short of majority. Between these two Lok Sabha elections, the BJP stepped up the Ayodhya movement that resulted in the demolition of the Babri mosque in December 1992, in a fit of mob frenzy. It was an attempt to semitise Hinduism and fundamentalise the Hindu electorate. In the first half of the 1990s, the party had gained power in the assembly elections in Uttar Pradesh, Madhya Pradesh, Rajasthan and Himachal Pradesh, but its governments either resigned (in U.P.) or were dismissed by the centre in the trail of the destruction of the Babri mosque. In the elections that followed a few months later, the BJP could regain victory only in Rajasthan. However, it won in some new states and formed governments in Delhi and Gujarat on its own and in Maharashtra in combination with the Shiv Sena. But it suffered a setback in Gujarat later, where a faction of the party led by Shankarsinh Vaghela rebelled against the party leadership and formed an alternative government in alliance with the Congress. A consolation of sorts came in the assembly elections in Haryana in 1996, where the Haryana Vikas Party (HVP)-BJP coalition government was formed. However, it is notable that these major changes in the electoral fortunes of the BJP have been mainly limited to the Hindi-speaking states, Maharashtra and Gujarat. Except for a spurt of initial gains in recent years in Karnataka, Kerala, West Bengal and Assam, the BJP remains a marginal political force in areas of the south and the east. This explains why, until recently, it remained a major player only in some states. In 1998, federal coalitional power came its way for the first time with the decimation of the Janata Dal as the pivot party and drew together the third-force parties which held the middle ground between the Congress and the BJP. More about this new coalition later.

Although there were always regional challenges to Congress dominance, regional parties have greatly increased in number since the 1980s. As the Congress, the party of the Indian national movement and independence, gradually declined, and as other 'all-India parties' failed to fill the void effectively, state or regional parties arose and grew in state after state. Indeed, most of the political formations recognised as 'national' parties by the Election Commission of India are only so in aspiration, for, their effective electoral and legislative strength is generally confined to no more than one or a few states.

The examples of long-standing regional parties include Dravida Munnetra Kazhagam (DMK) and All-India Anna Dravida Munnetra Kazhagam (AIADMK) in Tamil Nadu, Akali Dal in Punjab, National Conference in Jammu and Kashmir and the odd assortment of tribal and regional parties in the old state of Assam now divided into seven states. The political geography of hard-core regionalism is thus concentrated in the north-western, north-eastern, and southern rimlands around the Hindi-speaking states together with Maharashtra, Gujarat and Orissa where all-India parties had been particularly strong, including those that for all practical purposes are regional in their effective support-base but national in electoral aspiration.

Long decades of Congress dominance were only occasionally breached at the national level by multi-partisan and bi-partisan tendencies, e.g., during the Indira Gandhi minority government in the wake of the great Congress split (1969–71) and the ascendance of the Janata Party following the internal Emergency (1977–80). These reverses were easily offset by the restoration of the Congress until the end of the 1980s. It was only in 1989 that the Congress was first decisively beaten by non-Congress parties. A multi-party system of polarised pluralism with regional segmentation has since continued. This phase is characterised as the 'third' electoral configuration by the noted psephologist, Yogendra Yadav, distinguishing it from the first one spanning the general elections from 1952 to 1967 and the second one between 1971 to 1989. To quote Yadav:

> The most obvious and easily identified characteristic of the third electoral system is the change in the choice set available to the voter. … Clearly, the changes are so basic that we are justified in talking of a new party system. In the first two

> systems under the Congress era the voter exercised only the choice, whether to vote for or against the Congress. That is no longer the case, and not just because there are many non-Congress alternatives.[3]

Below the national level, the ground realities in state politics have also undergone a sea change:

> The vote for the Left Front in West Bengal and Kerala had long ceased to be merely an anti-Congress vote; it is more meaningful to see the Congress vote in West Bengal as anti-Left Front vote. In Delhi, Rajasthan and Gujarat the Congress has been replaced by the BJP as the natural party of governance. In Bihar, U.P. and Tamil Nadu any talk of Congress/anti-Congress vote is bound to invite ridicule today.[4]

In view of the electoral volatility, in retrospect it is apparently premature to designate any party as 'the natural party of governance' as the Congress once was. For instance, since Yadav wrote the above, Delhi and Rajasthan shortly thereafter were lost by the BJP to the Congress. Yet, there is no denying the fact that since 1989, the multi-partisan tendencies seem to be crystallising into a system.

The post-1989 period of Indian politics at the national level may be broadly chronologised into two phases: (1) National Front/United Front governments (1989–1998), and (2) National Democratic Alliance governments (1998-to-date). The former were Janata Dal-led left-of-centre coalitions, while the latter is a BJP-led right-of-centre front.

The Janata Party of the late 1970s defined itself in terms of a non-Congress and non-communist political formation. The major national party of the right wing, the erstwhile BJS, was indeed a part of it, but the regional political forces from non-Hindi rimlands were outside of it. The Janata Dal came to be formed during the preparations for the 1989 Lok Sabha elections by merging the main splinter of the Janata Party and Jan Morcha, a group of Congress deserters led by V.P. Singh, who resigned from the Rajiv Gandhi government in 1987. It differed from its earlier namesake in at least two crucial ways. For one thing, it was more receptive to the communist parties which V.P. Singh called its 'natural allies'. For another, it also built bridges with regional political formations from non-Hindi regions. At the core, its main support-base continued to be the OBC 'bullock capitalists'. This mainstay of the party was consolidated by the mobilisational strategy of 'mandalising' the electorate by the V.P. Singh-led National Front government by implementing job reservations in the central government for OBCs in 1990, as recommended by the Mandal Commission appointed by the Janata Party government in the late 1970s.

In organisational terms, the Janata Dal remained the confederal party of old whose stronger state units were loosely coordinated by a nominal national organisation.

Both National Front (NF) and United Front (UF) were an aggregation of 'third-force' parties holding the middle ground between the Congress on the one hand and the BJP on the other. The National Front included the Janata Dal (143 seats), Telugu Desam Party (TDP) (24), DMK (0), Asom Gana Parishad (AGP) (0) and Congress (Socialist) (1). Besides these parties in the *executive* or cabinet coalition of the National Front, its *legislative* coalition also included CPI(M) and the BJP, in the sense that they separately extended their support to the government from the parliamentary floor without joining the cabinet.[5] The unlikely BJP support to the NF government led by V.P. Singh may be explained in terms of the party's limited options and its anti-Congress stance. If the BJP was unable to form a government, neither would it allow the Congress to do so. In any case, this 'external' support proved to be the Achilles heel of the National Front. For, even though it was rocked by personality clashes between V.P. Singh, Devi Lal and Chandrashekhar and threatened by the unilateral decision of the prime minister to implement the OBC Mandal reservations, its final undoing came with the abrupt withdrawal of BJP support to the government in the wake of L.K. Advani's arrest in Bihar when he was heading the *rathayatra* from Somanath to Ayodhya as it was feared that it would provoke religious communalism.

At the core, the United Front was a replication of the National Front: Janata Dal (46 seats), Samajwadi Party (17), Telugu Desam (Naidu) (16), DMK (17), AGP (5) and Autonomous State Demand Committee (ASDC) (1).[6] It was no surprise that the same coalition partners—after the fall of the NF government in 1990 and their being in the opposition for a term between 1991–96 during the Rao Congress government—would shed the label of failure when another opportunity to form a coalition government came their way after the 1996 Lok Sabha polls. One major difference, of course, was the reduced strength of the Janata Dal in the UF owing to the breaking off from it the bulk of its U.P. unit led by an OBC Lohia-socialist, Mulayam Singh Yadav, who nonetheless, decided to keep his newly formed Samajwadi Party within the UF. Another change was that in the meantime, the TDP was also afflicted by a split that saw N.T. Rama Rao ousted as the chief minister of Andhra Pradesh. He was replaced by his rebel son-in-law, N. Chandrababu Naidu, with the bulk of the TDP behind him. NTR's second wife, Lakshmi Parvathi, stepped into the shoes of the patriarch after his death a few months later, but the party soon faded out. So, the storm blew over without much adverse effects either for the TDP or for the UF.

Like the NF, the UF was also a minority-coalition government dependent on outside support from the two communist parties and Congress. While the communists were 'natural allies' of the Janata Dal *à la* V.P. Singh, the Congress was a reluctant supporter of the UF, much like the BJP's backing of the NF, earlier. The rationale for the Congress support was because it wanted to keep the BJP out of bounds of power. Of the two communist parties, the CPI this time joined the cabinet, while the CPI(M) only participated in the coordination committee of the front. The Congress partook in neither, and relied instead on the ad hoc resolution of differences bilaterally by the prime minister and the Congress party president. As it happened, the two UF governments, both short-lived, managed to reconcile reasonably well its inter-party differences, including policy preferences of the left wing, through reconciliatory skills of the prime ministers and an open and dynamic coordination committee. The threats to power that it suffered twice, of which the last one unseated it, was due to pressures from its external ally, the Congress. The latter complained that its 'interests' were not properly attended to by the government and forced a mid-stream change of the prime minister, from H.D. Deve Gowda to I.K. Gujral in 1997. The Congress again raised a hue and cry when the Jain Commission, on inquiring into Rajiv Gandhi's assassination, submitted its interim report indicting the DMK government in Tamil Nadu for security lapses. Congress MPs stalled the proceedings of the parliament and the party president demanded the dismissal of the DMK ministers in the Gujral government in New Delhi. The core UF stood firm under the pressure. However, with the withdrawal of Congress support, the fate of the government was sealed and it bowed out of office in 1998. Thus, the UF regime witnessed two governments: one formed by Deve Gowda after 1996 and one formed by Gujral in 1997.

Similarly, the BJP-led National Democratic Alliance (NDA) that replaced the UF in 1998, have also had so far two governments: one formed in 1998 and one in 1999, both under the premiership of Atal Behari Vajpayee.

The 1998 Lok Sabha elections witnessed a political realignment that resulted in the shift of coalitional power from the left-of-the-centre United Front to a right-of-the-centre coalition led by the BJP and subsequently called the National Democratic Alliance. Like the United Front, the National Democratic Alliance too remained a minority coalition dependent for its survival on some allies from the parliamentary floor. The latter consisted of thirteen parties: BJP (182 seats), AIADMK (18), Samata Party (12), Biju Janata Dal (BJD) (9), Akali Dal (8), Trinamool Congress (7), Shiv Sena (6), Pattali Makkal Katchi (PMK) (4), M.G. Ramachandran Anna Dravida Munnetra Kazhagam (MDMK) (3), Lok Shakti (3), Haryana Vikas Party (HVP) (1), Janata Party (1) and Tamizhaga Rajiv Congress (TRC) (1).[7]

Inter-party relations in the BJP-led coalition have, in fact, been quite fidgety. Indeed, the coalition formed in 1998, fell prey to the tantrums of one of its major allies from the south, the chief of the AIADMK, J. Jayalalitha. She kept the coalition on tenterhooks from the beginning by delaying the promised letter of support to the president and kept everyone in suspense for days when the government was being formed. The imperious Jayalalitha and the impulsive Mamata Banerjee (the supremo of the Trinamool Congress) vied with each other to be the prima donna of the discordant show. The former, for example, clamoured for the reinstatement of the dismissed naval chief, Admiral Vishnu Bhagwat, who was removed for alleged violation of the principle of cabinet control of the armed forces. The latter vociferated for popular causes such as the rolling back of price increases and public expenditure cuts announced by the government and detection and deportment of illegal Bangladeshi migrants to India. The Samata Party was a more understanding ally, but it too joined Mamata and Jayalalitha in demanding central dismissal of the Left Front, DMK and Rashtriya Janata Dal (RJD) governments in Bengal, Tamil Nadu and Bihar, respectively, which were their regional adversaries in their concerned states. Inter-party differences in the coalition tended to be publicly aired in the press owing to the penchant of the BJP top brass to bypass the coordination committee in favour of bilateral mediatory conduits. In fact, Mamata once resigned from her membership of the coordination committee, complaining that it had become defunct. But it was Jayalalitha who ultimately withdrew support to the coalition and brought its government down. The unstated reason for her action was probably because the government was not doing enough to shield her from the series of corruption-related cases filed in the courts pertaining to her previous term as the chief minister of Tamil Nadu.

After the mid-term polls in 1999, which was concluded late because of the Kargil war with Pakistan and during which Vajpayee continued to head a caretaker government,[8] the NDA was returned to power in an expanded 16-party coalition: BJP (182 seats), TDP (29), Janata Dal (United) (21), Shiv Sena (15), DMK (12), BJD (10), Trinamool Congress (8), Indian Union Lok Dal (INLD) (5), PMK (5), MDMK (4), Shiromani Akali Dal (2), National Conference (4), Himachal Vikas Congress

(HVC) (1), Manipur State Congress Party (MSCP) (1), Loktantrik Congress (2).[9] Although the number of the BJP Lok Sabha seats remained the same as in the previous House, the NDA collectively improved its position to acquire a clear majority this time. All NDA constituents, excepting TDP and INLD (both in power in their respective states), joined the Vajpayee cabinet. The regional composition of the coalition remained by and large the same as in the past, barring the replacement of the AIADMK by the DMK, its rival in Tamil Nadu and also in the seat of government there.

In the wake of the failure of the UF experiment, most tellingly indicated by the precipitous decline of its leading party, the Janata Dal, the Hindu-right BJP has attracted to its coalitional fold, four categories of parties: (1) the Hindu nativistic Shiv Sena from Maharashtra and Sikh traditionalist Akali Dal from Punjab; (2) parties of Tamil linguistic regionalism/nationalism such as the AIADMK, MDMK and PMK; (3) Janata Dal splinters such as the Samata Party with is mainstay in Bihar (an ally since 1996 elections), BJD in Orissa, Lok Shakti in Karnataka, as also the rump Janata Party; and (4) Congress splinters such as Trinamool Congress in West Bengal, HVP in Haryana and TRC in Tamil Nadu. Thus, in the case of most of the BJP's allies the 'push' factor from the Janata Dal and Congress operated more strongly than the 'pull' factor from the BJP. The push factor that repulsed elements from the Janata and Congress mainly related to the autocratic ways of the dominant leaderships in the parent parties at the national and state levels. Thus, expediency, power and patronage are much more important than the glue of ideology in keeping the coalition going. Moreover, the parties in the coalition are also divided by a secular-religious cleavage. This has forced the BJP to put into cold storage its more controversial agenda such as the deletion of Article 370 of the Indian Constitution guaranteeing a special status to Jammu and Kashmir in the Indian Union, construction of a Ram *mandir* at the site of the demolished Babri *masjid* in Ayodhya and a common civil code for all religious communities in India replacing separate family laws.

However, there are some positive features in the NDA that better help in the unity of the coalition than there were in the UF. The BJP controls a larger number of seats than the Janata Dal did in the parliament in relation to their respective allies. Besides, organisationally and ideologically the main political force of Hindutva is more cohesive than the main political organisation of the OBCs. The Janata Party/Dal has always been excessively prone to factionalism and fragmentation. The BJP as the political wing of the Sangh Parivar is organisationally more institutionalised and centralised than the Janata Party/Dal ever was. The BJP is a federal party with a parliamentary bias as compared to the confederal Janata Dal with state units stronger than its weakly articulated central party organisation. Moreover, long years of being in the political wilderness as a political 'untouchable' in inter-party relations, the BJP has been more receptive to coalitional arrangements than the Congress, which was the natural party of the government till the 1980s.

To be sure, the larger Sangh Parivar is an amalgamation of various organisations besides the BJP such as the RSS, Vishwa Hindu Parishad (VHP), Swadeshi Jagaran Manch (SJM), Bharatiya Mazdoor Sangh (BMS), Bajrang Dal, etc. And, even in the brief period of political power, tension has developed between the BJP and its 'cultural' and front organisations. For instance, RSS-VHP-Bajrang Dal want the BJP to be more assertive on the Hindutva agenda and are critical of its moderate stance. Similarly, while the BJP-VHP are more compromising on globalisation, RSS-SJM-BMS are growing increasingly restive about such issues as reassertion of *swadeshi* and renegotiation of the World Trade Organisation (WTO) treaty to mitigate the adverse effects of globalisation on workers and peasants and indigenous industries. The BMS has also been opposed to indiscriminate privatisation of public-sector undertakings.[10]

Predictably, the top-level BJP leadership has been much more inclined to moderation and conciliation than the party rank and file and the cultural and front organisations. The prime minister did occasionally provoke controversies by his ambivalences like the time he said in the parliament that the nation wished for a

Ram temple in Ayodhya, the only question being when and where.[11] This was followed soon thereafter by his 'Kumarakom musings', a holiday resort in Kerala, which were much more liberal and conformed to the role of the State and coalition *dharma*.[12] His other top BJP ministerial colleagues, too, would tend to recede from the limelight after such controversial episodes. But the fires of Hindutva militancy are being continuously stoked by the top brass of the RSS and VHP and the BJP rank and file. RSS *sarsanghachalak* (head), K.C. Sudarshan, has constantly been articulating the view that foreign Christian churches in India must be replaced by a swadeshi church and that the minorities must Indianise themselves.[13] The VHP president, Ashok Singhal, has repeatedly clamoured for a deadline for the building of the Ram temple in Ayodhya. With the Sikh Akali Dal and predominantly Muslim National Conference being parts of the NDA government, anti-Christian feelings and attacks have become more frequent than the manifestations of other religious and caste clashes. These events have also affected inter-party relations in the NDA. The union civil aviation minister and JD(U) president, Sharad Pawar, demanded action against those involved in the violence, and the defence minister and Samata Party leader, George Fernandes, praised the social service activities undertaken by Christian missionaries in India.[14]

Yet, internal relations in the Sangh Parivar have been more or less successfully managed partly due to its ideological cohesion and commitment and partly owing to the force of power and patronage. Those, like the BJP general secretary, K.N. Govindacharya, and the U.P. chief minister, Kalyan Singh, who took more assertive stances on swadeshi and overt OBC identities, respectively, were sidelined by the prime minister.

Inter-party relations in the NDA, both in the parliamentary and federal arenas of politics, have been more volatile. Unity has been sought to be maintained by power-sharing arrangements in the union cabinet and in politics in the states. Major allies in the coalition have preferred to have autonomous spheres of influence either in a ministry or a state government. The BJP has kept for itself the key economic ministries—HRD, information and broadcasting, natural resources and external affairs—and allocated defence[15] and agriculture to the Samata Party; telecommunications and civil aviation to the Janashakti and JD(U), respectively; energy to the Shiv Sena, commerce to the DMK and railways to the Trinamool Congress.[16] The TDP took the speakership of the Lok Sabha. The TDP, INLD and BJD did not take any ministry at the centre and preferred instead a favourable federal deal for their respective states where they formed their governments. Relations between the BJP, on the one hand, and the National Conference, DMK and PMK, on the other, were strained owing to the differences on the issues of Kashmir autonomy and Tamil *eelam* (freedom) from Sri Lanka. The National Conference had the controversial Report of the State Autonomy Committee passed, which was earlier appointed by it by a special session of the Jammu and Kashmir assembly, but, which was subsequently rejected by the union cabinet.[17] The DMK chief minister, M. Karunanidhi, in the backdrop of the civil war in Sri Lanka, proposed a Czechoslovakia-like partition in the island republic along Sinhalese and Tamil lines, which the NDA government in New Delhi disowned, professing its commitment to the territorial integrity of India's maritime neighbour.[18] The PMK has always harboured known support for Tamil separatism from both Sri Lanka and India. Nevertheless, the National Conference and DMK have buried these differences and continue to stay in the NDA, though the PMK belatedly left the federal alliance to join the AIADMK-led alliance in Tamil Nadu.

One continuous refrain during the BJP-led coalition governments has been the BJP's alleged attempt to 'saffronise' the academic and research establishments. A conference of state education ministers and secretaries convened by the union human resource development minister, Murali Manohar Joshi, in New Delhi was marked by walkouts and protests by representatives of non-NDA state governments at the centre's attempt to undermine the secular national character of Indian education by a Hindu nationalist educational agenda.[19] The

Indian Council of Historical Research withdrew some outputs of a multi-volume research project from the Oxford University Press on the Indian freedom movement prepared by some Marxist historians under the general editorship of the eminent historian, S. Gopal, though he himself was not a Marxist.[20] The Indian Council of Social Science Research was backed by top officials and members with undistinguished academic credentials but known Hindutva leanings and who were lacking in commitment to social science research. The research journals of these organisations and other publications have been unofficially put on hold. The National Council of Educational Research and Training has replaced well-known Marxist scholars from their committee, which was responsible for the history textbooks, by Hindu traditionalists on the plea that they had been there far too long. The University Grants Commission has been working overtime for introducing astrology and 'Vedic mathematics' in the university curricula in the face of stiff opposition from scientists with more modern views. These events have created a great deal of furore in the academia and the press, but even the secular allies in the NDA have generally chosen not to raise any objections presumably for the fear of losing pelf and power.

The BJP governments in Gujarat, U.P. and Himachal Pradesh lifted the ban on government officers' joining and participating in the RSS—a move that was opposed by secular parties in these states and elsewhere. The president, K.R. Narayanan, marked a memorandum submitted to him by the Indian National Congress to the prime minister, Vajpayee, which sought more information on the lifting of the ban from the government. The union government itself did not remove such a ban for central and all-India services, but pleaded that the queries raised in the memorandum was within the constitutional jurisdiction of the state governments. Under pressure from the opposition and the president and fearing judicial intervention in the matter, the BJP national leadership finally persuaded the BJP state governments to withdraw the controversial edicts in the interest of the party.[21]

In the spring of 2001, the NDA government found itself under siege in the aftermath of a sensational exposé by

Tehelka.com journalists, who were masquerading as arms dealers. TV viewers watched in disbelief the BJP and Samata Party presidents accept cash donations to fix an arms-purchase deal. This also revealed how the nefarious system works by its involving political and bureaucratic functionaries in the Ministry of Defence and the Prime Minister's Office. Coming in the wake of irregularities in the telecom policy, privatisation of the public-sector undertaking, BALCO, and a stock-market scandal, Tehelka came as the proverbial last straw that forced instant resignations of the defence minister, George Fernandes, the BJP president, Bangaru Laxman, and Samata Party president, Jaya Jaitley. The NDA withstood this, despite the desertion of the Trinamool Congress on the issue, and the absence of DMK representatives from a mass NDA rally in Delhi. The government has stuck to the chair despite stalled parliamentary proceedings by the Congress which was mainly responsible for this. But as *India Today* wrote: 'Vajpayee's honeymoon with the country which began with his one-vote defeat (in the Lok Sabha) in 1999 is well and truly over.'[22] With five states going to the polls the following summer to elect their assemblies, a still further political chain reaction from Tehelka could well have been in store for the NDA. Significantly, West Bengal and Tamil Nadu, home turfs of the Trinamool Congress and DMK, respectively, were included in the five states where assembly elections were held.

Tehelka has also unsettled the internal equations in the Sangh Parivar. Vajpayee's growing ascendancy, especially since the 1999 mid-term polls, may now more easily be challenged by less liberal elements in the party and by the RSS/SJM/VHP elements. With senior, critical and sidelined BJP leaders such as Kushabhu Thakre and K.N. Govindacharya in attendance, RSS mounted a frontal critique of the government's economic policies, specially its 'reckless concessions for the entry of multinational companies.'[23] At a rally in New Delhi to kickstart a 'mass movement' against the WTO and 'anti-labour' policies of the NDA government, the president of the BJP-affiliated trade union, the BMS, and the founder of Bharatiya Kisan Sangh

(BKS) and SJP, Dattopant Thengdi, strongly criticised the labour law reforms hinted by the finance minister, Yashwant Sinha, in his 2001 budget speech. He went on to assail multinationals, and the privatisation of even profit-making public-sector undertakings (PSUs) including BALCO.[24] Moreover, trade unions in Mumbai observed a Maharashtra *bandh* on 25 April 2001, which was joined by the BMS and BJP ally, the Shiv Sena, as well, to protest against the economic policies of the NDA government.[25]

The electorally fatigued political class seemed reluctant to face another Lok Sabha election so soon. The opposition was badly organised and in less than full fighting form. Yet, the main opposition party, Congress, persisted in obstructing the parliamentary proceedings for weeks. It seems to be shedding its penchant for going to it alone as formulated at the Pachmarhi party conclave (1998) and making a strategic shift to coalition politics. It forged alliances with the TMC in Tamil Nadu and the Trinamool Congress in West Bengal; the latter deserted the NDA in a direct fallout of the Tehelka revelations. Both these parties had split up from the Congress in the past. Yet, doubts still persisted about the inexperience of the top Congress leader, Mrs Sonia Gandhi.

Rumblings of a different political realignment in the opposition camp was also heard in the Tehelka trail. The elements of the defunct National Front/United Front that have stayed unattached since the failed 'third-force' politics, have regrouped to form a new People's Front (Lok Morcha or Quami Morcha) as an alternative to both the Congress and BJP. The CPI(M) veteran, Jyoti Basu, is its president and the Samajwadi Party president, Mulayam Singh Yadav, its convener. It is comprised of the four major Left parties and the Janata Dal (secular). But it is likely to be weaker than the erstwhile NF/UF which included the Jana parivar plus the Left stream. Janata Dal splinters such as the RJD in Bihar, BJD in Orissa and Janata Dal (United), Janashakti, etc, are now scattered, some with the Congress and some in the NDA. Moreover, the People's Front parties hold different attitudes towards the Congress. Mulayam

Singh Yadav is strongly antithetical to the Congress. The Congress itself is lukewarm to the Left. Moreover, in the Tamil Nadu assembly elections (2001) the Left parties found themselves on the horns of a dilemma. While the CPI(M) and CPI were allied with the AIADMK-Congress-PMK alliance and were pitted against the DMK-BJP combine, they had to avoid being seen hobnobbing too much with the Congress in particular, as they had to confront it in neighbouring Kerala and West Bengal that were simultaneously going to the polls to re-elect their assemblies.

Electoral politics in India, today, are thus at the crossroads. They are bringing to the fore the intended and unintended consequences of some foundational theoretical issues that must be empirically worked out through democratic politics. The first of these issues emanates from the combination of parliamentary and federal principles of government attempted in the Indian Constitution. The 1980s and 1990s brought to the foreground the question of federalisation of the Indian polity in a way that was never witnessed in the past. A series of movements for greater state autonomy in terms of more powers and finances to the state governments surfaced both in the electoral and party arenas as well as the movements outside the space of the party system. In some states, some of these movements also took a separatist turn. Territorially based ethnic movements, specially in the north-western and north-eastern areas and Tamil Nadu, are reflections of the growing federal strains. The appointment of the first ever constitutional Commission on Centre-State Relations chaired by Justice R.S. Sarkaria in 1983, presented its monumental report in two volumes in 1987–88.[26] The signing of a series of ethnic accords in Jammu and Kashmir in 1975 and in Punjab, Assam, Mizoram and Tripura in the latter half of the 1980s,[27] and revival of Tamil nationalism in the 1990s are symptoms of the growing federal challenge that India must squarely face.

Moreover, the change in the party system from one-party dominance to a multi-party system since 1989 has altered the context of centre-state relations. This has resulted in greater facility for consultation between the two levels of the government and a reduction in the incidents of partisan misuse of president's rule in the states. The full implementation of the Sarkaria commission recommendations and of the ethnic accords would lead to a quantum leap in the direction of the federalisation of the system by instituting a series of points of autonomy in federal relations and consultation. India's parliamentary-federal Constitution provides a good institutional matrix within which the growing tensions of representation and institutional coherence, interests and identities, nationalism, regionalism and globalism can be resolved and accommodated. The unprecedented rise of regional parties and continuing fragmentation of the party system has underlined the problem of federal aggregation of political forces to ensure dynamic stability of parliamentary-federal governance. This problem is symptomatised in endemic governmental instability since 1989, necessitating five elections (1989 included) within the short span of a little more than a decade.[28] Functional viability of coalition governments is a major task that the Indian party system today must address.

The second set of theoretical issues raised by the contemporary electoral and party politics in India relates to the reconciliation of democracy and development, democracy and capitalism, economic and political systems and lifeworlds and nationalism and regional and global integration. The contemporary trends have exposed the growing disjuncture between Project Democracy and Project Development in a way that one is often said to negate the other.[29] Similarly, the macro impersonal structural imperatives and interests of the system are often perceived to be antithetical to the identities and micro concerns of the lifeworlds. It is, thus, on the seams of the systems and the lifeworlds that social movements emerge.[30] Likewise, local, national, regional and global interests often collide and engender conflicts that demand critical and creative resolution through a new politics that reconciles the conflicting concerns of autonomy and authority, liberalism and communitarianism, state and market. The answer to these questions must be found when the national state is under pressure both from below and above. It must respond constructively to the forces of localism and regionalism, on the one hand, and supra-national regionalism and globalism, on the other. Its task is made doubly difficult at a time when social and welfare spending are being cut to reduce deficit and allow freer play to the overly regulated market forces and to the weak institutions of the civil society. The challenges are heavy and onerous. Yet, the solution lies in greater democracy rather than less if we wish to ensure a development that is equitable and sustainable.[31]

Notes

1. See M.P. Singh, 1981, *Split in the Predominant Party: The Indian National Congress in 1969.*
2. M.P. Singh and Rajesh Kumar, 1992, *Lok Sabha Elections 1989: Indian Politics in 1990s.* M.P. Singh, 1994, *The India-Canada Relationship: Exploring the Political, Economic and Cultural Dimensions.*
3. Yogendra Yadav, 1999, *Economic and Political Weekly*, 2395.
4. *Ibid.*
5. David Butler, Ashok Lahiri and Prannoy Roy, 1991, *India Decides Elections 1952–1991*: 90–91; and News Services Division, All India Radio, 1991, *Lok Sabha Poll: An AIR Analysis.* Note that although DMK and AGP did not win any Lok Sabha seats, they happened to be the ruling parties in the states, of Tamil Nadu and Assam.
6. Election Commission of India, 1996, *Statistical Report on General Elections, 1996, the Eleventh Lok Sabha*, vol. 1.
7. Election Commission of India, 1998, *Statistical Report on General Elections, 1998, the Twelfth Lok Sabha*, vol. 1.
8. For a discussion of conventions regarding caretaker government and controversies surrounding the one led by Vajpayee, see M.P. Singh, 1999, *Indian Democracy at the Turn of the Century.*
9. Election Commission of India, 1999, *Statistical Report on General Elections, 1999, the 13th Lok Sabha*, vol. 1.
10. See V. Venkatesan, 'Politics: Unstable Equilibrium', *Frontline*, 2 February 2001: 31–32.
11. *The Times of India* (New Delhi), 15 December 2000. 'The Unmasking of Vajpayee', by Sukumar Muralidharan: '...Prime

Minister Vajpayee lets his mask of moderation slip—to reveal the visage of an unrepentant Kar Sevak and the outline of an underlying agenda', *Frontline*, 5 January 2001: 4.

12. In his musings published and reported in newspapers, the prime minister strongly condemned the demolition of the Babri Masjid as a flagrant illegality, adding 'the wrongs of the medieval past cannot be righted by similar wrongs in the modern times'. He went on to say, 'I wish to make it absolutely clear that the law will take its own course should any organisation attempt to disturb the status quo. The government will not remain a silent spectator and adopt delaying tactics as unfortunately happened eight years ago.' *The Pioneer* (New Delhi), 2 January 2001: 1.
13. *Asian News Digest*, vol. I, no. 42.
14. *Ibid*, vol. I, no. 30, 22–28 July 2000: 468.
15. Samata Party defence minister subsequently resigned in the wake of the Tehelka exposé.
16. The Trinamool railway minister, Mamata Banerjee, also resigned following the Tehelka episode demanding the resignation of George Fernandes.
17. The autonomy resolution demands the restoration of pre-1953 status of Jammu and Kashmir which amounts to reversing the federal integration of the state into India over the years and making it confederal. If accepted, the union will have nothing to do with the state except for defence, external affairs and communications. The head of the state would be called Sadr-e-Riyasat to be elected by the state legislature rather than appointed by the union government and the chief minister would be designated as the prime minister. For details, see *Asian News Digest*, vol. I, no. 28, 8–14 July 2000: 435. For the response of the union cabinet to the demand, see *Asian News Digest*, vol. I, no. 29, 15–21 July 2000: 450–51.
18. *Asian News Digest*, vol. I, no. 26, 24–30 June 2000: 403–04.
19. In the agenda paper circulated by the union HRD ministry, prior to the conference, the annexure included a blueprint of educational reforms by a 'group of experts' headed by P.D. Chittalangia, a Kolkata industrialist and patron of Vidya Bharati, the educational chain controlled by the RSS. Its recommendations included that the contents of education at all levels should be 'Indianised, nationalised and spiritualised'; Sanskrit learning should be made compulsory for students between classes III and X; amendment of Article 30 of the Constitution concerning the right of minorities to establish and

administer educational institutions of their choice so as to extend it to 'every section of citizens, whether based on religion or language', etc. Around 15 state education ministers opposed these proposals as a veiled attempt to inject 'the divisive ideology of Hindutva into formative educational influences.' In the face of boycott or abstention the controversial annexure to the agenda was withdrawn, Chittalangia's speech was cancelled, and the Saraswati Vandana at the invocation was replaced by the national anthem. See 'Cover Story: Taking Hindutva to School' by Sukumar Muralidharan and S.K. Pande in the *Frontline*, 20 November 1998: 4–10.

20. The historian K.N. Panikkar told a press conference in Chennai that the two volumes of the *Towards Freedom* project edited by him and Sumit Sarkar were withdrawn by the ICHR from the publisher because they included documentary evidence that the Hindu Mahasabha collaborated with the British war measures during the freedom struggle that controverts the current Hindu nationalist and swadeshi campaign.

    S. Gopal, the group editor of the project contradicted the contention of the ICHR that the manuscripts had been sent to the publisher directly without routing it through the proper channel, i.e. the ICHR. See *Asian News Digest*, vol. I, no. 13, 26 March–1 April 2000: 199.

21. *Asian News Digest*, vol. I, no. 15, 9–15 April 2000: 228.
22. *India Today*, 26 March 2001: 31.
23. *Frontline*, 13 April 2001: 13.
24. *The Hindu* (New Delhi), 17 April 2001: 1.
25. Star News, Star TV, 25 April 2001.
26. The Commission on Centre-State Relations (1987–88).
27. P.S. Datta, 1995, *Ethnic Peace Accords in India*.
28. Rekha Saxena, 1998a, *The Pioneer*, 1998b, *Mainstream*, 1999, *Denouement*, vol. 9.
29. Rekha Saxena, 1998c.
30. Jurgen Habermas, 1987, *The Theory of Communicative Action*, vol. 2, *Lifeworld and System: A Critique of Functionalist Reason* and *Telos*, vol. XLX.
31. For problematising some of these concerns in terms of the impact of global and regional integration on the Indian parliamentary federal system, see M.P. Singh's paper to the *International Seminar on Comparative Federalism*, 2002.

CHAPTER TWO

Gearing up to the 1996 Polls and their Conduct

The Horizon

The eleventh Lok Sabha elections were held in a context marked with considerable anxiety about governmental stability. Since 1989, the country had seen three governments in six years. All of them were minority governments and the terms of two of them, very short. The National Front government survived for eleven months and the SJP government for four months. It was only the Congress government that was able to complete its full term, half of it as a minority government and the remainder as a majority one, and this was made possible by the accretion to the ruling party's strength by elections in Punjab and the merger with it of some sections of opposition parties. The Punjab elections as well as defections from the opposition ranks had caused anguish to the soul of the nation because of low participation of the voters and the permitting of opportunistic political realignments in the parliament by the prime minister, perhaps for the first time in India's parliamentary history. The Congress government had also survived the vote of no-confidence through huge bribes to JMM MPs which were subsequently exposed culminating in court cases. Even though the Congress government eventually managed to muster majority status, there was widespread anxiety that the following elections were unlikely to result in a clear victory for any party. The spectre of another hung parliament haunted the nation.

The passing away of one-party dominance led to mixed reactions. While the growth and strength of the opposition had fostered optimism for the democratic future of India, the absence of any viable alternative to the Congress created anxieties. Neither did the Congress appear poised for a regeneration nor did any alternative party appear to cross the threshold to a majority status within the framework of party government, nor did any coherent coalition government present itself as a prospective government for India, at least within that foreseeable time. All known stable parliamentary-federal governments other than India have been governed by a set of disciplined parties in a two-party system with a national leadership in the parliament. Only India and Japan had initially operated with one-party dominant systems in a multi-party configuration. With the end of this system in India, there was no clear forethought as to how India's parliamentary-federal system would operate with dwarf national parties, increasingly fragmented along state lines, and state-based regional parties. Parties in the United States do operate with a state-based organisation, where they meet in national conventions every fourth year for the selection of presidential candidates by state delegations. But then, the USA is a presidential-federal system whose structural logic is different from a parliamentary-federal system. A presidential-federal system can operate with a highly regional and even fragmented party system as the federal executive does not require a congressional majority for its stability. The stability of the parliamentary executive, the cabinet, is contingent on the majority support from a cohesive and disciplined party or parties. Coalition governments in Europe and even in some Indian states have shown that governmental stability and a coalition government are inherently not antithetical. However, India's experience with coalition governments at the centre, at least so far, does not inspire much confidence.

For these reasons, the 1996 elections were held in an atmosphere of anxiety and uncertainty. There was another dimension to the background of the polls. This was partly a by-product of the growing federalisation of the political system and partly that of judicial activism. Owing to the impact of federalisation, independent inter-governmental agencies such as the Election Commission had acquired a new earnestness and assertiveness, putting its weight in favour of free and fair elections and party reforms. T.N. Seshan, who initiated this activist phase of the commission as the chief election commissioner had ruffled the feathers of almost all parties. He found in the appointment of two additional election commissioners, an attempt, on the part of the government, to clip his wings. He resisted the move as unconstitutional, aimed at compromising the independence of the commission. He kept the additional commissioners M.S. Gill and G.V.G. Krishnamurthy without work almost for a year and appealed to the Supreme Court to protect the autonomy of the commission. While the court approved a number of other decisions of Seshan, it did not invalidate the government's action in making the Election Commission a multi-member body. Besides, judicial activism resulted in speedy investigations and judicial actions in a number of cases such as H.D. Shourie's public interest litigation in Common Cause vs. Union of India and Others (1996) and the hawala scandal, which has direct implications for political parties and elections.

The Poll Schedule

In the parliamentary tradition, e.g., in England, the dissolution and the timing of fresh elections at the expiry of the parliamentary term is considered to be the prerogative of the prime minister; even a minority prime minister who has lost the confidence of the House of Commons is not denied dissolution by the monarch.[1] It may be regarded as an index of the growing federalisation of the Indian political system that extensive consultation among the governments and the Election Commission and opposition parties precede the finalisation of the date and schedule of elections. On 29 February 1996, the Election Commission wrote to the prime minister inviting his views on the dates for the holding of elections. Around the same time a delegation of five political parties—the CPI(M), Janata Dal, CPI, Forward Bloc and Samajwadi Party—waited on the Election Commission and submitted a memorandum which urged it to recall that in September last year, all major parties except the Congress had expressed the view that elections should be held between the end of February and early March. The Congress had then preferred polls in February.[2]

On 6 March, a discussion between the prime minister, Narasimha Rao, and senior ministers and officials on election dates indicated the government's preference against simultaneous elections to the Lok Sabha and Vidhan Sabha in Uttar Pradesh and Jammu and Kashmir so as not to overstrain security and administrative resources.[3] By available indications, the opposition parties would have preferred simultaneous elections in these states under president's rule along with those whose assemblies were about to complete their terms.[4] The announcement of elections was preceded by a controversy over the chief election commissioner T.N. Seshan's two meetings with the prime minister alone without the knowledge of the other two election commissioners. One of them, G.V.G. Krishnamurthy, took strong exception, saying that this was likely to create misgivings with regard to the independence of the functioning of the commission, which is committed, as a constitutional authority, to the nation to hold free and fair elections without being under the influence of the ruling party and for that matter, under the government. This came on the heels of Krishnamurthy's reservations against Seshan's unilateral advice to President Dr Shankar Dayal Sharma to alter Seshan's foreign travel plans in view of the election schedule.[5]

On 19 March, the Election Commission recommended to the president and governors of six states to notify the elections according to the following schedule:

TABLE 2.1
Programme of Elections, 1996

Notification	27 March 1996
Last date for filing nominations	3 April 1996
Scrutiny of nominations	4 April 1996
Withdrawal of nominations	6 April 1996
Polling	8 April 1996, to be completed in four phases: 27 April, 2, 7, 23 and 30 May 1996.
Dates before which the elections shall be completed:	
1. in all states except J&K	14 May 1996
2. in J&K	30 May 1996
Hours of polls	7.00 a.m. to 5.00 p.m.
Counting of votes	To be completed in three phases on 8, 9 and 23 May 1996

Source: Election Commission of India (1996), vol. 1:1; the schedule of counting of votes from contemporary newspapers.

By-elections to 14 assembly constituencies spread over six states were also announced and they were to be held simultaneously. The chief election commissioner (CEC), accompanied by the two election commissioners (ECs), also clarified that the model code of conduct for the parties, candidates and governments would go into effect immediately ('from this very hour') and sought cooperation of all concerned to ensure a free and fair poll.[6]

On 19 March, the Election Commission rejected the government's proposal to simultaneously hold parliamentary and assembly elections in Jammu and Kashmir and then the general elections in the rest of India in June. The commission was particularly worried about any delay in the general elections. The unanimous decision of the three commissions left the home secretary, K. Padmanabhaiah, with no alternative. They felt that postponing the general elections would not be proper in view of the prevailing atmosphere in the country and would damage the credibility of the commission. The government's case was based on the report of the union government's officials who had visited

Jammu and Kashmir and had said that the negotiations between the government and militants were at a crucial stage and that the election schedule suggested by the government would be the better option. This did not, however, convince the commission.[7]

At various stages of consultation between the government and the commission, there had appeared sharp differences, with the government's insistence on an early poll and the commission's concern about the feasibility of free and fair elections in view of the background of terrorism in the state and the emerging political scenario. As it turned out, it was decided first to hold the parliamentary elections delinked from the assembly polls. Seshan, commenting on this step, explained it thus:

> in coming to the conclusion to hold elections to the Lok Sabha constituencies in Jammu and Kashmir, the Election Commission has taken into full account the difficulties which have persisted in the states during the last several months, the several discussions held by the commission with officials of the Ministry of Home Affairs, the central government and the indications received therefrom as to the conditions presently prevalent in the state. The commission is conscious of its duties to ensure the democratic process everywhere in the country as well as the legal provisions.[8]

The Electorate

The enormity of the task of administering elections in the largest democracy of the world may be gauged from the fact that at least 59 crore voters were eligible to cast their ballot in the 1996 elections. The state-wise break up of elections is given in Table 2.2. The range of variations, state-wise, was 10,08,26,305 in Uttar Pradesh and 34,111 in Lakshadweep, with the median of 80,58,941 in Delhi.

A comparison of the size of the electorate in 1996 with that in 1991 shows that over 94 million new voters were added to

TABLE 2.2
Size of the Electorate, 1991 and 1996

S. No.	State/Union Territory	No. of Electors 1991	No. of Electors 1996
1.	Andhra Pradesh	4,26,17,973	4,95,01,274
2.	Arunachal Pradesh	5,19,315	5,44,440
3.	Assam	1,18,73,952	1,25,87,659
4.	Bihar	5,04,53,647	5,84,38,317
5.	Goa	7,54,319	8,69,093
6.	Gujarat	2,48,82,508	2,85,29,094
7.	Haryana	97,25,897	1,11,52,856
8.	Himachal Pradesh	20,76,182	35,36,517
9.	Jammu and Kashmir	.	44,55,709
10.	Karnataka	2,88,39,296	3,18,10,069
11.	Kerala	1,96,57,976	2,06,73,867
12.	Madhya Pradesh	3,77,08,721	4,39,27,252
13.	Maharashtra	4,86,31,193	5,52,54,414
14.	Manipur	12,32,149	12,90,990
15.	Meghalaya	9,42,513	10,92,753
16.	Mizoram	4,14,412	4,08,094
17.	Nagaland	8,14,836	8,74,518
18.	Orissa	1,98,04,564	2,24,19,118
19.	Rajasthan	2,65,13,502	3,03,88,357
20.	Sikkim	2,01,704	2,29,160
21.	Tamil Nadu	3,99,17,777	4,24,88,022
22.	Tripura	15,61,085	16,47,908
23.	Uttar Pradesh	7,94,54,881	10,08,26,305
24.	West Bengal	4,13,92,460	4,55,83,054
25.	Andaman & Nicobar Islands	1,69,120	2,11,226
26.	Chandigarh	3,72,792	4,50,599
27.	Dadra & Nagar Haveli	75,009	94,909
28.	Daman and Diu	57,892	70,202
29.	Delhi	60,73,156	80,58,941
30.	Lakshadweep	31,665	34,111
31.	Pondicherry	5,93,305	6,33,635
	Total	49,83,63,801	59,25,72,288

Source: Election Commission (1991 Statistical Volume and 1996, vol. I).

the electoral rolls five years later. At least over six million of these new voters were not all young, for the 1991 column does not report the voters in Jammu and Kashmir and Punjab where elections were not held in that year. However, the rest of the expanded electorate were most likely greenhorns with somewhat new orientations and political preferences. This added an element of imponderability, pregnant with new patterns of political behaviour.

Administration of Elections

On the recommendation of the Election Commission, the state governments had already decided to give multi-purpose photo-identity cards to each voter. However, the election commissioner M.S. Gill said in Ahmedabad on 1 March that while the idea was not shelved and though the country had already spent 1,000 crores on it, it would not be possible to implement the scheme in 1996. Some states such as Tamil Nadu, West Bengal, Bihar and Assam had lagged behind in getting the cards ready. The commission by its insistence on cards would not like to deny the constitutional right of the people to exercise their franchise. He noted with satisfaction that states such as Gujarat and Maharashtra had nearly completed the process.[9]

The Election Commission had also ordered the videography of major events during the electioneering. Besides, it was also seized with the problem of the misuse of the government-controlled media by the parties in power at various levels. This problem was also covered by the model code of conduct. The commission also prepared, in consultation with recognised political parties, the telecasting and broadcasting of electoral messages by parties on Doordarshan and A.I.R.

There has been a widespread feeling and demand among political leaders that the current legal ceiling on election expenses incurred by candidates ought to be revised as they had by now been rendered unrealistic. The EC had already recommended a revision upwards to Rs 15 lakhs for a parliamentary constituency in major states and Rs 6 lakhs for an assembly one—subject to the proviso that these amounts be inclusive of the expenditure by the candidates individually as well as though political parties and well-wishers. However, since no reforms have been legislated in this regard so far, the existing ceiling of Rs 4.5 lakhs for a parliamentary constituency and a smaller figure for an assembly constituency was supposed to have been in force in 1996. However, a Supreme Court judgment in this regard clarified that all expenses by the candidate, his party or anyone else shall be presumed 'to have been authorised by the candidate or his election agent under explanation 1 to Section 77 of the Representation of the People Act.'[10]

Over the years, there has emerged a consensus on the idea of state funding for recognised parties in elections, but, no concrete step in this direction has been taken. The government sources discounted the prospects of the proposal's coming into effect in the ensuing elections. The finance minister, Dr Manmohan Singh, told *The Times of India*, on 8 March that the home minister, S.B. Chavan, had been negotiating with various political parties in this connection but without any final agreement so far. Dr Singh was quoted as saying: 'We will be willing to fund the elections provided that there is a feasible formula evolved by political parties.' He had suggested at a cabinet meeting that one possible way of providing the funds for the purpose could be by taking away Rs 25 lakhs from the Rs one crore that each MP is allocated for the local Area Development Scheme in his constituency. The idea did not appeal to his cabinet colleagues and hence it was not put across to the opposition. The government, however, was still toying with the idea as late as 8 March and wished to introduce in the current session of the parliament an amendment to the Representation of the People Act, providing for a reduction in the poll campaign period from 20 to 14 days and the raising of the poll expenses ceiling.[11] The idea of limiting the campaign period did not find favour either with the opposition or with the Election Commission, at any rate, for the 1996 elections. The ceiling revision proposal was generally acceptable. As it turned out, none of the contemplated bills were introduced in the parliament.

On 5 April, the commission, sounded a warning to all parties and candidates to adhere strictly to the existing election expenditure limits, and referring to the recent Supreme Court judgment, the election commissioner G.V.G. Krishnamurthy, told press reporters that defaulters would be disqualified. He said that most parties had consistently failed to file returns under the Income Tax Act compounding the problem of unaccounted money in party financing of elections. He went on to say that the Supreme Court verdict in Common Cause vs. Union of India and Others (1996) had created a new atmosphere in which the various relevant Acts and Article 141 of the Constitution would be more strictly enforced. In particular Article 324 of the Constitution had been interpreted very broadly by the court and under a relevant clause of the Representation of the People Act been given a legal nod requiring political parties to maintain their audited annual accounts.[12]

In the course of the hearings of the case and in the wake of the judgment, it became clear that except for the AIADMK, DMK and two communist parties, no other party had been filing returns of income as required under the Income Tax Act. The Supreme Court bench wondered why the income tax department did not issue notices to the parties regularly in this regard. The parties had defaulted in their returns for all the years from 1 April 1979, till the assessment year 1990–91 and thereafter to date. The bench observed: 'It is thus obvious that there had been total inaction on the part of the government to enforce the provisions of the income tax laws relating to filing income by a political party'.[13] On 7 April, with a view to curbing misuse of black money in elections, the Election Commission directed the chief electoral officers, political parties, revenue secretaries and expenditure observers to monitor poll expenses in accordance with the orders of the Supreme Court. The parties were asked to send the details of expenses by 31 July for scrutiny by the commission. Parties were also required to declare their bank balance as on 19 March at the end of the election. The revenue secretary was directed to inform the commission about the status position of the filing of income tax returns by recognised national and state parties by 22 April. The commission's own expenditure observers were advised to make their independent estimates of expenses item-wise. The directive issued by the commission said, quoting extensively from the Supreme Court verdict:

> A political party, which is not maintaining audited and authenticated accounts and has not filed the return of income tax for the relevant period, cannot ordinarily, be permitted to say that it has incurred or authorised expenditure in connection with election of its candidates in terms of explanation 1 to Section 77 of the Representation of the People Act.[14]

The constitutional provision for the delimitation of constituencies after every decennial census, was frozen by the Constitution's 42nd Amendment Act, 1975, until 2001. The last delimitation was based on the 1971 census. In the meantime, anomalies have appeared that have distorted the numerical size of the electorate in various constituencies causing, often, a glaring discrepancy. As Era Sezhiyan[15] suggested, any legislation which puts a ceiling on expenses must take into account, as does the British law in this regard, the size of the electorate in each constituency.

The 1996 Lok Sabha elections was generally perceived as more peaceful than past elections as also less turbulent than apprehended. Under a 1996 amendment in the Representation of the People Act, 1951, the commission appointed 1,667 observers for the entire country, generally three for each Lok Sabha constituency, who reported directly to it and were authorised to ask the returning officers on the spot to postpone declaration of the completion of the elections in their respective jurisdictions or postpone the counting of votes until the Election Commission so desired after considering the flash reports of its observers in the field. The Election Commission also permitted

TABLE 2.3

Eleventh Lok Sabha Elections, 1996, Numbers of Observers Appointed, Total No. of Polling Stations where Repolls were Ordered, and Total No. of Violent Incidents

S. No.	*State/Union Territories*	*No. of Observers*	*Repolls*	*Violent Incidents*
	States			
1.	Andhra Pradesh	139	139	—
2.	Arunachal Pradesh	3	—	—
3.	Assam	42	222	82
4.	Bihar	176	1,274	992
5.	Goa	3	—	—
6.	Gujarat	79	—	—
7.	Haryana	30	25	—
8.	Himachal Pradesh	8	—	—
9.	Jammu and Kashmir	16	—	8
10.	Karnataka	83	—	9
11.	Kerala	50	—	26
12.	Madhya Pradesh	123	2	—
13.	Maharashtra	160	—	—
14.	Manipur	5	12	1
15.	Meghalaya	5	—	—
16.	Mizoram	2	—	—
17.	Nagaland	2	—	—
18.	Orissa	67	27	34
19.	Punjab	29	—	—
20.	Rajasthan	77	48	12
21.	Sikkim	2	—	35
22.	Tamil Nadu	121	145	35
23.	Tripura	4	1	7
24.	Uttar Pradesh	284	130	—
25.	West Bengal	127	18	81
Union Territories				
26.	Andaman & Nicobar Islands	1	—	—
27.	Chandigarh	2	—	—
28.	Dadra & Nagar Haveli	1	—	—
29.	Daman and Diu	2	—	—
30.	Delhi	21	—	—
31.	Lakshadweep	1	—	—
32.	Pondicherry	2	1	—

Source: Election Commission of India, Letter No. 485/STATS/6/96, Dated: Delhi, 2 September 1996, to the Director of this UGC Research Project.

temporary, disciplinary authority over the administrative services of the state which were engaged in poll-related duties during the period of the electoral exercise.

However, the conduct of the polls in 1996 was not entirely satisfactory. As Table 2.3 shows, in as many as 1,919 polling stations, repolls had to be ordered and 1,423 violent incidents were reported nationwide. Most of these aberrations were reported from Andhra Pradesh, Assam, Bihar (by far the most violent), Haryana, Kerala, Manipur, Orissa, Rajasthan, Tamil Nadu, Uttar Pradesh and West Bengal. By and large, the southern and western regions were relatively less prone to violence. Surprisingly, the north-west and the north-east areas, generally known to be more agitated, were remarkably peaceful during the elections, presumably owing to heavy deployment of the centre's paramilitary forces and the state police forces. Interestingly, the deployment of the centre's forces that used to be a bone of contention in centre-state relations prior to the 1980s has ceased to be so in the last two decades, with state governments themselves pressing the centre for the legions of the centre's police forces. But the states continue to clamour for more revenue resources to administer their constitutional responsibilities, law and order being one of them.

Conclusion

We may conclude this chapter with a note on the Election Commission's entrenchment into the Constitution, parliamentary enactments and case laws. Until pre-1989 Lok Sabha elections, the commission functioned as a one-man body comprising the chief election commissioner appointed by the president of India, acting on the advice of the government of the day under Article 324 of the Constitution. In 1989, just before the Lok Sabha elections, the United Front government added two election commissioners to the body besides the chief election commissioner. Following the 1989 polls, the status quo ante was restored, but since 2 October 1993, it has again become a three-member body enlarged by the appointment of two election commissioners, first under an ordinance and subsequently under an act of the parliament. Two factors appear to have led to this development. First, there has been an enormous expansion of the electorate by the lowering of the voting age from 21 to 18 years in the mid-1980s. Elections since 1989, have also become more frequent owing to the high incidence of mid-term parliamentary elections, to say nothing of the 'delinking' of Lok Sabha and Vidhan Sabha elections since 1971. Second, Seshan, the then chief election commissioner, had contended in the Supreme Court in his protest against the enlargement of the commission to the disadvantage of the chief election commissioner after his appointment, that he had been the victim of the ire of all political parties which were piqued by his strict enforcement of the election laws and the model code of conduct. Rare was a party, indeed, that did not lash out at Seshan. In T.N. Seshan vs. Union of India (1995), the court, however, unanimously upheld the parliamentary enactment of equating the status, power and authority of the two election commissioners with that of the chief election commissioner and the stipulation that the body should seek to function, as far as possible by consensus, and failing this, by majority. This reversed the Supreme Court's earlier decision in S.S. Dhanoa vs. Union of India (1991) that the election commissioners could not be placed on the same footing in terms of power. The court went on to say: 'The Election Commission discharges a public function. ECs form part of the Election Commission unlike the RCs [Regional Commissioners]. Therefore, they must have a say in decision making. If the CEC is considered to be superior in the sense that his word is final, he would render the ECs non-functional or ornamental. Such an intention is difficult to cull from Article 324. It is not possible to accept the argument that the ECs' function is only to render advice to the CEC.'[16] The Election Commission itself has now settled for a three-member set-up, but does not favour expanding its size further as such a move, in its opinion, would 'hamper the expeditious manner in which it has necessarily to act for conducting the elections peacefully and in a free and fair manner.'[17]

The constitutional provisions relating to the conduct of elections are supplemented by the Representation of the People Acts, 1950 and 1951, as amended subsequently. In the opinion of the Supreme Court, 'Article 324, in our view, operates in areas left unoccupied by legislation and the words "superintendence, direction and control" as well as "conduct of all elections" are the broadest terms.'[18] Neither the Constitution nor the parliament has laid down any detailed provisions governing the organisation and the working of political parties, leaving them largely to evolve as a matter of convention. This has not happened. Political parties were nominally registered before 1989 by the Election Commission under its Election Symbols (Reservation and Allotment) Order, 1968, contingent on their securing one per cent of the valid votes polled in the state/union territory either in the Lok Sabha or Vidhan Sabha election. Since 1989, parties have been registered by the commission under Section 29(A) of the Representation of the People Act (RPA), 1951, as inserted by the RPA (Amendment 1989). This provision continues to be casual and sloppy to the extent that it does not even prescribe the minimum number of members nor stipulates adherence to their constitutions to establish and register a party. This has resulted in the mushrooming of parties and fragmentation and atomisation of the party system. This obviously needs to be tightened up.

The Election Commission is a crucial constitutional agency, endowed with a great deal of autonomy and full of immense reformist potential in the context of India's parliamentary-federal system. It mediates between the politically sovereign electorate and the constitutionally divided parliamentary authority and federal power. It regulates the electoral and party systems that play the most vital role in linking the State and the civil society and translates social dominance into governmental authority. Its efficacy and accountability is central to public political participation, representation and legitimacy. Hence, the care taken by the Constitution to ensure the autonomy of the

Election Commission from executive interference and political pressures and its evolving role in inter-governmental administration of elections, regulation of political parties and coordination between the State and the civil society would appear to be entirely consistent with the constitutional design and values underlying the Indian political system.

Notes

1. Robert Blackburn, 1990, *The Meeting of Parliament*: 64.
2. *The Times of India*, 1 March 1996: 10.
3. *The Times of India*, 7 March 1996: 8.
4. *The Times of India*, 20 March 1996: 9.
5. *The Hindu*, 17 March 1996: 1.
6. *The Hindu*, 20 March 1996: 1.
7. *The Times of India*, 20 March 1996: 1.
8. *Ibid*.
9. *The Hindu*, 20 March 1996: 2.
10. Common Cause vs. Union of India and Others (1996).
11. *The Times of India*, 9 March 1996: 7.
12. *The Hindu*, 6 April 1996: 1.
13. *Ibid*: 8.
14. *The Times of India*, 8 April 1996: 1.
15. Era Sezhiyan, 'Ceiling on Election Expenses', *The Hindu*, 2 March 1996: 8.
16. T.N. Seshan vs. Union of India, 1995.
17. Election Commission, 1997, *Agenda and Notes: Meeting with Recognized National and State Parties*: 2.
18. Mohinder Singh Gill vs. Chief Election Commissioner and Others (1978).

CHAPTER THREE

Candidate Selection in 1996

Indian political parties are a weak link between the State and the civil society. The Constitution did not even mention parties until the Anti-Defection Act, 1985, was incorporated into the Xth Schedule. And that too, only incidentally. Parties are mentioned in the Representation of the People Act, 1950, but their organisation is left to the rules and regulations formulated by themselves. In the absence of a firm, legal framework, parties become easy prey to personal whims and caprices and unbridled dynastic and oligarchic cliques on the one hand and raw inputs from primordial loyalties in the society. Ideology and party organisation take a back seat. Parties have generally turned into no more than electoral machines and personal instruments.

Rajni Kothari has appropriately observed: 'The litmus test of electoral politics in India has always been the selection of candidates by different parties when elections are round the corner.'[1] Candidate nomination is of crucial importance for at least the following reasons. First, the battle before the ballot determines the quality of the electoral input into the political system. The screening of representatives at this stage makes the parties the filtering mechanism in the polity. Second, the ideological and organisational efficacy of parties is also contingent on the process of political recruitment.

Two dimensions are important here in the context of candidate selection by parties. As parties, like any other organisation, are an authority structure, it is important to probe into the process through which decisions are made in nominating candidates. The role of local, state and national-level party units in the process is of relevance. Moreover, there is the equally important aspect of the political careers and socio-economic backgrounds of candidates selected. Their profiles determine the human element in the party leadership, at least, for the next five years.

Indian National Congress (INC)

The Congress constitution as amended at the Delhi Session of the AICC on 22 July 1990, provides for a Central Election Committee (CEC) to be set up by the Congress Parliamentary Board (CPB) and a Pradesh or Territorial Election Committee to be elected by the General Meeting of the Pradesh Congress Committee (PCC) or TCC. The CEC is to consist of the Congress president and seven other members including the leader of the Congress party in parliament with the Congress president as the chairman. This body is entrusted with making the final selection of candidates for state assemblies and the parliament and with conducting election campaigns. The final decision of the CEC is made on the recommendations of the PEC (Article XXV, Clauses A and B). The constitution is silent on the participation in the process by District/City/Block/ Constituency Congress Committees which come within the jurisdiction of the PCCs.[2] In the past, Congress constitutions as well as the actual selection process mentioned, involved the sub-pradesh Congress units in the selection process.[3]

In 1996, the selection process did not proceed in strict adherence to these provisions of the party constitution. Since the Congress party under Rao never constituted a CPB, the final selection was actually made by the Congress Working Committee which was converted into an ad hoc CEC with a few more invitees added to it. It was in this manner too that the selection of candidates for the assembly elections held in 1993 and 1994 was done.[4]

In the run-up to the 1996 Lok Sabha elections, Rao appointed AICC screening committees for different states to conduct the preliminary exercise preparatory to the final decision by the ad hoc CEC. To stymie his rivals, he appointed forty members of these screening committees in such a way that those whose loyalties were suspect would be hamstrung by Rao's supporters, and he also strategically placed his loyalists in major states. For example, Sharad Pawar and Ahmad Patel, named for the screening committee for Orissa, would be countervailed by the strong, Rao-loyalist chief minister of the state, J.B. Patnaik. G.K. Moopanar, who had been of late opposing Rao's inclination to align with Jayalalitha's AIADMK, was put in the screening committee for Delhi, presumably to keep him away from his home state but close to Rao's national seat of power. The Rajasthan PCC president, Ashok Gehlot, was directed by the central party to step down if he wished to recontest. A party general secretary in AICC said: 'Rao's next move will be to get the PECs to pass resolutions that in the event of a dispute, they would leave the matter to the Congress president.'[5]

Rao tried to favourably tilt the balance in his favour in the PCCs which were particularly factionalised. We can put in this category, Maharashtra, Bihar and Uttar Pradesh, all three then under non-Congress governments. Pawar and union home minister, S.B. Chavan, having agreed on renominating thirty Maharashtra MPs, were still fiercely fighting over the rest, with smaller factional leaders like A.R. Antulay and V.N. Gadgil instigating Rao to allot a ticket to Balasaheb Vikhe Patil, who had sued Pawar for corrupt electoral practices in 1989 and had for a brief period deserted the party.[6] Sharad Pawar managed to capture the bulk of the nominations for his faction. When the Maharashtra Pradesh Congress Committee (MPCC) launched the campaign for 1996, senior state party leaders such as former CMs and union ministers and central party functionaries such as Sudhakarrao Naik, A.R. Antulay, and V.N. Gadgil were conspicuous by their absence.[7] The Bihar PCC was badly divided into three major factions led respectively by (1) the former chief minister, Dr Jagannath Mishra, and PCC president, Sarfraz Ahmed, (2) union social welfare minister, Sitaram Kesari, and Tariq Anwar, and (3) union minister, Ram Lekhan Singh Yadav. Vying with one another to win Rao's favour they came with daggers drawn. The PCC unit in Uttar Pradesh was considerably weakened by the desertion in the summer of 1995, by rebels led by Narain Dutt Tewari to form the All India Congress (Tewari) along with Arjun Singh in neighbouring Madhya Pradesh. They were protesting against the authoritarianism of the prime minister and the party president's stepmotherly treatment to the party unit in U.P., and the soft stance of the centre towards the SP-BSP government in the state. Jitendra Prasada, the PCC president, who had been emerging as the major factional leader in the main party as a protégé of Rao was marginalised by Rao's appointment of Devendra Dwivedi, the former additional solicitor-general as an AICC general secretary.[8]

Madhya Pradesh Congress Committee became the scene of the greatest upheavals over the nomination of candidates. The state had been won back by the party from the BJP in the previous assembly elections and had become the first Congress-ruled state in the post-Nehru era where the Congress Legislature Party had exercised its autonomy in electing Digvijay Singh as the chief minister. More than half of the seven Congress leaders (besides those from the opposition) chargesheeted in the hawala case happened to be from this state. All were denied party tickets. All, excepting one, rebelled and threatened to oppose the official Congress candidates as independents. Madhavrao Scindia went to the extent of forming a regional party, Madhya Pradesh Vikas Congress. While Kamal Nath was placated by being offered a Congress ticket for his wife from his constituency, he, however, declared: 'No Congress leader except Madhavrao Scindia will be allowed to campaign for my wife.'[9] H.K.L. Bhagat, the party boss in the Delhi Pradesh Congress Committee, also revolted when he was not renominated because of the hawala case against him. He finally relented and was named the official spokesman of the AICC, a job he was never seen subsequently to perform.

AICC guidelines for selecting candidates in 1996 exhorted the Pradesh Election Committees (PEC) to give due weightage to the recommendation of the District Congress Committees (DCCs). However, most DCCs were so factionally divided that they recommended five or six names for each constituency.[10] Consensus in such deeply divided committees is a slow process. Given the time, the choices may have been further narrowed down. But the AICC poll schedule gave such little time to the PECs and party committees further down the line that it appeared humanly impossible to fabricate any meaningful consensus.[11]

The selection process as it actually came to unfold itself revealed two broad patterns. First, the PCCs with even a slight regional base and autonomy exercised some degree of participation in the process. This appeared to be true of the party units in Haryana, Madhya Pradesh, Maharashtra, Karnataka and West Bengal. Congress units in these states, and though seriously factionalised, preferred to fight it out among themselves, while jealously guarding their authority in the matter. The second pattern was typical of the states such as Andhra Pradesh, U.P. and Delhi. These units hardly took any time to abdicate their responsibility and authorise Rao to do the job on their behalf.

Two characteristics seemed to have dominated the deliberations of the INC in the selection of candidates: one, age with an accent on new entrants to the legislatures, and two, exclusion of candidates with criminal records and association with the hawala scandal. Besides, the AICC guidelines also emphasised adequate representation of minorities, weaker sections, women, youth and labour.[12] Addressing the general body meeting of the Congress Parliamentary Party on 13 March, the prime minister hinted that aspirants in the age group of 40–55 could get the lion's share in nominations. Of the total membership of 260 in the outgoing Congress Parliamentary Party, 160 were reported to be in this age group. The party sources indicated that it planned to enhance their proportion to more than two-thirds.[13]

In Karnataka, the State Congress Election Committee was reconstituted in mid-March accommodating most senior leaders. The PCC executive was scheduled to consider the recommendations of the election committee which in turn was to have deliberated on the list of nominees, to be given by the third week of March by the Block and District Congress Committees. A senior state party leader guessed that 60 per cent of sitting MPs would be renominated, with five new faces for the constituencies lost by the party in the previous Lok Sabha election and three for those where the incumbents were not inclined to contest or were dead. The AICC observer for Karnataka was Santosh Mohan Dev, a union minister. The AICC reportedly had its own computerised data sheets on the state with vital statistics on possible candidates and constituencies.[14] The list of candidates finally approved by the central party leadership created some measure of discontent among the state party leaders. Particularly sore was the former chief minister, Veerappa Moily, who sent a fax to the prime minister protesting against nine changes made in the list recommended by the state party unit as the replacements were allegedly weak. The Moily supporters accused Janardhan Poojary, one of the AICC general secretaries from Karnataka, of 'hijacking seats in Karnataka for his favoured ones sacrificing party interests.'[15] The final list in Karnataka revealed that 14 out of 20 sitting MPs were renominated and, in all, 12 new faces were introduced.[16]

In Kerala, prolonged negotiations were witnessed for candidates for both the assembly and parliamentary elections as well as for the party's allies in the UDF and the seat adjustments with them. The faction led by the chief minister, A.K. Antony, rejected the Karunakaran faction's demand for the sharing of seats between the two factions in accordance with the ratio followed in 1991.[17] It may be recalled that Karunakaran had assumed the office of chief minister following that election and had lost it to Antony mid-stream owing to factional feuds and central intervention. The seat-sharing negotiations among the UDF constituents were initially deadlocked with the Kerala

'Congress' groups (regional parties) led by T.M. Jacob and R. Balakrishnan on the one hand and Mani on the other.[18] The alliance was finally saved. The list of assembly candidates unanimously recommended by the state party unit were approved by the central party leadership within ten minutes. But, for some disputed seats with a minimum of two to four candidates, the process was tardy. With the date of filing nominations at hand, all those whose names figured in the list prepared by the PEC were advised to file in their nomination, pending final clearance by the central party leadership.[19]

The West Bengal Congress unit was among the most deeply divided, where unlike in Bihar, the party still continued to be the major opposition. The two factions, one led by Somen Mitra and the other by Mamata Banerjee, both waged proxy wars on behalf of the two national-level leaders, union minister, Pranab Mukherjee, and Siddartha Shankar Ray, the erstwhile Indian ambassador in Washington and former chief minister of West Bengal. The central party leadership was reportedly trying hard to make the two factions agree on the composition of the PEC and a compromise formula on ticket distribution. The central party leaderships recipe for the PEC's composition was 3+3+6 —three representatives from each of the two factions and six neutrals.[20] The final Bengal list turned out to be 'a mixed bag of old-timers and new entrants.' The delays in finalising the list at both the state and national levels created anxieties about timely filing of nomination papers, though the PCC officials on their return from New Delhi after protracted negotiations and bargaining claimed: 'The Congress has outdone itself in finalising the list of nominees.'[21]

Some state Congress leaders such as the Madhya Pradesh chief minister, Digvijay Singh, the PCC president in the same state, Parasram Bhardwaj, and Rajasthan Congress Committee president, Ashok Gehlot, put the central leadership in a dilemma by lobbying for the inclusion in the selection process of ministers chargesheeted in the recent hawala case. Digvijay Singh argued that it was their winnability that ought to be the main criterion. He remarked: 'Merely filing of the chargesheet does not make these politicians criminal. The cases are going on in the court and one is innocent till proved guilty.'[22] Rao himself had, at one point, observed that one was innocent until proved guilty and had hinted to his partymen to come forward with this suggestion.[23] The party finally decided to keep the seven hawala-accused ministers out, but conceded to accommodate their relatives and nominees, except for Madhavrao Scindia who floated a new regional party, Madhya Pradesh Vikas Congress, and Kalpnath Rai who resigned from the party and filed his nomination as an independent candidate from Tihar Jail where he was in judicial custody as an undertrial for his having provided shelter to an accused in the Mumbai bomb blast.[24]

In Haryana at least 50 per cent of sitting MLAs were denied renomination and a sizeable number of defectors were ticketed. The Haryana chief minister, Bhajan Lal, along with the PCC president, Dharmapal Singh Malik, were reportedly in a dominating position in the party, and it was because of the intervention of Rao himself that three dissident MPs opposed to the chief minister were renominated.[25]

The state party units that were in agreement on the list of candidates to be submitted for approval to the central party leadership, but which finally authorised Rao to do the choosing, were not necessarily weak units. Only Uttar Pradesh could be put in that category with persistent electoral reverses in the 1990s, and a major split led by N.D. Tewari in 1995. But this unanimous decision by the PEC to relinquish its role in candidate selection was an entirely recent feature. In the halcyon days of the party in the Indira Gandhi era, too, this pattern of behaviour was not unknown in the state that has been perhaps most centrally oriented, having provided many prime ministers, both Congressmen and non-Congressmen. The prime minister, P.V. Narasimha Rao, did not, however, accept the offer of the UPCC's PEC. He, instead, appointed an ad hoc committee consisting of the AICC observer in Uttar Pradesh, UPCC president, UPCLP leader and the chairman of the campaign committee to shortlist the candidates, pending the final approval by the CEC.[26] The Andhra Pradesh Congress Committee also referred the applications for party tickets without even shortlisting them. This was probably because of the deference shown to Rao, the patriarch, by the partymen in his home state.[27] This process of selection of candidates in the state by the party led to uncertainties and some dissatisfaction among the rank and file.[28] The Delhi Pradesh Congress Committee, too, followed suit, with the Delhi chief, Deep Chand Bandu, announcing: 'Mr Rao is aware of the situation in Delhi and we will go by his decision.'[29]

The AICC guidelines pointed out that the principal criterion in renominating sitting MPs would be their performance in their respective constituencies. Moreover, it also clarified that no sitting MP would be permitted to shift from his or her constituency 'except in very special cases.'

About renominating the hawala-tainted ministers, the party at first seemed to be on the horns of a dilemma, even Rao being in two minds about it. However, finally, it was decided to keep them out of the list. One compromise made in this regard was to concede to the demand to nominate the kith and kin of such ministers.

There was evidence of balancing the tickets in terms of caste arithmetic, especially by some PCCs. The UPCC, for example, made a bid to favour upper castes in the nomination process. The list recommended by the PEC included 15 Brahmins and 13 Rajputs. With candidates for nine seats still undecided, 30 of the 76 candidates declared came from the upper castes. Besides, there were 18 scheduled caste candidates and 11 OBCs. In addition, the party fielded nine Muslim candidates in the constituencies dominated by the minority community.[30]

The All India Indira Congress released the first list of 41 candidates for Gujarat, Madhya Pradesh, Punjab, Jammu and Kashmir and Tripura following the meeting of its Central Parliamentary Board. Its general secretary, P.R. Kumaramangalam, said that the party was still negotiating alliances with like-minded secular and democratic parties excepting Congress(I) and BJP.[31] Its second list included five candidates for Delhi including Haroon Yusuf, chief of the party's youth wing, and Manoj Prabhakar, the star cricketer.[32]

Bharatiya Janata Party (BJP)

The BJP decided to contest 475 out of the 542 Lok Sabha seats, leaving the remainder to allies in seat adjustments, mainly with the Shiv Sena, Akali Dal, Haryana Vikas Party and Samata Party. The guidelines circulated by the BJP national office among state units outlined three main criteria to be considered while selecting the party candidates: one, loyalty to the party, two, non-involvement in criminal and economic offences, and three, probability of electoral success. The party also appeared inclined not to renominate about 15 to 20 per cent of the sitting MPs. There was also no clear decision regarding the nomination of sadhus or *sants* as party candidates.[33]

The BJP and its major ally and senior partner in the Maharashtra coalition government, the Shiv Sena, had reached an agreement earlier about the sharing of 36 Lok Sabha seats. An agreement on the remaining 12 seats was also hoped for soon.[34] However, a dispute between the two parties at one stage forced the BJP to put off the release of the list of candidates. The bone of contention was the Thane seat which was represented in the last Lok Sabha by Ram Kapse of the BJP. The party sources said that the BJP would be willing to give up its claim over the seat and accommodate Kapse elsewhere.[35] The Shiv Sena chief, Bal Thackeray, announced that the Sena would contest 20 seats and the BJP 28.[36]

The BJP-Samata Party alliance in Bihar decided to divide the 54 Lok Sabha seats in the state between them in the ratio of 32:22, respectively. In Haryana, the BJP-HVP alliance, likewise, decided to allocate six seats to the former and four to the latter. The rank and file BJP members in Haryana were sore about the admission of the dissident Congressman, Colonel Ram Singh, into the party, though he was generally considered to be a big catch for the party on the eve of elections. The party rank and file was also agitated over the selection of candidates for the seven Delhi seats, especially the Delhi Sadar constituency. There were demonstrations on this account in the party headquarters.

The BJP-Samata party list in Bihar reflected the intricate caste arithmetic in the state. In contrast to the predominantly Yadav/OBC look of the Janata Party in Bihar, the BJP and Samata Party relied heavily on nominating Baniyas, Brahmins and Kurmis. The BJP gave five tickets to the Baniyas, four to the Brahmins, three to the Bhumihar Brahmins, one each to a Koeri and a Rajput. Besides, the BJP nominated two Yadavs and no Muslims. Both the parties gave short shrift to the so-called 'MY' (Muslim-Yadav) factor of the Janata Dal, chief minister, Laloo Yadav.[37]

The process of nomination in the BJP represented a fine balance between centralisation and autonomy to state party units. The final selection was made by the Central Election Committee of the National Council but different state units especially those in Gujarat, Delhi, Karnataka and Bihar appeared to have dealt with the nitty-gritty of the process. In Gujarat, the party committee coordinating the governmental and organisational wings was converted into the state election cell of the party. Its meeting was attended by a national party observer and its recommendations formed the basis for the decision of the central election committee of the party. The central observer in Gujarat pointed out that the image of the aspirants was to be the main criterion for the selection of candidates. Besides this, no definite norms had been set regarding the nomination of the sitting members. Party sources clarified that, by and large, the sitting members willing to contest would be given the nod. Even Shankarsinh Vaghela was renominated, who had been, during the previous year, the kingpin of the revolt in the BJP legislature party in Gujarat that led to the fall of the Keshubhai Patel government and his replacement by Suresh Mehta. The Sangh Parivar was also reportedly displeased with Vaghela. The state election cell was deeply divided on many nominations, in some cases, even eight to ten names being recommended for one seat. The matter was finally referred to the party's high command for finalisation. This stalemate explains why practically all the sitting members were renominated to avoid controversies.[38]

The BJP election committee in Karnataka had four to five rounds of meetings before it was ready to send its recommendations to the Central Election Committee. The degree of unanimity in the State Election Committee—on 17 out of 28 constituencies—appeared to be much greater in Karnataka than in Gujarat.[39] The central party observer in Karnataka, Sushma Swaraj, was quite optimistic about the party's prospects in the state where it had emerged as the second-largest party in the last assembly elections.

The twenty-member Delhi Pradesh BJP election committee, had a marathon meeting chaired by the Delhi party chief, Kedar Nath Sahani. Each member was subsequently consulted individually by Sahani to suggest names. The panel prepared included more than one name for each of the seven Lok Sabha seats in Delhi. The panel was submitted to the central party for the final selection.[40] The finally approved panel included high-profile candidates for the various seats, but the party cadre protested about the selection of one particular candidate.[41]

The BJP decided not to contest two Lok Sabha seats in Uttar Pradesh, one of them to accommodate the Samata Party leader, Chandrashekhar, a former prime minister. The Samata Party president, George Fernandes, had put in a word to the BJP president, L.K. Advani, in this regard. The BJP-Samata Party alliance in Bihar decided to share the Lok Sabha seats in Bihar allocating 32 seats to the BJP and 22 to the Samata Party. The two parties also planned to undertake joint campaigning in the state. The BJP-HVP alliance in Haryana divided the Lok Sabha seats in the state such that six would be contested by the former and four by the latter. In Rajasthan the party refielded eight sitting MPs.[42]

The Third-Force Parties

The selection of candidates in the Janata Dal in 1996, appeared to be even more decentralised than in the days of the Janata Party and the early days of the Janata Dal under the leadership of V.P. Singh. Party units in Bihar, Karnataka and Orissa acted as more or less independent units with a very tenuous central organisational framework provided by the party offices in New

Delhi and Patna under the recently selected National Party president, Laloo Prasad Yadav, the Bihar chief minister. Even the finalisation of the party manifesto was considerably delayed and so was the final list of candidates owing to the lack of agreement among the leaders of the three major state units. About Karnataka, Sharad Yadav, who was in charge of the party's campaign, said in so many words that the list would be decided by the state party unit. This occurred just a day before the last date for the withdrawal of the nominations. He also announced that his party would not put up any candidates against Madhavrao Scindia and Kamal Nath, the two Congress rebels in Madhya Pradesh.[43]

Among the three Janata Dal state units, Bihar and Orissa appeared to have selected candidates by giving the final say to Laloo Prasad Yadav and Biju Patnaik, respectively. The Karnataka unit went through several rounds of discussion by the State Parliamentary Board. The broad indications were that the party was inclined to field Lingayat candidates in predominantly Lingayat constituencies and Vokkaliga candidates where the latter predominated. The party leadership favoured backward and minority candidates for some constituencies on the foregoing demographic criterion.[44] The Orissa Janata Dal chief, Biju Patnaik, said that the JD-CPI-CPI(M) alliance would continue in the coming elections.[45]

The Samajwadi Party's parliamentary board in Uttar Pradesh also went through a three-day deliberation to finalise the list of its candidates. The SP leaders blamed the JD national chief and Bihar chief minister, Laloo Prasad Yadav, for tinkering with SP-JD seat-adjustments. The SP chief and U.P. chief minister, Mulayam Singh Yadav, had a meeting on their own initiative with V.P. Singh who was in Lucknow around that time. Yadav reportedly turned down V.P. Singh's idea of a broad JD-SP-BSP combine to defeat the BJP and Congress. He would have no truck with any party dealing with the BSP (which had been instrumental in the fall of SP-BSP coalition government). The SP and the BSP appeared to be vying with each other to appeal to the Muslim voters by nominating disproportionately larger number of Muslim candidates in their party lists.[46]

The CPI(M) politburo in New Delhi discussed at a two-day meeting the candidate selection as well as the party's electoral alliances with other parties. A member expressed satisfaction that 'the third front looks like it is taking off after talks between JD and Samajwadi Party in U.P.' There were strong indications that the party would renominate most of the sitting MPs. It reneged on its earlier proposal of a norm of a maximum of two terms in the Lok Sabha for its candidates—a norm that it had already implemented for its Rajya Sabha members. Significantly, its list for the West Bengal assembly inducted 68 new faces. Its leading Lok Sabha members like Somnath Chatterjee, Basudeb Acharya, Nirmal Chatterjee and Saifuddin Choudhary and others had already had more than two terms in the Lok Sabha. They would not be hampered by a two-term ceiling now. Interestingly, Saifuddin Choudhary, who had been dropped from the party's central committee the previous year, presumably for his alleged independence from the party line, was not to be denied the party ticket for the Lok Sabha. His election to the state committee of the party was apparently interpreted by the central leadership as strong support for him from the state unit.[47]

The CPI(M) list for Kerala was officially released in Thiruvananthapuram by the state party secretary, E.K. Nayanar. There was indication of an unprecedented infusion of young blood in the parliamentary as well as assembly candidates. Its first list of nominees for 65 assembly seats included 29 new entrants. Eleven Lok Sabha seats were reserved for the SFI and DYFI. Candidates for 11 assembly seats were still undecided. Most of them were in Muslim-dominated constituencies and the delay was attributed to the inability of the party to forge an alliance with the Indian National League. The two-term norm for assembly members was subsequently slackened but there were 14 candidates with such a background being renominated.[48]

The CPI(M) list for other states released in New Delhi included 16 candidates from nine states including three constituencies in Maharashtra, Rajasthan and Himachal Pradesh where the party would be making its debut. The second and the final list was to cover states such as Kerala, Tamil Nadu, Andhra Pradesh and Karnataka. In Uttar Pradesh and Bihar, the party planned to contest a slightly increased number of constituencies though not significantly large in comparison to other parties.[49]

The CPI released its list of Lok Sabha candidates in Patna, Bihar. The party generally tended to retain its sitting members. As against eight seats contested in the previous election, it planned to contest 15 this time. It also wanted to negotiate the continuance of its alliance with the Janata Dal and CPI(M) in Bihar. A party leader said that the objective was to win as many seats as possible in combination.[50]

Regional Parties

The Telugu Desam (Naidu faction) appeared inclined to renominate the sitting members. Its first list of eight candidates for the Lok Sabha included only two new faces. The chief minister, Chandrababu Naidu, said that his party would have alliances only with two communist parties and would contest all the seats over and above those that were adjusted with them. He discounted media reports about the good response to Mrs Lakshmi Parvathi, the leader of the breakaway faction and the widowed second wife of NTR, in coastal Andhra and Telengana.[51]

The first line of candidates released by the Asom Gana Parishad in Guwahati included 40 assembly and three Lok Sabha seats. Most of the sitting MLAs were renominated. The party finally planned to contest 90 assembly and 10 parliamentary seats. The party had already finalised election understandings with the CPI, CPI(M) and Autonomous State Demand Committee (ASDC).[52]

The Jharkhand Mukti Morcha (Soren group), which had three seats in the tenth Lok Sabha, planned to field candidates for 15 seats in Bihar, six in West Bengal and Orissa and one in Madhya Pradesh. Shibu Soren and his deputy Suraj Mandal would seek election from Dumka and Godda constituencies, respectively, in the Santhal *parganas* in Bihar.

Conclusion

To sum up, the process of selection of candidates in various major national parties in 1996, showed more common features than variations. The top-heavy organisational features and practices in the Congress and BJP continued, although these were combined with significant trends of federalisation of the power structures in both these parties. But this federalisation stopped short at the state level and did not reach out to the grass-roots or local-level parties, if any. Also, the central party leadership sought to at least partly checkmate the state or regional leaders and their factions through the tactics of sending loyal observers to reconcile state-level disputes, factionalising the state party organisations, and differentially using central power and patronage. The final say in the matter in any case notionally/legally rested with the central party leadership, which it can and did give, at least in some instances, especially where it was not likely to be very unpopular with state and local-level party leaders and voters in a particular constituency, more in terms of ethnic configuration than democratically participant public opinion. Moreover, central intervention was more frequent and tenable where the state-level party leadership was itself divided and could not unanimously agree upon a list of panels of party nominees to be approved for party tickets. Given the fact that both the Congress and BJP had been known to be highly centralised parties—the former dynastically and the latter in terms of Hindu *sangathanism* ('organisationalism')—the evident federalisation in candidate selection in 1996, coupled, of course, with central control might appear puzzling. This may, however, be attributed to the fact that the heir-apparent of the Nehru dynasty, Sonia Gandhi, was still in her self-imposed isolation, but, was keeping contact with members of the Congress party. In any case, Rao was in command of both the

Congress government at the centre and the all-India party organisation. Although he had consolidated his power in the government and the party, and had held organisational elections in the party in 1992, after a lapse of twenty years under Indira and Rajiv Gandhi, he could not afford to totally ignore either the dynastic loyalists or Congress chief ministers and regional satraps. In the BJP's case, the opening for federalisation came from the ascendant electoral fortunes of the party both nationally and regionally, albeit with some ups and downs in some states. This prompted the party leadership to be more accommodative, some may say, promiscuous, and the RSS-VHP ideologues of Hindutva to be politically more pragmatic towards parliamentary politics. Moreover, power for the BJP came first at the state level and only subsequently at the national. Moreover, several weighty alliances of the BJP with regional parties, some ruling in coalitional frameworks with the BJP (e.g., Shiv Sena, Haryana Vikas Party, etc), also exercised a downward pull in the power hierarchy of the national party.

In contrast to the trend of federalisation of the candidate-selection process in the Congress and BJP, the Janata Dal and communist parties displayed a penchant for a confederal pattern of decision making in which the real power was exercised by the state units of the parties with minimal or formal federal coordination. Regional parties were by definition state-based in that regional satraps wielded personal, charismatic and dynastic power with the masses, but with their ears much closer to the ground realities in terms of ethnic arithmetics and grass-roots clientelism.

Finally, in terms of the characteristics of the candidates selected, we need fuller information to offer more detailed findings than the major patterns barely visible here. Among the old-timers most parties were inclined to renominate the sitting MPs unless a change became unavoidable for whatever reasons. Yet, a comparison of the party candidates in 1991and 1996, on the basis of the detailed constituency-wise electoral results reported by the Election Commission, showed that the overall ratio of the new candidates—in comparison only with the immediate previous election—to the old in 1996 was uniformly higher in all major parties; only in the CPI(M)/CPI could the renominations be compared favourably with the new candidates fielded: 51 to 59 (Table 3.1). The onrush of new political recruits in 1996 was not an indication of old, institutionalised parties replacing their old guard by greenhorns; this was, indeed, a function of weakly institutionalised parties without a full-fledged national spread and which sought to cover as much ground as possible with candidates of whatever credentials. This surmise is also supported by the generally adverse success rate of the total candidates fielded by parties: national or all-India parties, 22.17 per cent; state or regional parties, 28.16 per cent and registered (unrecognised) parties 0.38 per cent. Only the CPI(M) and BJP have a more impressive track record: 42.67 per cent and 34.18 per cent, respectively. The relevant statistics for other all-India parties are as follows: the INC, 26.47 per cent; the Janata Dal, 23.47 per cent; and the Samata Party 9.88 per cent.[53]

TABLE 3.1
Number of Renominated and New Party Candidates in the Lok Sabha Elections, 1996

Party	*Renominated*	*New*
BJP	163	275
INC	180	310
JD	34	153
CPI(M)/CPI	51	59
TDP	6	28
DMK	5	13
AIADMK	2	4
AGP	3	8
Shiv Sena	3	18
BSP	11	133

Note: Based on the comparison between constituency-wise results of the Lok Sabha elections in 1991 and 1996, in the Election Commission Reports (1991, vol. Statistical; and 1996, vol. III).[54]

Notes

1. *India Today*, 30 April 1996: 35.
2. Apparently these are left to be filled in by AICC directives to PCCs/DCCs, etc.
3. Ramashray Roy, 1987, *Perspectives on Indian Politics*, Chap. 4. See also W.H. Morris-Jones (1968, *Politics: National and International*: 36–37), who observed that in the first four general elections the process of CEC's consultation with lower-level party organisations in candidate selection was gradually elaborated, developing the practice of sending AICC observers to the PEC level in 1961 and making the PEC the direct recipient of applications without the intermediation of DCCs for screening and onward transmission to the CEC.
4. *The Hindu*, 19 March 1996: 11.
5. *Outlook*, 3 April 1996: 35.
6. *Ibid.*
7. *India Today*, 30 April 1996: 23.
8. *Outlook*, 3 April 1996: 35.
9. *India Today*, 30 April 1996: 22.
10. *The Hindu*, 21 March 1996: 11.
11. *Ibid.*
12. *The Times of India*, 16 March 1996: 7.
13. *Ibid.*
14. *The Hindu*, 20 March 1996: 11.
15. *The Hindu*, 6 April 1996: 1.
16. *The Hindu*, 4 April 1996: 5.
17. *The Hindu*, 28 March 1996: 5.
18. *Ibid.*
19. *The Hindu*, 3 April 1996: 5.
20. *The Hindu*, 21 March 1996: 11.
21. *The Times of India*, 2 April 1996: 6.
22. *The Times of India*, 22 March 1996: 7.
23. *The Hindu*, 19 March 1996: 11.
24. *The Times of India*, 22 March 1996: 7 and *The Hindu*, 14 April 1996: 1.
25. *The Hindu*, 4 April 1996: 4.
26. *The Hindu*, 23 March 1996: 4.
27. *The Hindu*, 23 March 1996: 7.
28. *The Hindu*, 1 April 1996: 6.

29. *The Times of India*, 27 March 1996: 5.
30. *The Hindu*, 4 April 1996: 4.
31. *The Hindu*, 28 March 1996: 11.
32. *The Hindu*, 3 April 1996: 11.
33. *The Times of India*, 23 March 1996: 7.
34. *Ibid.*
35. *The Times of India*, 1 April 1996: 6.
36. *The Hindu*, 13 April 1996: 5.
37. *The Hindu*, 3 April 1996: 4.
38. *The Hindu*, 28 March 1996: 7.
39. *The Hindu*, 24 March 1996: 5.
40. *The Hindu*, 29 March 1996: 2.
41. *The Times of India*, 31 March 1996: 1.
42. *The Times of India*, 31 March 1996: 7.
43. *The Hindu*, 6 April, 1996: 1.
44. *The Hindu*, 30 March 1996: 5.
45. *The Hindu*, 30 March 1996: 5.
46. *The Hindu*, 16 March 1996: 4.
47. *The Hindu*, 3 March 1996: 6.
48. *The Hindu*, 1 April 1996: 6.
49. *The Hindu*, 29 March 1996: 7.
50. *The Hindu*, 29 March 1996: 4.
51. *The Hindu*, 30 March 1996: 5.
52. *The Hindu*, 29 March 1996: 7.
53. There are obviously some discrepancies in the accounts of renominations and nominations of new recruits based on press reports and those based on a more systematic calculation of the Election Commission Reports. This is presumably a function of the penchant of the press to focus more on prominent and partial lists released from time to time. The complete data reported by the Election Commission also has an inherent 'validity' problem (Are we measuring concepts we intend or something else?) in the sense that a large number of new candidacies in 1996, may not really reflect the essence of the variables concerned. For the category of 'new' candidates may conceal defectors from other parties as well as non-serious new candidates fielded in large numbers by all parties to cover as much nationwide ground as possible in the context of party-system fragmentation and atomisation in the 1990s.
54. Election Commission, 1996, *Stat. Rep. on Gen. Elections, 1996, the Eleventh Lok Sabha*, vol. I.

CHAPTER FOUR

Election Manifestos in 1996

The cynical view considers Indian politics as a naked game of power and an unprincipled spoils system in pursuit of the interests of the self and of one's followers. This perception is engendered and reinforced by recurrent scams with apparent and obvious political linkages and motivation, by the politics-crime nexus, and examples of conspicuous consumption and acquisitiveness of legislators and ministers during their incumbency. The image of politics as an avenue of social service which was prevalent during the freedom struggle and early decades of independence has suffered serious erosion. Election manifestos in this backdrop are generally regarded as an empty ritual that is not taken seriously either by the parties and politicians themselves or by the voters. An average reader of the manifestos is also often, lost in a great deal of similar themes harped on by various parties such as their giving top priority to the issue raised by the Mandal and Sarkaria commissions and issues of national security and integrity; poverty alleviation, more jobs and less inflation; cheap rice and safe drinking water; universal literacy and education, mid-day meals for children in schools, etc. Prohibition is another theme which features in the poll promises of parties with increasing frequency apparently to woo the newly mobilised women voters.

Yet, manifestos are not an entirely worthless exercise. It helps parties, their leaders and the rank and file to define or redefine themselves, do a stocktaking and offer ideological or pragmatic anchorage and packages to their members and voters. The press and parliamentary/legislative elites pay a great deal of attention to and scrutinise the manifestos formally released by top-level party leaders. Public opinion polls that mushroomed in the 1990s, also revealed that the average Indian voter is not as issue-blind as has often been assumed. An increasingly more independent and vigilant Election Commission under T.N. Seshan and his successors is also giving greater attention, in recent years, to party manifestos, finances and organisational elections in accordance with their constitutions and by-laws. Violation of the electoral code of conduct for parties for non-compliance to the laws of the land is penalised in such legislations, as the Representation of the People Act (1950 and 1951), Income Tax Act (1956), and the Companies Act (1961).

Federalisation and the Panchayati Raj

The political change in India, today, may be synoptically subsumed under the label of federalisation of the predominantly parliamentary system under the 1950 Constitution. Our constitutional system is based on the combination of parliamentary and federal principles with the former component, much like in the Canadian Constitution, predominating. Both Canada in 1867 and India in 1950, began their constitutional odysseys with a predominantly parliamentary system combined with federalism. And, both have subsequently been undergoing a process of federalisation through judicial interpretation, changing political culture, reconfigurations in the party system and slow growth of federal conventions. Revival of the panchayats in India in the early 1990s, through constitutional amendments along with the development of sub-state regional development councils in Darjeeling, Bodo districts and Jharkhand have added a third tier in the evolving multi-level federalism in the country.

The manifestos of major political parties* for the 1996 Lok Sabha elections was addressed to this dimension of political change. With the exception of the Congress, all other major parties promised more federalisation. The BJP, Janata Dal and CPI undertook to implement the major recommendations of the Sarkaria Commission in this context. The CPI(M) also did the same without mentioning the Sarkaria panel. More specifically, the BJP underlined the need to bring about the balance of resources in favour of the states, the end of misuse of Article 356 by the centre, the introduction of a constitutional obligation on the union government to seek two-thirds majority of parliament for the dismissal of a state government, consultation with the state governments before appointing governors and activation of the Inter-State Council. Besides, it proposed to set up a commission to examine the formation of smaller states such as Uttaranchal, Vananchal, Vidarbha and Chhattisgarh; set up regional development councils in Ladakh, Jammu and Kashmir; abrogation of Article 370 of the Constitution to remove the asymmetry in Jammu and Kashmir's relationship with the Indian union; and review of the manner of appointment of other constitutional functionaries.

The Janata Dal proposed to strengthen the Inter-State Council and National Development Council to ensure a more regular and effective coordination between the states and the centre so as to make India 'a truly federal Republic.' It also promised the review of Article 356 and governor's powers to promote responsible federalism. The party also favoured a reallocation of financial resources and administrative powers to enable the states to discharge their responsibility to the people adequately. Moreover, the party would appoint a commission to examine the demands of smaller states and to remove economic backwardness and political deprivation in backward regions of some states.

*In most cases the original texts of party manifestos in the 1996 Lok Sabha elections have been directly used. Newspaper reports have been used only for those whose texts could not be procured or readily translated into English or Hindi.

The CPI(M) also favoured a restructuring of centre-state relations with increased powers and revenue resources to the states, removal of regional imbalances through legislative measures and 'protection' of the federal character of the Rajya Sabha by barring membership of persons from outside the respective states they represent. The CPI, too, proposed a restructuring of centre-state relations along the lines proposed by the CPI(M) above. It decried the partisan use of Article 356 and advocated that the fate of a state government must be decided on the floor of the state legislative assembly. The CPI also advocated the revival of the Inter-State Council. Moreover, it wished to retain Article 370 in relation to Jammu and Kashmir and promised rectification of the erosion in the autonomy of that state that had already taken place. The party also intended to hold dialogues with insurgents or militant movements in the Northeast without any precondition.

There was considerable agreement among parties across the board on political and financial empowerment of the local political systems, with, of course, some differences in terms of specifics. The BJP would bring about further constitutional amendments in this direction beyond the 73rd and 74th amendments. The Congress would implement the recommendations of the Committee of MPs and Experts on matters such as the extension of constitutional provisions with regard to panchayats and nagarpalikas to scheduled areas, the instituting of district planning boards under Article 243ZD of the Constitution, and increasing functional and financial autonomy of local bodies under the existing constitutional amendments. The Janata Dal was critical of the tendency of state governments to postpone elections of local self-governing institutions. It was in favour of curbing the discretionary powers of the state governments over panchayats and wished to provide finances through state governments to them commensurate with their functions. Moreover, it wished to introduce reserved representation to the OBCs in panchayats. The CPI(M) and CPI promised to devolve greater powers to the institutions of grass-roots democracy. Besides, the CPI(M) preferred that all funds to panchayati raj institutions flow through the state governments.

This was obviously to counter the tendency of the Congress governments at the centre to attempt to establish direct links with district administration and panchayat elites instead of through the state governments. The Samata Party welcomed the 73rd and 74th constitutional amendments and promised to liberate the cooperative movement from bureaucratic controls and restore them to the people.

The National Conference manifesto for the 1996 Lok Sabha elections (it did not contest the Vidhan Sabha elections held a few months earlier) made the restoration of 'undiluted autonomy' and assertion of Article 370 of the Indian Constitution its main poll plank. It put the blame for alienating the people of the state from the national mainstream on the union government, specially since the dismissal of the Farooq Abdullah government by the centre in 1990. Among other things, the National Conference emphasised the imperative of power-sharing among the three regions of the state—Kashmir Valley, Jammu and Ladakh—with a view to balanced sub-regional development in the state.[1]

As usual, the Akali Dal stream in Punjab remained greatly factionalised, but among these, the Akali Dal (Badal) clearly emerged as the main party. Its election manifesto, drafted by a sub-committee chaired by former chief minister, Surjit Singh Barnala, who incidentally was also the chairman of the sub-committee that had drafted the controversial 1973 Anandpur Sahib Resolution, made the following its main planks: the question of state autonomy, inter-state riverwater dispute, territorial claims for Punjab and favourable policy outputs for Sikhs and other communities in Punjab including farmers, traders, industrial and agricultural sectors and school-going boys and girls. While there were similarities between the Anandpur Sahib Resolution and the election manifesto, some notable differences were also there. For one thing, while the former had called upon the Congress government at the centre 'to vacate the gross injustice and discrimination done to Punjab in the distribution of Ravi-Beas waters,' the latter rejected all the previous agreements, decisions, allocations and arrangements which deprived Punjab of its water. For another, the Anandpur Sahib Resolution was overtly for Sikhs only, while this manifesto was more sensitive to the pluralities in the Punjab society. The two documents take a similar stance on the transfer of Chandigarh and other Punjabi-speaking areas to Punjab and the demand for the enactment of an All-India Gurudwara Act by the centre.[2]

The ruling TDP appealed to the Andhra Pradesh electorate to give it a strong representation in parliament so that it could share power in the federal coalition government and in inter-governmental councils and to ensure devolution of more powers to states and greater autonomy of the media and autonomy of the judiciary (TDP, 1996).

Having been out of power for a long time, the DMK struck a strident note when it used regional autonomy and Tamilian ethnicity to mobilise the critical mass of the state population which was disgruntled by the ruling AIADMK. In a state-level conference of the party in January 1996, the DMK appeared to shed its moderate stance of the mid-1960s, when its separatist demand was dropped, and now sought to revive aggressive regionalism by demanding Kashmir-type status for all other states to prevent India's 'disintegration'. Another demand made at the conference was for Tamil to be made an official language to counter the imposition of Hindi as the link language between the centre and the state. Ethnic chauvinism was also evident at this conference in references made to the Jayalalitha's and Rajni Kant's non-Tamil origins.[3]

The party's manifesto itself, going by press reports, appeared to be more moderate and oriented towards the problems of governance and issues of public policies. It promised an open, transparent government; an ombudsman empowered to probe into corruption charges against the chief ministers, ministers and senior government officials; an investor-friendly government; the acceptance of foreign capital but without corruption-generating commissions and underhand dealings; the setting up of a permanent trade-fair centre; self-employment for the urban poor and rural youth; and the Anna Renaissance scheme in at least one block in each constituency with self-sufficiency in all respects.[4]

Being a splinter party from the Congress, the Tamil Maanila Congress, seemed almost like a regional version of the Congress. It campaigned basically as a regional party with national orientation. At its first state-level conference after the elections, resolutions were passed which emphasised, protection of the rights of the farmers, assurance of Tamil Nadu's just share of the Cauvery waters, suitable economic policies to attract more investments in the state, administrative reforms, public policies to meet the basic needs of the poor and downtrodden and due investments in the social sectors for education, housing, medical care and public distribution system, reservation for scheduled castes and other backward classes, and protection of human rights. The motto of the TMC was proclaimed to be 'a prosperous Tamil Nadu and strong India.'[5]

The Asom Gana Parishad manifesto promised to introduce social-security assistance to all sections of the people living in the state and to seize all the unlicensed arms to curb terrorism. While releasing the manifesto, party president, Prafulla Kumar Mahanta, said that his party, if voted to power, would take adequate political, administrative and economic measures to restore confidence to all common Indian citizens in Assam.[6]

The Haryana Vikas Party led by former Congress minister and union minister, Bansi Lal, displayed in its manifesto the concerns of a regional party dominated by the Jat peasantry and its agrarian interests and rural values. The main points in its manifesto included clean administration and all-round development of the state, adequate supply of drinking water and electricity to all districts in the state, the demand for the implementation of the Eradi Commission Report on river water sharing among neighbouring states, construction of the Ganga-link Canal from Haridwar to Karnal, agreements for the purchase of more power for the state from the National Thermal Power Corporation and electricity boards of other states, total prohibition in the state, the introduction of the Crop Insurance Scheme, strengthening of the panchayati raj, implementation of the Fifth Pay Commission's Report for state employees, and reforms to make education more employment oriented.[7]

The growing trend of regionalisation and sub-regionalisation in the country in the 1990s is reflected in the fact that few state and sub-state units of some national parties like the Congress party, issued state or micro-region-specific manifestos, e.g., the Haryana Pradesh Congress Committee and Congress in the Jharkhand districts of south Bihar. The Delhi Pradesh Congress Committee also had similar intentions, but, the idea was finally abandoned owing to internal differences in the state unit.

The post-election 14-party United Front (comprising the Janata Dal, Federal Front, Left Front parties) formulated—after the elections and the formation of their government—a common minimum programme committed 'to advance the principles of political, administrative and economic federalism.' In pursuit of this objective, the document proposed a dual strategy. First, it proposed to implement the major recommendations of the Sarkaria Commission through legislative and administrative measures. More specifically it intended to initiate immediate action on the following matters: greater autonomy to the states to enable them to determine their own plan priorities within the framework of the national Five-Year Plans and the handing over of most of the centrally sponsored schemes to the state governments; prompt presidential assent to state legislations on subjects in the State List; reactivation and energisation of the NDC and Inter-State Council.[8]

Second, the UF government promised to expeditiously appoint a powerful committee 'to review and update the recommendations of the Sarkaria Commission' and to examine the devolution of financial powers to the state governments. Besides, the common minimum programme also proposed to amend Article 356 of the Constitution which provided for president's rule in states, particularly in the light of the recent decisions of the Supreme Court (i.e. S.R. Bommai and Others vs. the Union of India, 1994). Moreover, it pledged further devolution of administrative and financial powers to panchayats and nagarpalikas beyond those envisaged in the 73rd and 74th constitutional amendments.[9]

After the strident demands for regional or state autonomy by constitutional reordering, especially in the 1980s, the changes in the party system ending Congress predominance in 1977 and 1989 and the series of Congress debacles in the states in the early 1980s, partly defused the pressures. The tenor of the Sarkaria Commission Report was probably partly influenced by these developments. Appointed by Prime Minister Indira Gandhi in 1983, under mounting regional pressures to look into these demands, its report submitted in 1987–88 did not go beyond its exhorting a fundamental change in political culture and elite behaviour for the development of healthy, federal conventions and minor constitutional amendments. The non-Congress National Front government, too, did not implement all the recommendations of the Sarkaria panel, except for constituting the Inter-Governmental Council under Article 263 of the Constitution. The common minimum programme of the United Front government seemed to go beyond the Sarkaria panel as well as the National Front. It turned out, however, to be a rhetorical exercise, as it failed to specify any constitutional changes beyond the amendment of Article 356 so as to preclude its misuse by the centre and was thus consistent with the 1994 Supreme Court verdict, which validated the dismissal of the BJP state governments in the wake of the 1998 demolition of the Babri Masjid in Ayodhya. It sought to establish the principle of judicial review of a presidential takeover of a state government and declared the dismissal of some other state governments in the preceding period as unconstitutional (these cases came up for consideration in the apex court together). In the past the courts were reticent on the issue. To the extent that the judicial deterrent and review is now available, the proposed amendment may not only be superfluous but may also be undue tinkering with the basic law. The federal agenda of the United Front government may indeed, be better pursued through administrative and fiscal measures.

As Harish Khare[10] aptly observes in the following:

> If the regional parties are smart, the first thing they would want to do is to get the central government to start the process of devolution of fiscal powers to the states. This demand for devolution of fiscal powers is entirely consistent with the ideology of the economic liberalisation—a centre retreating from the commanding heights of the Indian economy cannot pretend to be an overzealous guardian of the states' behaviour. It was in the name of centralised planning that the centre over the years drained the states of their most yielding fiscal resources.

Economic Growth and Liberalisation

The Nehru strategy of economic development with a dominant role for the state came in for review by the mid-1980s prompted by the widespread and persistent failure of the public sector in industry and appreciable success of the agrarian sector under private ownership. The trend of economic liberalisation and retreat of the welfare state in the western world and the political arrival of a new generation of elites in India, less enchanted by socialist ideology, indeed more socialised in western, liberal values than the Nehru-Indira generation also contributed to this development. The 1980s witnessed the slow appearance of economic liberalisation mainly premised on deregulation of the economy and partial disinvestment of public-sector undertakings in India. An accelerated pace of this policy with the additional component of partial structural readjustment that affected the relative position of public and private sectors was stepped up by the Congress minority (later majority) government of P.V. Narasimha Rao in 1991. However, by international comparison, even the Rao-Manmohan Singh package of liberalisation is fairly cautious and tempered by continued adherence to political liberalism hitched onto subsidies and welfare.[11]

The BJP manifesto decried the 'Licence-Quota-Permit Raj' and recognised the expanding role of the market. But this did not prevent it from emphasising the continuing role of the state in the interest of equity and justice. But, on the other hand, it sought the reduction of the role of the state and size of the bureaucracy. In a similar vein, the BJP sought to combine swadeshi and globalisation. Swadeshi was defined as:

> a self-reliant India, asserting its national economic interests, not as autarchy, but as a prerequisite to meeting the challenge of globalisation; of preserving our identity without compromising our sovereignty or self-respect. We reject unbridled consumerism and believe in adherence to sustainable consumption and growth.[12]

The BJP also favoured the forging of India's membership in regional trading blocs for export promotion. It believed in minimising dependence on foreign saving and investment. While the public sector was preferred only in areas sensitive for national security and as a countervailing force to the private sector, foreign investment and multinational corporations were welcome in the infrastructural, export, high technology and consumer-durables sectors, preferably with domestic partners.

The BJP's industrial policy was guided by economic sovereignty, modernisation and decentralisation. It emphasised the continued role and relevance of the small-scale industry. It proposed to hike the annual income-tax exemption limit to Rs 60,000/- (more than double the existing limit) and to grant tax concessions to intellectuals and professionals. It would also strengthen the universal public-distribution system or concessional ration shops.

The Congress election manifesto baldly promised to continue and strengthen the policy of economic reforms initiated by it in 1991. This relative quiescence compared to its 1991 manifesto may be attributed to the greater magnitude of its electoral reverses since 1991 than its successes in state assembly elections and being blamed for this by the rank and file because of the economic reforms and the loss of the pro-poor image of the party. Further economic reforms were, indeed, put on hold for this reason during the 1996 national elections in the latter half of the Rao regime. Besides, owing to its nationalist and socialist heritage, the Congress has always been a rather cautious, economic liberaliser in the first place.

Nonetheless, the Congress in 1996, had come a long way since the days of Nehru and Indira Gandhi. It had turned the national economic self-reliance of old on its head by redefining 'true self-reliance' in terms of some additional and alien new points of view:

> The capacity of the country to save more and invest more.
>
> The potential of the country to create more jobs and generate more incomes.
>
> *The capacity of industry and agriculture to absorb more investment and better technology [from abroad].*
>
> *The capacity of the country to pay for the import of capital goods and raw materials.*
>
> *The capacity of the government to pay for the import of essential articles like fertilisers, edible oils and petroleum products to meet the needs of the people.*
>
> *The capacity of the government to pay the national debt and to pay the interest charges.*[13]

Economic self-reliance premised on import substitution, domestic saving and investment and technological development had obviously been abandoned.

Through its new economic policy and structural readjustment, the Congress target was 'to achieve a higher trajectory of economic growth, efficiency and competitiveness in all production sectors and achieve 8 to 9 per cent growth in GDP per annum.'[14] The party waxed eloquent on its achievements in the past five years in the government, in the economic spheres (and other fields), but its silence on the most stirring economic questions of its position regarding, Dunkel Draft and GATT, MNCs, disinvestment in public-sector undertakings, etc, were more eloquent than its claims of achievement and promises. While its manifesto was veiled with regard to the above mentioned, it was no less tightlipped on the 'restructuring of the public sector' which was declared to be 'the highest priority.'[15] Its statement on science and technology was also silent on the issue of the import of high technology from abroad. But the sections on power and telecommunication did make laudatory references to its past decision of opening up these sectors to private domestic and foreign investment but gave no clues to its future intentions. Small-scale industries faced an uncertain future in the era of economic liberalisation, but the Congress reiterated that it was 'deeply conscious' of its 'critical role' in the economy and claimed to have, established a Small Industry Development Bank (SIDBI), legislated timely payments to entrepreneurs and strengthened banking facilities in about 100 locations where such units were densely clustered.[16]

In the agricultural sector, the accent of the Congress manifesto was on the promotion of capitalist farming; the issues which concerned small and marginal farmers and their anxieties over Dunkel and GATT were conspicuous by their absence which was something of a break with the party's past fixation on the *kisans* (peasants) in the Gandhi-Nehru-Indira days. The party referred with satisfaction to, the record level of food production of 19.1 crore tonnes in 1994–95, the major thrust being given to horticulture with an outlay Rs 1,000 crores in the Eighth Plan against Rs 24 crores in the Seventh Plan, increase of agricultural exports from about Rs 5,000 crores in 1990–91 to over Rs 10,000 crores in 1994–95 and freeing of agriculture 'from controls of domestic and international trade.'[17] The party also promised delicencing of the sugar industry and computerisation of land records, rural industrialisation and reduction of the urban-rural gap.

The only departures from the economic liberalisation policy in agriculture, appeared to be promises of price incentives or minimum-support price for farm produce and input subsidies that would improve the relative profitability of agricultural productivity. The party seemed to think that distributive land reforms had reached a plateau. It believed that the higher agricultural production 'has in turn led to higher wages, enhancing the purchasing power of the rural poor.'[18] It also proposed to strengthen the universal public-distribution system of fair-price shops.

The economic programmes of the two major communist parties—CPI(M) and CPI—reflected both the extent of their social democratisation and political liberalisation as well as their points of contrast to the Congress and BJP. They had come a long way from their earlier adherence to the Soviet or Chinese models of communism. Their current economic policies were reminiscent of the Nehru model of Indian democratic socialism. They differed from the BJP brand of swadeshi in their greater concern for economic betterment and political empowerment of the working class and, especially in the case of the CPI(M), regional pluralism and composite nationalism.

The CPI(M) was highly critical of economic liberalisation, privatisation and globalisation. The CPI also echoed these views. Both supported reforms in the public sector to make them efficient and competitive and autonomous from governmental control and interference rather than their dilution or dismantling. The CPI(M) was opposed to the decision of the Rao government to privatise the power, telecommunication and financial sectors. It advocated a 'new policy to strengthen indigenous industry and domestic capacities.' It sought an 'end to preferential treatment to foreign investors' and pleaded that the 'entry of foreign capital' should be 'decided on national priorities and technology needs.' Its case for the nation's 'economic sovereignty and self-reliance' included refusal of any amendment to the Indian Patent Act of 1970, for it would 'erode India's sovereign right to develop domestic R&D.' In sum, the CPI(M) was for the reversal of the policy of 'unbridled liberalisation which undermines our sovereignty.'[19] The CPI were inclined to defend the interests and concerns of small- and medium-scale industries.

Both the CPI and CPI(M) mentioned the objective of their extending distributive land reforms to a further degree. Both showed a greater concern for the marginal peasants and agricultural workers than the Congress or BJP. The CPI promised to allocate 50 per cent of the budget for the agrarian sector. It also assured subsidised inputs of irrigation, power, credit, etc, to small and marginal farmers. It promised to balance the need for a remunerative price for agricultural produce and the availability of food at a reasonable price to the consumers. The CPI(M), too, made most of these promises. Both parties favoured comprehensive central legislation guaranteeing minimum wages and social security to workers.

The Samata Party's manifesto reflected a rural and egalitarian bias. It was, in some ways, reminiscent of the socialist parties of yesteryears and communist parties of today. It was highly critical of the 'state's abdication of its role in promoting national self-reliance and economic growth with justice and equity.' To quote: 'The free-market system cannot but be unjust on the one hand and most unstable on the other. In the absence of any corrective measures, the market system only accentuates disparities further.'[20] The disparity that loomed large, in its perception, was that which existed between the agricultural and industrial sector. It would allocate 50 per cent of plan resources to the former 'every year until the deficiency of infrastructure and social services are adequately made up.'[21] Its plan for agriculture would put special emphasis on 'protection of the Indian farmer from the provisions of GATT/ WTO.' It believed there was scope for the extension of cultivable land and distributive land reforms. 'A family of five persons that engages in agriculture will be left with a maximum of three times the unit of land that a family can cultivate without employing hired labour or mechanisation.'[22] Its bête noire seems to be what the Rudolphs[23] have called the 'bullock capitalists.'

The United Front's common minimum programme was an exercise in tightrope walking. On the face of it, it did not seem very different from the policy of economic liberalisation and development followed by the Congress government headed by Rao, if only with a somewhat greater accent on agrarian interests and the public sector, with a peasant and industrial working-class bias (bullock capitalist). This similarity between the economic programmes of the right-centrist Congress and centre-left United Front might be explained in terms of compulsions of minority and coalition governments and of electoral politics in a less developed economy.

The common minimum programme proclaimed growth with social justice as its 'motto' and self-reliance since independence as an 'article of faith'. It promised that the Ninth Five-Year Plan commencing in 1997, would be formulated within six months aiming at annual GDP growth rates of seven per cent and industrial growth of 12 per cent. Investment in the infrastructure would be increased to six per cent of the GDP and fiscal deficit lowered to below four per cent. It would continue the process of deregulation and decontrol but made no mention of privatisation. Its endeavour to strike a fine balance between economic and political liberalism is indicated by pronouncements such as these: (1) There is 'ample room for public investment as well as private investment'; (2) the bulk of investment would flow from domestic sources but there was scope for foreign direct investment at the rate of 10 billion dollars a year, but not in low-priority areas; (3) 'when it is required to face competition, domestic industry will be assured of a level-playing field'; (4) the corporate sector should elicit the enthusiastic contribution of the working class, which formed the 'backbone of the industrial sector' to the nation's economic development; (5) the public sector, with reforms, would continue to be an 'important component' of the Indian economy, with the efficient ones being encouraged to become 'global giants'; (6) disinvestment in the public sector would be transparent and on the advice of a disinvestment commission; (7) sick industries would be rehabilitated and revived and interests of workers protected; (8) the public-distribution system would be strengthened, but the affluent sections would be excluded from its ambit.[24]

Social Sector and Welfare

Platitudes notwithstanding, the development of the social sector in terms of investments in education, public health, sanitation, public transportation, etc, have been a neglected dimension of planned socio-economic transformation in India. Similarly, despite the intentions of the makers of the Constitution and planners, India could be described as a welfare state only in name. Unlike the western capitalist economies, where a revision or retreat began from the more fully fledged post-war experiment of a welfare state under the impact of the conservative winds of political change, in India, ironically, the advent of economic liberalisation and structural adjustments in the economy retarded the denouement of a welfare state in its infancy. However, compulsions of electoral politics in an economy of scarcity make all political parties, including those favouring economic liberalisation, adopt a posture of political liberalism by providing welfare to the poor, working classes, women, scheduled castes and tribes, students and youth, army jawans, employees and consumers of essential commodities, minorities and other backward classes. All party manifestos repeat these pledges, mostly in vague generalities or through gross investment figures of non-comparative incomprehensibility, with monotonous regularity.

A remarkable degree of consensus seemed to pervade the programmatic spectrum of the party system in 1996, on poverty-alleviation programmes, strengthening of the public-distribution system and exclusion of the affluent sections from availing of it, SC/ST/OBC reservations in government jobs and reservations for SCs and STs in legislatures and for women in panchayats. The Janata Dal and Samata Party manifestos in addition promised the right of work to all Indians. The former also favoured extension of job reservation to the private sector of the economy. The Janata Party's obsession with reservations in the name of social justice now verged on mania. It was opposed even to the exclusion of the 'creamy layer' in the OBCs and the restriction of reservations of all types to a maximum of 50 per cent of available openings, both stipulated by the Supreme Court. This prostitution of the reservation policy is against the spirit of the Constitution under compulsions of electoral and economic greed. In the telling metaphor of Andre Beteille, it is like using the crutch of reservation as a stick, with which to beat the constitutional design. Even the Congress that held the Mandal Commission Report in abeyance during its reign through the 1980s, and the communist parties that did not have anything to say on this report in their 1989 manifestos, rushed to ride the Mandal bandwagon once the V.P. Singh government implemented it and triggered a veritable caste war in north India in 1990.

A party of socialistic and OBC orientations, the Samajwadi Party made an appeal for the unity of the 'Socialist, Left, and democratic forces' to establish 'social democracy' in India. Its manifesto clearly expressed itself against the new economic policies of liberalisation as well as the Dunkel proposal and the GATT agreement which, in its view, undermined national self-reliance and autonomous development prospects of Indian agriculture. It advocated that agriculture ought to be treated at par with industry, with 80 per cent of the budget to be allocated for rural development. Its industrial policy would restrict heavy industries to only basic and infrastructural sections and provide special concessions to agro-based and swadeshi industries.[25]

The manifesto of the Bahujan Samaj Party, a party of 'SC reservation aristocracy', sought to highlight four major objectives in its platform: abolition of what it calls 'Manuvadi' social and political establishments allegedly premised on the cumulative inequalities and hierarchic traditional social system and its replacement by a humanistic and egalitarian society; annihilation of the 'Goonda-Mafia raj' and anarchic forces; promotion of secular forces; and development schemes for scheduled castes and tribes, OBCs, Muslims, and farmers and traders.[26]

Political parties in India must come to grips with the caste-class nexus, but it has to be done within the framework of the law of the Constitution and social science research of contemporary social realities in the country. It is an index of an absolute intellectual and ethical bankruptcy of party ideologues, Marxists included; their learning at the feet of Ambedkar is understandable, but not at the feet of Lohia and Mandal with their political perceptions shaped by the pre-Green Revolution India. Reservations are fast becoming a serious threat to constitutionalism, and the rule of law of special quotas—politically motivated by a brute and crude majority— practically devour the open category premised on universal equality.

The ongoing, economic reforms obviously must come to terms with the need of adequate investment in the social infrastructures such as education and public health to accelerate the desirable effects of the human resource development. Moreover, the reforms cannot proceed in terms of exclusively economic rationality. The historical linkage of agrarian and industrial capitalism and democracy creates the imperative of reconciling the conflicting claims of the economic market of consumers and corporate firms, on the one hand, and the political market of voters and interest groups and parties, on the other. This cannot be accomplished by political populism. It can only lead to economic and political chaos. The only way out of this morass is a happy marriage of public law and morality.

Secular-Communal Divide

The composite, secular Indian nationalism has been bedevilled by the competing religious communalism of the Hindus, Sikhs and Muslims since, at least, the beginning of modern politics in 19th-century British India. This was at the root of the partition of the country by the retreating colonial power in 1947. India cannot be said to have turned the corner yet, as far as the bane of religious communalism and separatism is concerned. But secularism continued in 1996, to be a stronger and more desirable force in the country.

Communalism pervades the Indian party system at two levels. Overtly, it has produced a secular-communal divide among parties, which led to a virtual isolation, in 1996, of the BJP; such isolation was mitigated only during the anti-Emergency consolidation against the authoritarianism of the Congress or coalition situations such as those in the wake of the 1989 and 1991 parliamentary elections, when even left parties joined hands with the BJP in the electoral or parliamentary arenas.

With the prospect of a proletarian revolution receding to the background, the communist left wing persuaded itself about the feasibility of a bourgeois, democratic revolution by rubbing shoulders with the so-called bourgeois parties. The undivided CPI's support to Nehru, its support in the post-1964 split of the CPI [producing the CPI(M)] during the Emergency, and the CPI(M)'s joining forces with all non-Congress 'secular and democratic' forces during and after the Emergency were all premised on this interpretation. In the aftermath of the 1996 elections, the BJP emerged as the largest single party and even basked in the glory of presidential favour forming a government for about two weeks, but, except for lesser allies such as the Shiv Sena, Akali Dal, Samata Party and Haryana Vikas Party, it found itself miserably isolated. Failing to gain larger allies to forge a parliamentary majority, the BJP government headed by Atal Behari Vajpayee resigned after a nationally televised parliamentary debate, forestalling the voting on the motion of thanks, which is tantamount to a no-confidence motion, for the president's address to the joint session of the parliament on behalf of the minority government. But during its brief spell in power, the BJP and its more liberal prime ministerial mascot ('the right man in the wrong party' supported by M. Karunanidhi) gave enough signals of further moderation in the party's ideological platform.

The second level at which communalism pervades Indian politics is somewhat covert, but more pernicious and often explosive. This is evident in the communal and caste arithmetic indulged in by practically all the parties in the electoral politics of vote-banks. The phenomenon of recurrent communal riots and the politics of 'protecting' the minorities, instituting commissions of inquiries into violent incidents and the issues of punishing those inciting or indulging in them are all parts of this broader communal politics. Some recent examples of this include inquiries into the Bhagalpur riots; anti-Sikh Delhi riots after the assassination of Indira Gandhi and the role of some Congress leaders in inciting these riots, which led to a number of court cases and the internment of a union minister and capital punishment for a few. This also included inquiries into the Mumbai chain-bomb blasts (covering as well, the subsequent riots) by the Shrikrishna Commission appointed by the Congress government in Maharashtra, though it was disbanded by the successor BJP government, only to be recommissioned at the request of Prime Minister Atal Behari Vajpayee.

The manifestos of all parties, including the BJP, explicitly committed themselves to the protection of minority communities and human rights. However, while other parties declared secularism as a foundational value of the Indian Constitution, culture and nationalism, the BJP declared that it 'will be guided by its policy of "justice for all, appeasement of none".'[27] The terms 'secularism' or 'positive secularism' (the latter was used by its 1989 manifesto) are eschewed by the BJP manifesto of 1996, which, however, declared:

> The BJP subscribes to the view that human dignity, justice for all and protection of the individual from the tyranny of the State are among the basic tenets of Hindutva. We are committed to upholding the human, democratic and civil rights of every individual, irrespective of the person's caste, creed, religion or gender. But we will not allow this commitment to be used as a shield by those who commit inhuman atrocities and thus forsake their claim to human rights.[28]

The BJP was distinguished from the other parties by its insistence on the replacement of the Minorities Commission by the comprehensive National Human Rights Commission (at present both are in existence), a uniform civil code for all religious communities, 'equality for all and discrimination against none on grounds of religion in matters of education by amending Article 30 of the Constitution', ban on all foreign funds to all organisations and on fraudulent religious conversions, abolition of Article 370 of the Constitution relating to the special status of Jammu and Kashmir in its relation to the Indian union and a commission of inquiry like the Neogi Commission 'to inquire into the activities of foreign missionaries and other organisations that have been receiving foreign funds.'[29] Most of these items did not only not find a place in the manifestos of other parties, but the Congress and Janata Dal rejected the proposals for a common civil code and abrogation of Article 370 of the Constitution, unless these measures were willingly accepted by the concerned sections of the population. The Congress claimed credit for peace in Punjab and a new beginning in Jammu and Kashmir. There was also a consensus among almost all non-BJP parties for a binding judicial arbitration of the Ayodhya dispute under Article 138(2) of the Constitution (the previous reference by the Congress government was for advisory opinion of the Supreme Court under Article 143). The CPI(M) manifesto specially promised an immediate legislation that separated religion from politics, a move made but subsequently withdrawn by the Rao minority government when its comprehensive legislation against misuse of religious, caste and linguistic divisions in politics had to be diluted under the pressure of the Mandal mania of the Janata Dal and Left parties. Mandal and mandir issues appeared destined to bedevil Indian politics even into the years ahead. The 1996 manifesto of the BJP continued to be committed to the construction of a Shri Rama Mandir at Ayodhya in the name of 'cultural nationalism'.

The Common Approach and Minimum Programme of the United Front (1996) proclaimed:

> United Front is founded on the plank of secularism and democracy. The United Front declares that secularism means that there should be separation of State and religion and also notes that it is that definition that has been accepted as correct by the Supreme Court in numerous decisions. Attempts by sectarian and communal forces to erode the multi-ethnic, multi-religious and multi-linguistic character of our society will be strongly resisted.[30]

It was also committed to (in terms of specifics) refer the Ayodhya dispute to the Supreme Court under Article 138(2), implement the Protection of Places of Worship Act, 1990, and maintain personal laws of religious communities unless there was a desire for reforms in the communities concerned. The UF-CAMP went on to pledge a determined effort

> to bring every section of the society together to build a strong, modern, forward-looking, liberal and democratic society imbued with a scientific temper and an aspiration for material progress.[31]

The secular-communal divide is basically a conflict between the concept of a secular and plural multi-cultural Indian nationalism and a concept of 'one nation, one people, one culture' premised on Hindutva as 'a unifying principle which alone can preserve the unity and integrity of our nation.'[32] The BJP leaders and their RSS mentors tend, however, to explain that their use of the term Hindutva goes beyond Hinduism as a religious identity and is coterminous with the territorial extent of India such that any religious community residing therein is part of this broader phenomenon of Hindutva.

Ironically, *Ayodhya* literally means a non-warring city and the *Ramayana* and *Ramcharitamanasa* are less war-like epics than the *Mahabharata*. The fire of Hindutva is fuelled by the psyche of historical and geographical victimhood and exigencies of contemporary electoral politics. Constitutional ethics, federalisation, effective governance and a mass movement against religious fundamentalisms are the only ways out of the misuse of religious, caste, tribal and linguistic divisions in Indian politics.

Corruption

Corruption has been one of the major issues in Indian politics right from at least the early post-independence days. Initially, it was administrative corruption that figured prominently in the administrative reforms discourse, but, by the early 1970s, political corruption and the need to combat it moved to the forefront of the political discourse, when the *Nayanirman* movement in Gujarat and the JP (Jayaprakash Narayan) movement at the national level made it the focal point of protest. This subsequently snowballed into the anti-Emergency consolidation of non-Congress parties and movements into the formation of the Janata Party, and the first-ever unseating of the Congress government in New Delhi. The issue of political and administrative corruption epitomised by the Bofors and other deals for defence supplies, again, became the central issue in the electoral defeat of the Congress government of Rajiv Gandhi in 1989. Under pressure of the press and the parliament, the Congress minority government of P.V. Narasimha Rao, appointed in the early 1990s, an administrative committee headed by the then home secretary N.N. Vohra, to look into the problem in general. Its report emphasised the grim reality of the politician-bureaucrat-criminal nexus on a fairly large scale.[33] It is also evident from press reports that practically all parties, the more ideologically oriented left-wing CPI(M) and the right-wing BJP included, harbour criminals and underworld dons in their ranks. Moreover, in the 1990s, especially since the increased pace of economic liberalisation by the Rao government in 1991, there have occurred, with nauseating frequency, scams after scams that have involved both the Congress and non-Congress governments alike. The Joint Parliamentary Committee and the administrative, and judicial inquiries appear to make little progress and the political scene gets more murky. The stream of what W.H. Morris-Jones[34] called the 'saintly idiom' of political culture and leadership seems to have been depleted. It has been drawn into a pernicious nexus between business and politics of the reigning political establishment through a combination of intimidation and temptation. The only silver lining in this bleak scenario has been judicial activism in cases like the hawala scandal, where huge payments were made to leaders from practically all national parties (except for the communists and regional parties); and the payments made to the MPs of the Jharkhand Mukti Morcha allegedly to vote against the no-confidence motion against the Rao government in 1993, the fodder scam in Bihar, etc.

The issue of corruption predictably figured in all major party manifestos in 1996. While others proposed some specific measures against corruption, the CPI(M) preferred to set store by an appeal to the wisdom of the voter with a call to defeat the 'hawala government' of the Congress. The enactment of a Lokpal (Ombudsman) Bill, which would not spare even the prime minister, was an item that recurred in the BJP, Congress, Janata Dal and CPI manifestos. Some other items included by these parties, but not invariably by all, were legislations aimed at the conflict of interests between the public and personal lives of ministers and civil servants and the declaration of personal and family assets by public men on entering office.

The Common Approach and Minimum Programme of the United Front (1996) pledged its commitment to 'a corruption-free and clean administration.' It outlined the following specific measures of steps in this direction: (1) an expeditious Lokpal Bill covering the office of the prime minister as well: (2) a law requiring all MPs to declare their assets annually to the lokpal; (3) a review of the amendment in the Official Secrets Act, 1923, with a view to bring 'openess and transparency in governance'; (4) a speedy legislation on freedom of information to the people at all levels; (5) ministerial discretionary quotas of allotment of amenities to be abolished and replaced, but, where such quotas are absolutely necessary, a decision to be taken by a committee in accordance with published rules and guidelines and a publication of a quarterly of the decisions in a medium comparable to the gazette.[35]

Electoral Reforms

Going by the prevailing state of political parties and electoral malpractices, it is surprising that party and electoral reforms, especially the former, have received such scant attention. Almost all parties, except to some extent the communist parties and BJP, including the centrist and regional parties, are so blighted organisationally that any rigorous definition of parties would accept them with difficulty within its purview. These parties do have their constitutions but they are followed more in the breach than in the observance. They mostly operate with ad hoc committees appointed from the top. There is no proper audit and account of party finances. They are subjected to the personalised power of the party boss and some of them are afflicted also by dynastic domination. Local and constituency party organisations hardly exist nor do the rank and file have much say in the nomination of party candidates for elections. Lacking a strong ideological sense of direction, they are also afflicted with factionalism on non-issues and a politics of defection for ministerial positions and the scourge of bribes. Surprisingly, none of the party manifestos in 1996, addressed these problems, except for some bland and unspecified proposals for an amendment of the anti-defection law.

The issue of electoral reforms of sorts figured in manifestos of all parties in 1996, barring the Congress. In view of the fact that most parties referred approvingly to the Dinesh Goswami Committee constituted by the National Front government which submitted its report in May 1990, it would be appropriate to take a good look at its recommendations. The main points of suggested reforms may be summarised as follows:

1. A three-member Election Commission and appointment of the chief election commissioner in consultation with the chief justice of India and the leader of the opposition and the appointment of other election commissioners in consultation with the CEC.
2. A fresh delimitation of constituencies on the basis of the 1981 census and a rotation of seats reserved for SCs/STs.
3. Issuing of multi-purpose photo-identity cards to voters.
4. Disallowance of the contesting by candidates from more than two constituencies.
5. The raising of security deposits of independent candidates

and forfeiture of security deposits of all candidates failing to secure less than 1/4th of the votes polled.

6. A statutory status to the model code of conduct formulated by the Election Commission.
7. Introduction of the electronic-voting machine.
8. Legislative measures against booth-capturing, rigging and intimidation of voters.
9. Limited state funding in kind to recognised political parties, to begin with.
10. Transportation of voters, carrying of firearms, sale and distribution of liquor on poll day to be cognisable electoral offences in law.
11. Restriction of disqualification of candidates under the anti-defection law to voluntary resignation and violation of party whips only in the instances of vote of confidence, money bills and vote of thanks to the president.
12. A review of the electoral system by a standing committee of the parliament and by an expert committee.[36]

Not all these points were covered in the party manifestos here reviewed; themes were selectively included by different parties. Indeed, all these recommendations are worthy of serious consideration and thought.

Chapter V of the Dinesh Goswami Committee Report has made recommendations relating to political parties and candidates. The main reform here proposed is the deletion of section 29(A) of the Representation of the People Act, 1951, concerning registration of parties. The matter, instead, should be delegated to and solely decided by the Election Commission under the Election Symbols (Reservation and Allotment Order, 1968). The committee did not feel the necessity to recognise electoral alliances of political parties or to change the present procedure of allotment of symbols.[37]

Even the Goswami committee report does not address the full range of party reforms required to deal with the problems of party decay briefly mentioned above. The V.M. Tarakunde Committee on Electoral Reforms appointed by Jayaprakash

Narayan in August 1974 on behalf of the Citizens For Democracy, at least, partly addressed these problems though they had not become as acute then as they have, today.

An important recommendation of the Tarakunde committee was that there should be a law requiring all recognised political parties to keep audited accounts of sources of all income and details of expenditure, with false accounts being a punishable offence. More recently, a committee headed by Justice V.R. Krishna Iyer (Rtd.) recommended in May 1994, among other things, that a law should ensure inner-party democracy in all political parties. It also reiterated a legal sanction for proper audit and accounts. Besides, it proposed the appointment of a commissioner to examine and decide whether a political party was promoting communalism or was in any way acting against the Constitution.[38]

The Common Approach and Minimum Programme of the United Front (1996) promised a bill on electoral reforms 'reflecting the consensus already arrived at' to be introduced in the first budget session of the eleventh Lok Sabha.

Environment and Ecology

Concern for ecology and environment is steadily growing in India. But the issue did not seem to have featured in the party manifestos of 1996 in a big way, not even to the extent which was evident in the administration and the press. The manifestos of the Congress Party, CPI and Samata Party did not even mention it. Only the BJP, Janata Dal and CPI(M) manifestos devoted some space to the problem. The BJP promised to formulate a national environment policy seeking to strike a balance between development and ecology in consultation with the states. The Janata Dal manifesto emphasised the need for 'development to be sustainable and equitable' and 'in harmony with the environment.' It went on to say that 'the planning process must ensure long-term security of ecology, livelihood and community life for all sections of society.'[39] The CPI(M) manifesto laid stress on the integration of the environment policy with 'the needs of rapid and sustainable economic development.' It also promised, action against the illicit activities of contractors who were depleting forest resources, introduction of strict control of industrial pollution and technology hazardous to the health of workers and their neighbourhood and rehabilitation of persons displaced by development projects.[40] The CAMP of the United Front government (1996) combined the ideas expressed in the Janata Dal and CPI(M) manifestos. Besides, it proposed to recruit millions of young men and women, imbued with idealism, into a Development Corps to be deployed in public work such as afforestation, repairs of canals and waterways.

National Security and Foreign Policy

There was a remarkable consensus on foreign policy among parties in their manifestos for the 1996 elections. The broad areas of agreement included friendly relations with neighbours without compromising India's national integrity and security, the desirability of joining regional groupings and trading blocs, a refusal to yield to international pressure to sign the discriminatory Non-Proliferation Treaty and Comprehensive Test Ban Treaty, South-South Cooperation, reforms in the United Nations with a permanent seat for India in the Security Council, creation of a just and equitable international order and a foreign policy consistent with India's national interest. Besides, cultivation of good relations with the USA, Russia and China, along with other world and regional powers was also emphasised by almost all parties. The communist parties, however, cautioned against the imperialist US designs and made nostalgic references to the need to revive the Non-Aligned Movement. The BJP and JD also lamented the anti-India tenor of American foreign policy but favoured India's continuing the effort for good Indo-American relations without sacrificing India's vital national interest. The Janata Dal proposed the revival of the National Security Council formed in 1990 by the National Front government which was proposed to be replaced, by the Congress government in 1991, by a new system claimed to be more consistent with the parliamentary system of government. At the apex of the new institutional arrangement was the Cabinet Committee on National Security with three cabinet sub-committees on internal security, defence, and foreign policy. The CAMP of the United Front (1996) government did not diverge from the policy-frame outlined above. Its fine balancing was reflected, for example, in its resolve to strengthen the Non-Aligned Movement as also to participate in UNCTAD so that it could articulate the views of the developing countries.

Responses of Some Pressure Groups

Some interest groups keenly observed and evaluated manifestos of some of the major political parties from their own perspectives and widely publicised their assessment. For example, the Indian Council for Enviro-Legal Action (ICELA) passed an eight-point resolution backed by eminent environmentalists, jurists, doctors and scientists at a one-day national workshop on 'Hazardous Waste—A Major Threat to Life and Environment' held in New Delhi on 23 March 1996. One of the points in the resolution demanded inclusion of environmental protection as one of the main objectives in the manifestos of all parties. They also proposed that the union government should establish an Independent National Environment Commission headed by a judge from the Supreme Court and consisting of two technical experts to look into public grievances concerning controversial developmental projects. At the conference, the Magasaysay-Award-winning eminent lawyer, M.C. Mehta, emphasised the need for constituting the right to information and transparency in government decision making to ensure public participation and effective environment protection.[41]

Two major chambers of commerce and industry, FICCI and ASSOCHAM, also commissioned studies to scrutinise major party manifestos. Their main grievances against political parties related to the failure of the manifestos to squarely address the on-going economic reforms. The FICCI paper was critical that the manifestos lacked a 'well-honed' strategy for tackling fiscal deficit, the infusion of liquidity into the system, implementing reforms at the state level, privatisation of PSUs and the introduction of transparent, simplified, speedy and objective regulatory procedures for approval of projects involving foreign investment. 'Rhetoric on poverty alleviation or a deluge of semantics on employment generation', the FICCI analysis emphasised, 'are not enough to give a clear policy thrust to social issues.'[42]

The two apex chambers were also critical of the BJP manifesto, even though, they felt, that it was in some cases more specific on some economic issues (e.g., the setting up of a disinvestment commission for PSUs, raising of the income-tax exemption limit to Rs 60,000, etc), but it was also vague and very general in its approach on issue-specific measures such as abolition of double taxation on dividends and scrapping of the TDS which resulted in depletion of bank deposits and the methods needed to put an end to black money.[43]

Besides the industry, the National Academy of Agricultural Sciences made a vigorous attempt to get their demands included in the election manifestos of major parties. Releasing its document *An Agenda for Food-Secure India*, the eminent scientist Dr M.S. Swaminathan requested all parties to profess commitment to the end of hunger and malnutrition. The agenda demanded 'sustainable food security' and conservation of natural resources such as land, water, forests, bio-diversity, oceans and atmosphere.[44]

Conclusion

Our analysis, based on the manifestos of major national and regional parties in the 1996 Lok Sabha elections, examined the ideological spectrum of the Indian party system along the following dimensions: (1) federalisation and panchayati raj, (2) economic growth and liberalisation, (3) social sector and welfare, (4) secular-communal divide, (5) corruption, (6) electoral reforms, (7) environment and ecology, (8) national security and foreign policy, (9) responses to party manifestos by some pressure groups such as industrialists, agriculturists and environmentalists. Our study revealed a great deal of ideological convergence as well as persisting polarities. The programmatic centre, previously occupied by the Congress and Janata Dal, has considerably shrunk, with the Congress itself moving to the right on economic policies. However, despite the polarisation of the right and the left on economic issues (e.g., economic liberalisation and restructuring), common areas of agreement emerged as reflected in the CAMP of the United Front consisting of the Janata Dal and major communist and regional parties. The legislative coalition between the United Front government and the Congress supporting it from the parliamentary floor was also indicative of the same trend. Moreover, regionalisation of the party system, symptomatised by the rise of new regional parties and the continuing salience of the older regional parties as well as the emergence of state-autonomy demands and movements in different parties of the country, did not create insurmountable divisiveness in coalition-building and governance. Fundamental cleavages did, however, surface and continued in the party system in the 1990s on social and cultural issues symbolised by the Mandal and mandir-masjid issues. These deep cultural cleavages were contained by moving neither forward nor backward or maintaining a stand-off, but by judicial intervention and recourse to constitutional emergency in a state under president's rule (Article 356). The Indian parliamentary-federal democracy and its party system that made a transition from a one-party dominance to a multi-party system of polarised pluralism have successfully constitutionalised revolutionary communism. Their success in constitutionalising militant communalism is yet to be decisively demonstrated. We must keep our fingers crossed.

Notes

1. *The National Herlad*, New Delhi, 3 September 1996, LARRDIS newspapers clipping file no. 324 3B, Parliament Library.
2. *The Tribune*, 26 April 1996.
3. *The Hindustan Times*, 31 January 1996.
4. IIPA Library, New Delhi, press clippings file on political parties, newspaper's title illegible.
5. *The Hindustan Times*, 16 July 1996.
6. *The Statesman*, 12 April 1996.
7. *The Tribune*, 11 April 1996.
8. *The United Front Common Approach and Minimum Programme*, the text reprinted in *The Hindu*, New Delhi, 6 June 1996: 7.
9. *Ibid.*
10. Harish Khare, 'A New Deal in Federalism', *The Hindu*, 9 June 1996: 11.
11. cf., James Manor, 1995.
12. BJP, 1996, *Election Manifesto 1996*: 18.
13. INC, 1996, *Election Manifesto, General Election 1996*: 8–9 emphases added.
14. *Ibid*: 33.
15. *Ibid*: 27.
16. *Ibid*: 26.
17. *Ibid*: 14–15.
18. *Ibid*: 15.
19. CPI(M), 1996, *Manifesto, Eleventh Lok Sabha Elections*: 11.
20. Samata Party, *Manifesto 1996*: 4.
21. *Ibid*: 15.
22. *Ibid*: 15–16.
23. Lloyd Rudolph and Susanne H. Rudolf, 1987, *In Pursuit of Lakshmi: The Political Economy of the Indian State*: 49–55.
24. United Front Common Approach and Minimum Programme, 1996.
25. Samajwadi Party, 1996.
26. BSP, 1996, *Uttar Pradesh Vidhan Sabha Elections.*
27. BJP, 1996, *Election Manifesto 1996*: 64.
28. *Ibid*: 65.
29. *Ibid*: 64–65.
30. UF-CAMP, 1996, *New Age Weekly*: 7.
31. *Ibid.*

32. BJP, 1996, *Election Manifesto 1996*: 15.
33. Morris-Jones, 1967, *Politics: National and International*: ch. 2.
34. Vohra Committee Report, 1993.
35. UF-CAMP, 1996, *New Age Weekly*: 7.
36. *Report of the Committee on Electoral Reforms*, 1990: chaps. 2, 3, 4.
37. *Ibid*, ch. 5.
38. Lok Sabha Secretariat (1994).
39. Janata Dal, 1996, *Janata Dal Election Manifesto 1996*: 25.
40. CPI(M), 1996, *Manifesto: Eleventh Lok Sabha Elections*: 16.
41. *The Hindustan Times*, New Delhi, 24 March 1996, LAARDIS newspapers clipping file no. 324, 3B, Parliament Library.
42. *The Financial Express*, New Delhi, 19 April 1996; *The Pioneer*, New Delhi, 23 April 1996; LAARDIS, newspapers clippings file no. 324, 3B, Parliament Library.
43. *Ibid*.
44. *The Pioneer*, New Delhi, 25 March 1996, LARRDIS, newspaper clippings file no. 324, 3B, Parliament Library.

CHAPTER FIVE

Electoral Campaigns in 1996

An electoral campaign is a part of the broader strategies of political mobilisation, economic development and governance. Only it becomes intense and condensed around election time and zeroes in on the most salient issues, personalities and parties in the period of formal campaigning in the legally defined election schedule. Every action of a democratic government during its incumbency is motivated by electoral considerations, reaching an apogee in the period strategically close to the polling, often accompanied by the malaise of electoral bribing. Hence, the recent insistence of the Election Commission that governments ought to desist from their announcing welfare doles, laying foundations of construction projects and transferring or promoting officials immediately before elections. That decisions and non-decisions of governments do not go unnoticed and without response from voters is indicated by such psephological concepts as 'incumbency factor' (it could be both negative and positive, but in recent, Indian electoral experience it is mainly the former), 'bandwagon effect', etc.

The tendency for a campaign mentality to spill over and fill the entire space of an electoral mandate of five years has particularly heightened in the post-Nehru era. This has happened especially in two varying contexts since the 1970s. First, the Indira era heralded the onset of personalised plebiscitary elections marked by nationwide, uniform electoral waves or landslides. The uniformity of electoral response across the nation was, to be sure, also the hallmark of the Congress party under Nehru. But there was a difference. Congress dominance in the Nehru era was characterised by regularity of organisational elections in the party and autonomy of state legislatures and governments. By and large, Indira Gandhi changed all that and initiated some new trends besides. This is succinctly summarised by the Rudolphs:

> Instead, she tended to rely on plebiscitary methods: direct, unmediated mass appeals enabled by ample funds (often of dubious provenance) and government's monopoly over the electronic media, the national name, recognition and magic that the Nehru dynasty uniquely possesses, and the continuing but declining identification of Congress with both independence and *sarkar* (government in the generic sense).[1]

This directly led to the widely accepted thesis on the crisis of political institutions in the post-Nehru-Shastri era that followed the undoing of 'the remarkable institutionalisation of the party at the state and district levels that had been the distinguishing mark of the Congress since 1920, when Mohandas Gandhi built a political organisation unparalleled in the third-world countries.'[2]

In the altered context of the late 1980s to the mid-1990s, two additional factors contributed to the perpetual mobilisation and electoral campaign mentality of political parties: (1) the recency of the decline of Congress predominance and the ambition of all major parties to either re-establish or wrest power in the ensuing uncertainty; and (2) the onset of the era of minority or coalition governments, or both, with the Damocles' sword of governmental instability hanging over each government formed since 1989. Of the six governments sworn in during this period only one, the Congress government led by P.V. Narasimha Rao, could at the time of writing (January 1998) be said to have completed its mandate, that too by encouraging splits in other parties to swell its own parliamentary strength and alleged bribing of some opposition party MPs to vote for the government in a no-confidence motion in the parliament. One of these governments, all minority coalitions or single-party governments supported by some opposition parties from the parliamentary floor, lasted for about eleven months, one for four months, one for less than two weeks, one for ten months, and the last of these—the United-Front minority government headed by the Janata Dal's I.K. Gujral—for seven months, and finally around the end of the year they made way for the mid-term polls in early 1998.

One of the most important recent developments in the administration of elections has been the activist role of the Election Commission, first with the initiative of the chief election commissioner, T.N. Seshan, and subsequently jointly by Seshan and election commissioners, M.S. Gill and G.V.G. Krishnamurthy. They were added to the commission, despite the determined but abortive administrative and judicial fight put up by Seshan earlier, and who kept the ECs virtually without work for months together during the pendency of the case in the Supreme Court. Reversing its own judgment in S.S. Dhanoa vs. Union of India (1991), which had conceded that the CEC was more than just the first among the equals, the court ruled in the case of T.N. Seshan vs. Union of India (1995): 'If the CEC is considered to be superior in the sense that his word is final, he would render the ECs non-functional or ornamental. Such an intention is difficult to cull from Article 324.'

Much like judicial activism, the more autonomous and assertive role of the Election Commission may be attributed primarily to the transformation of the party system from one-party dominance to a multi-party configuration and the attendant federalisation and regionalisation of politics. The Election Commission, of course, has always enjoyed considerable autonomy under the Constitution as a federal agency independent of direct control of either the central or the state governments. However, in the era of one-party dominance, not all chief election commissioners were inclined to use the constitutional position and powers of the commission as assertively as Seshan did. Besides, the reluctance of successive governments to introduce comprehensive electoral and party reforms resulted in a veritable reduction of the whole electoral process to a farce because of corruption and criminalisation of politics. Without some reforms, a veritable collapse of the electoral system would have taken place.

The union government intended to reduce the election campaign period, in 1996, from 20 to 14 days by amending Section 30 of the Representation of the People Act, 1951, by a presidential ordinance. The government's case was premised on the recommendations of the Dinesh Goswami Committee on Electoral Reforms for shortening the campaign period in the interest of reducing electoral expenses. Also, according to the home ministry officials and security agencies, the move was likely to facilitate effective arrangement for VIP security and reduce pre-poll violence. The government's move was opposed by the JD, CPI and the CPI(M) in a memorandum to the president. The Election Commission also expressed its opinion against the idea on administrative grounds. It pleaded its inability to get the ballot papers ready and make other arrangements for the poll so soon. Finally, the idea was dropped.[3]

As in previous elections, the Election Commission arranged to prepare, in consultation with parties, a schedule for the broadcast and telecast of electoral campaigns by recognised political parties on AIR and DD by a draw of lots. The campaign on these media commenced on 11 and 15 April, respectively. Each party was allotted 15 minutes to get its message across the nation. The commission also used the DD and AIR to promote public awareness about various candidates in the field and the do's and don'ts of correct voter behaviour. The commission was particularly concerned about the lack of sufficient information about the candidates and the rules, owing to an unusually low-key campaign, a fallout of strict enforcement of the election expenditure ceiling as well as the Supreme Court's then ruling which insisted that the above ceiling included the expenditure incurred by the candidates as well as his parties.

The Election Commission pressed into service a team of 1,500 observers equipped with video cameras and other gadgets who were to travel all over the country to monitor the campaign for possible violation of election laws and regulations and the model code of conduct. The commission also ordered the chief electoral officers of the states and the union territories to ensure video recording of 'critical events' for evidence.[4]

The Election Commission's *Model Code of Conduct for the Guidance of Political Parties and Candidates* (1991) enjoins guidelines upon all concerned, with a view to ensure a clean and orderly campaign and peaceful conduct of the polls. It covers what parties and candidates say of each other, meetings, processions, do's and don'ts on the polling day and at polling booths. It draws attention to the appointment of observers by the commission throughout the country and encourages the contestants to bring any specific complaints to its notice. It takes the convenience of citizens into account in order to protect them from noise pollution, prevent the use of their walls and premises for unwanted posters and hoardings, and to prevent traffic jams resulting from political processions. For the party in power, the model code of conduct exhorts ministers not to use their official tours for their electioneering work and to avoid using the official machinery from the time of announcement of the poll schedule by the commission. The government shall not:

(a) Announce any financial grants in any form or promises thereof; or
(b) Lay foundation stones, etc, of projects of schemes of any kind; or
(c) Make any promise of construction of roads, provision of drinking-water facilities, etc; or
(d) Make any ad hoc appointments in government, public undertakings, etc, which may have the effect of influencing the votes in favour of the party in power.[5]

The code is also against the use of discretionary grants by ministers and monopolisation of open public spaces, rest houses, etc, and advertisements in the mass media at the cost of the public exchequer.

This code of conduct was evolved by the Election Commission with the consensus of the recognised political parties. It is obviously based on public morality and ethics. It does not have legal sanction, except for the actions that lead to a breach of some public law. Thanks to the vigilance and assertiveness of the Election Commission in recent elections, the code of conduct is now being taken more seriously by parties and candidates.

BJP Campaign

While *bandhs* and rallies have, over time, become widely used methods of electoral campaigns and political mobilisation in general, *yatras* or *rathyatras* in the 1990s are a distinctively BJP contribution to mass politics and go beyond the election period in the armoury of political parties in India. Besides their vague association with ancient, Vedic symbolism of *ratha* (chariot) and pious, traditional activity of *teerthayatra* (pilgrimage), the BJP yatras, done in cosy cars suitably bedecked by the top leadership of the party, cover long distances involving thousands of miles and large segments of the public. The *surajya* (good government) rathayatra mounted for the 1996 Lok Sabha election campaign was flagged off by Vajpayee in Ernakulam in Kerala on 9 March and ended at the Delhi-Gurgaon (Haryana) border on 23 March. The second leg of the surajya yatra began after 6 April, the last day for the withdrawal of applications, and covered the five Hindi-speaking states, which is the region of greater electoral success for the party as well as the site of the demolished Babri mosque and the proposed Ram temple.

A low water-mark of the surajya yatra was its passage through Andhra Pradesh. In the course of his drive through nine Lok Sabha constituencies in seven districts, Advani made over 30 stops for public meetings and receptions. But unlike the *janadesh* (mandate) yatra of September 1993, through 10 districts, when the people had turned up even at midnight whistle stops, the response this time was disappointing. Reference to the hawala scandal and other national issues evoked poor response. Advani attempted to make amends by raising local issues at the prompting of state leaders.[6]

A reference may also be made here to the *parivartan* (change) yatra of the Shiv Sena-BJP government in Maharashtra led by the then chief minister, Murli Manohar Joshi, and deputy chief minister Gopinath Munde that culminated in a rally in the Shivajee Park in Mumbai on 16 March. It was organised on the first anniversary of this government's being in power and thus had broken the hold of the Congress for the first time in the state. The poor public response to it was explained away by the dismayed organisers in terms of complacent planning, the absence of crowd-pullers like Bal Thackeray and Vajpayee, the world cup matches and the mistake made in not choosing Chaupaty as the venue. The absence of Thackeray and Vajpayee and others was presumably intended to convey the autonomy of the Maharashtra government and the legislative wing from national and state party organisational bosses of the BJP and Shiv Sena.

In addition to candidates and campaign workers of the BJP, the party's electioneering was joined by the Vishwa Hindu Parishad, especially women, using emotive issues such as Kashivishwanath and Krishna temples at Varanasi and Mathura, respectively, and cow-slaughter. About 5,000 VHP and vahini activists were to campaign in Uttar Pradesh alone and about 1,000 in Gujarat. Other states that were to be intensively covered were Madhya Pradesh and Rajasthan which were already receptive to the RSS and BJP.[7] Electronic mass media reports also suggested and which was also confirmed by the rebel, Gujarat BJP leader, Shankarsinh Vaghela, that the RSS and VHP activists had campaigned against him in reprisal for his factional activities in the state culminating in the fall of the Keshubhai Patel government and its replacement by a successor BJP government led by Suresh Chandra Mehta after a prolonged reconciliatory effort by Vajpayee.

The BJP campaign in Delhi's seven parliamentary constituencies was conducted by, besides the generally illustrious candidates and Delhi state party leaders, Vajpayee and the film actor and newly elected Rajya Sabha member, Shatrughan Sinha, the latter on the penultimate day of canvassing. Thanks to the Election Commission, Delhi's walls were spared the usual war of posters and cutouts of candidates, and its citizens, the noise of loudspeakers. Some press reports referred ruefully to a 'campaign without frills, thrill, frolic, mirth and revelry' this time, noting that only Sushma Swaraj's and Manoj Prabhakar's canvassing managed to be somewhat more colourful and provided some flavour of the pre-Seshan elections. In the local campaign there was greater accent on *padayatras* (walks), *nukkad* (street-corner) meetings, and door-to-door contact than rathayatras and business-like car drives. To advertisements in the print and electronic mass media were added 'telelinks' in the capital where people could dial in to know about any party's view on different issues.

An RSS meeting on 6 March 1996 in Delhi, attended by other members of the Sangh Parivar such as the VHP, Bajrang Dal, Swadeshi Jagaran Manch, and chaired by sarsanghachalak Rajendra Singh, decided to project its distinctive ideology in a concerted attempt to emphasise Hindutva and acknowledge Advani as the leader.[8] The BJP made it known that it intended to play the Ram mandir card again. The party identified five principal campaign issues for the second leg of Advani's (the party president) surajya yatra in the Hindi-heartland: (1) Hindutva, (2) Ram temple in Ayodhya, (3) Vajpayee as prime minister, (4) national security lapses of the Rao regime, and (5) plight of farmers and the promise to restore farm subsidies.[9]

Congress Campaign

The Congress campaign was marked by a series of meetings in the party chaired by Rao at the AICC office and addressed by Ahmed Patel, one of the party's general secretaries. A Sankalp rally, addressed by Rao, was held in the Red Fort grounds in

Delhi, and electioneering exercises across the nation were pursued by Rao and some other important leaders. The Delhi campaign was virtually launched by flagging off a procession by general secretary, B.P. Maurya, which went through the areas of outer Delhi and culminated at the Red Fort for the Sankalp Rally on 24 March. The conveyor of this rally was the Congress candidate from the outer-Delhi Lok Sabha constituency, Sajjan Kumar. Rao in his speech at the rally emphasised the positive aspects of the economic and political achievements of his administration and the welfare schemes for the people. Hoardings, banners, and cutouts of Nehru, Indira Gandhi, Rajiv Gandhi and predictably Rao were much in evidence through the route and at the venue of the rally. Public enthusiasm was, however, reportedly missing.[10] Other notable rallies included the ones addressed by Rao at Kurukshetra in Haryana, Udaipur in Rajasthan, Berhampur in Orissa and the Lucknow rally organised by the UPCC president, Jitendra Prasada and his cohorts in Begam Hazrat Mahal Park. Stability and development were the main themes of the Congress campaign. 'Give me stability, I will give you prosperity', Rao often proclaimed. The labour cell of Delhi Pradesh Youth Congress mounted the *yuvashakti rath* to garner support for all the seven Congress candidates in Delhi.

Video and print media were apparently more extensively used by the Congress in their campaign than the other parties. The Pradesh Congress Committee presidents were called to a meeting at the AICC office in New Delhi on 13 February and were supplied with audio and video cassettes in Hindi and ten other languages. At the two-day District Congress Committee President's meeting in New Delhi, each participant was given 125 audio and video cassettes. In November in the previous year, Pranab Mukherjee and V.N. Gadgil had instructed party organisations in different states to recommend a list of newspapers in which Congress-campaign advertisements in Hindi and other Indian languages could be published.[11]

Besides these activities above, the intensive campaigning in the constituencies was apparently carried out by individual candidates. Public meetings, door-to-door contact, padayatras, grievance-hearing sessions, etc, all formed part of the canvassing. One of the highlights of the Congress campaign, as also of some other parties, was the wooing of the voters by film stars such as Dilip Kumar, Sunil Dutt, Jitendra, and Rajesh Khanna with his wife and daughter. As in the previous recent elections, the Congress campaign also relied on some reputed professional advertisement agencies. It is difficult to measure the actual impact of celluloid campaigning and the role of advertisement agencies in the absence of the relevant survey data. Broadly, it reflects the failure of the party organisations and leaders and their resorting to these short-cuts in an attempt to succeed. Ironically, the role of the celluloid factor in politics in the north was apparently not as pervasive as in the south. This may presumably be for the reason that the Hindi-film industry seems to be less rooted in the culture of the north than the film industry of the south. The former tends to become more cosmopolitan and commercial. The Bengali film industry appears to be more authentically rooted in the cultural ethos of its region, but it generally eschews direct political involvement.

Janata Dal Campaign

With the National Front being defunct for years, dialogues among the JD, Left Front and some regional parties resulted in piecemeal but conflicting electoral alliances. It tried to orchestrate some semblance of coherence on issues, which was reflected in a belated common appeal to the electorate. It emphasised concern over communalism, price-rise, privatisation and the failure to enact a Lokpal Bill. But the various parties of the third force did not do any appreciable amount of joint campaigning. Individual parties mostly campaigned on their own in their respective areas of influence and power depending on their own available resource of leadership. In Andhra Pradesh, the Left parties decided to ally with the TDP (Naidu), while the Janata Dal allied with the TDP (Lakshmi Parvathi). The Left parties were concerned about the split in the TDP and the breakdown of the SP-BSP understanding. But their anxiety and efforts, if any, to improve the situation in this regard did not yield any results. In Tamil Nadu, a combination of the MDMK, JD and CPI(M) was formed and efforts were being made to bring in the Indira Congress, PMK and CPI. The idea was to put up a concerted fight against the Congress-AIADMK alliance, which was weakened by the revolt of a rebel Congressmen in the state who floated a separate regional party, the Tamil Maanila Congress, to protest against Rao's decision to ally with Jayalalitha despite the expressed views of the majority faction of the party led by P. Chidambaram and G.K. Moopanar. There was also talk of the Indira Congress being admitted into the National Front, as the party was already cooperating with the NF-LF in various states. The CPI(M) continued to keep the Indian National Muslim League led by Ibrahim Sulaiman Sait in Kerala at arm's length, for, as the CPI(M) general secretary, Harkishan Singh Surjeet said, his party would not join hands with communal parties.[12]

The assembly elections of 1993, indicated the decimation of the Janata Dal and its slide from the position of being second after the Congress, which was the largest, but, often not the majority party. Of the three Janata-ruled states, only Bihar re-elected a Janata government for a second time in 1994, the first one being in 1990. Karnataka was lost to the Congress in 1995, but, was regained in 1994 and in Orissa, too, the Janata Dal yielded the reins of power to the Congress in 1995. Prospects for the JD looked better in the run-up to the 1996 Lok Sabha elections, for, besides the Karnataka and Bihar gains, the Left persisted in its effort to bring Mulayam Singh Yadav back to the Janata parivar and keep the myth of the NF-LF alliance going despite the evident disintegration of the National Front.

For observers, accustomed to the presence of centralised all-India parties dominating the parliamentary scene, the Janata Dal (and, for that matter, the communist parties, but the former even more so) appears like an aberration. This was not only because of the lack of full integration despite a formal merger, among the four (later five) constituent parties that formed the Janata Party in the backdrop of the Emergency and the imminent 1977 elections, it was even more so because of the growing regionalisation of the JD to such an extent that its ruling state units operated practically independently of its national organisation, whose activities were minimal and intermittent.

Having lost power in Orissa in the previous year, the 1996 campaign of the Janata Dal appeared lacklustre. Some of its leaders left for 'greener pastures' and it was afflicted with bitter factional fights between its patriarch, Biju Patnaik, and greenhorn, Srikant Jena. The former, chargesheeted by the successor Congress government in two cases, complained: 'We don't have the kind of money the Congress have.' The JD was in alliance with the CPI. The Congress braved it alone, but the BJP withdrew its candidate from Berhampur, where Prime Minister Rao was seeking election from a second constituency besides Nandayal in his home state, Andhra Pradesh.[13]

The Janata Dal in Karnataka launched its campaign in Bangalore on 5 April 1996, with the state unit leaders' invoking divine grace in three temples. H.D. Deve Gowda confided that he had worshipped in the name of 'Karnataka Praja' (people of Karnataka). The JD state unit president, C.M. Ibrahim, defended temple visits as an act of self-purification before seeking the people's mandate.[14] The national JD campaign may be said to have been kicked off in Patna on 18 March 1996 at the mega 'Garib rally' where besides its national party president, Laloo Prasad Yadav, others such as V.P. Singh, Deve Gowda, R.K. Hegde, Ram Vilas Paswan, S.R. Bommai addressed the impressive gathering in the Gandhi Maidan. The JD leaders at the rally were joined by Chaturanan Mishra of the CPI and H.S. Surjeet of the CPI(M). Festivity and hundreds of welcome arches throughout the city marked the procession and the rally, though the crowd was smaller than some recent public meetings organised by the JD chief minister of Bihar. The audience also appeared to be restive and largely indifferent to speeches. A couplet recited at the rally reads as follows:

> *Bahaar ho Barsaat ho; garmi ho ya thanda*
> *Lal Kila par 15 August ko Laloo fahrayega jhanda.*[15]

The Patna rally was followed by another national rally addressed by Yadav and other leaders of the JD. The theme which marked the entire campaign of Yadav in Bihar, was his asking the electorate to vote for him to enable him to become the prospective prime minister of India. For the JD campaign in Bihar, especially in towns and road-side villages, Yadav 'conjured up a low-budget circus of sorts, complete with parrots, elephants, camels and dwarfs.'[16]

With the most popular JD national leader, V.P. Singh, first opting out of the race (until December 1999) and subsequently agreeing to only minimally canvas in U.P. and elsewhere, the main burden of whatever can be said to be the JD national campaign (outside its three regional strongholds in Bihar, Karnataka, and Orissa) fell on Yadav. Besides covering all the 54 constituencies in Bihar in 10 days, Yadav's campaign trail included Uttar Pradesh, Madhya Pradesh, Karnataka and West Bengal. Remarked a close observer:

> A marked change in the JD leader's campaign this time is the toning down of his earlier anti-upper-caste rhetoric. Besides, as the JD president, Laloo has to tread carefully this time and take the National Front-Left Front (NF-LF) constituents along with him if he is serious about the 'march to Delhi.' In keeping with his latest slogan, he tells his electorate that if the NF-LF were to come to power, Dalits and Backwards would rule the country for the first time.[17]

Left-Front Campaign

Despite being all-India parties, the campaigns of the major communist parties appeared to be basically regionally oriented, their spheres of influence or power being restricted to West

Bengal, Kerala, Tripura and Bihar (in case of the CPI). But, the CPI(M) general secretary, Harkishan Singh Surjeet made greater efforts to transcend regional boundaries. The lesser left parties were even more region-bound. Not that the communists lacked ambition to acquire national power. It was rather the trend in electoral politics in the country that kept them confined to areas of their initial successes. Their plans to extend operations beyond, since the first Congress debacle at the centre in 1977, did not take them very far. But the Left Front enjoyed an unbroken spell of power in West Bengal since 1977, and has held power alternately with others in Kerala and Tripura.

The CPI(M) campaign in West Bengal started earlier than those of other parties, beginning with street-corner meetings and going on to big rallies. The campaign mainly emphasised the achievements of the Left Front government and decried the hawala scam and the new economic policy. Its objective was to stall the division of the anti-Congress and anti-BJP vote.[18] The Left Front's main anti-Congress refrain in elections since the 1970s has been Siddartha Shankar Ray's 'murderous rule in West Bengal'. With Ray himself in the field after his stint as India's ambassador to the USA and facing the opposition of the Naxalite factions of some influence in the district of his Berhampur constituency, 'the LF's campaign' 'acquired an extra edge.'[19]

Some hurried, pre-emptive decisions taken by the Left Front government, before the formal notification of elections dates by the Election Commission and done, possibly, to prevent action by the commission, revealed a shrewd grasp of the political scenario. Thus, about 4,50,000 government employees and about the same number of school teachers, municipal and corporation staff were paid a long-delayed dearness allowance. Several lakh pensioners were granted enhanced pension. And, about 40,000 group D casual employees were regularised.[20]

The Left Democratic Front in Kerala was initially handicapped a bit by a split in its Janata Dal allies, but the rebels were won over and the Front stayed unified in the campaign.

The Congress-led United Democratic Front, on the other hand, remained bedevilled by the Antony-Karunakaran rift. Besides, the electricity crisis affecting the industries and domestic users also worked against the incumbent LDF government in a state where the electorate had invariably alternated parties in recent elections. The Nairs who have traditionally voted for the Congress and UDF appeared during the campaign inclined to vote for the LDF this time. The organisation of fisherfolk, All Kerala Dheevara Sabha, headed by V. Dinakaran withdrew its support to UDF, owing to, on available indications, the Antony-Karunakaran feud. Dinakaran who is considered particularly close to union minister, K. Karunakaran, and the chief minister, A.K. Antony, contested from Shertallai, where the Dheevar Sabha reputedly controlled a 50,000 vote-bank. The LDF also tried to dent the upper-caste vote of the Congress by promising 10 per cent reservation for the economically poor, irrespective of caste.[21] Parliamentary and assembly elections were held simultaneously in Kerala and the campaign appeared to be going well for the LDF at both the levels.[22]

In Tripura, the ruling CPI(M) in power at the state and district levels, activated its cadres in towns and remote villages for its campaign. But a sort of vacuum was created at the highest level of leadership, when the former chief minister, Nripen Chakraborty, was expelled and the then present chief minister and legendary tribal leader, Dasarath Deb, was rendered less active owing to his prolonged illness. This was the first test of the greenhorn, young leadership of the party. The party campaigns were held in the shadow of the Congress sweep in the recent municipal elections in the state capital bagging 14 out of 17 seats. However, the Congress was beset with factionalism and its erstwhile ally in state politics, TUJS, had recently broken the 14-year alliance. Other all-India parties such as the BJP, JD and Indira Congress (Tewary) did not have much of a base in the state, but they hoped to gain some manoeuvrability if the contest between the two major parties was going to be a closely fought one.[23]

TDP Campaign

In Andhra Pradesh, the election campaign was dominated by the issue of the inheritance of the NTR legacy between the two TDP factions. NTR's son-in-law chief minister, Chandrababu Naidu, and NTR's widowed, second wife, Lakshmi Parvathi, fought fiercely over the legacy, even though it was the former's revolt that had led to the fall of the NTR government and installation of a new one led by Naidu in August 1995. The Naidu party gave preference in ticket distribution to backward-caste candidates, while the Parvathi party preferred upper-caste Reddys and Kammas. In the campaign, Naidu was able to press into service a vibrant party organisation which assigned responsibilities to the MLAs in overseeing the electioneering. It also seemed to have enough funds. An experienced political manipulator, Naidu was also backed by his CPI and CPI(M) alliance partners. Lacking adequate funds and experience in politics, Parvathi's campaign was less organised but more eloquent, counting on public sympathy as the widow of NTR. The support of the electoral allies such as the JD and Naxalite People's War Group were either too distant or irrelevant in electoral politics.[24] Both groups kicked off their campaign from Tirupathi ceremoniously and went on to enlist the services of filmstars. The N. Taraka Rama Rao *Chaitanaya Ratham* and the *Praja Chaitanaya Ratham* of the Parvathi group rolled out a month ahead of Naidu's hectic helicopter electioneering, 'but (the latter) failed to match the excitement stirred up by Parvathi's campaign.'[25]

DMK-Tamil Maanila Congress Campaign

The electoral campaign in Tamil Nadu was described by one observer as 'by far the most exciting electoral potboiler', with a veteran film script-writer engaged in a fight to the finish with the prima donna of the Tamil screen of yesteryears. Going by the turnout of crowds during the campaign, one could see that Karunanidhi had already won half the battle. The Karunanidhi-led DMK's prospects, were further improved by an almost total desertion of the state Congress unit which was rebelling against Prime Minister Rao's decision, in the face of opposition by the dominant faction in the state unit, to align with Jayalalitha's AIADMK. The Congress rebels led by G.K. Moopanar and P. Chidambaram floated a regional party called Tamil Maanila Congress (TMC) and quickly forged an alliance with the DMK. If Jayalalitha had emerged as the inheritor of the MGR legacy, Karunanidhi was the survivor of two major splits in the original DMK, including the one in the 1970s that led to the formation of the AIADMK by M.G. Ramachandran. Jayalalitha was vitiated by, the reputation of her leading an allegedly corrupt and inefficient government, her arrogant ways with party managers and alliance partners, a perceived anti-Dalit image and her poor campaign skills. The DMK campaign was strengthened by the skilful oratory of Karunanidhi and the backing of filmstar, Rajnikant, whose fan clubs were active in the DMK-led front poll campaign and who had a sway over the young voters. Its weak points were Karunanidhi's past unpopularity with sections of the electorate, his inclination to politically favour his son M.K. Stalin, the relative unfamiliarity of the TMC's electoral symbol in rural areas and apprehension of the dividing of the anti-DMK vote by other fronts.[26]

Samajwadi Party Campaign

The Samajwadi Party of Mulayam Singh Yadav in Uttar Pradesh in the 1993 assembly elections had strenuously resisted pressure to join forces with the Janata Dal, and the Congress had hurriedly extended support from outside to the SP-BSP minority-coalition government, while the BJP provided the main opposition. By June 1995, the SP-BSP relations had soured and the BSP broke away from the SP to form its own exclusive minority government backed by the BJP from the legislative floor. Since his ouster from power, Yadav toured 28 of the 66 districts of U.P. and held fairly impressive rallies there. During this election, the SP finally decided to join forces with the Janata parivar with persuasion, among others, from the national leaders of the Left Front. Observers noted that the SP campaign had a headstart over other parties and its candidate could hope to benefit by the consolidation of the OBC-Muslim vote-bank, thanks to the SP-JD alliance.[27]

Haryana Vikas Party Campaign

The Haryana Vikas Party had to contend with three other contenders in the state—the Congress, Samata Party and BJP. The Congress, ruling the state at the time of the election, was led by Bhajan Lal. Initially, a minister in the Janata Dal government of Devi Lal in the state in the late 1970s, Bhajan Lal manouevred himself to become the Janata Party chief minister of Haryana, and later when the Congress government of Indira Gandhi returned to power in New Delhi, he managed to take almost his entire cabinet and legislature party into the Congress. The erstwhile Samajwadi Janata Party, led in the state by Devi Lal (former Lok Dal/JD chief minister of Haryana and JD deputy prime minister) and at the centre by Chandrashekhar (former BJP prime minister), merged with the Samata Party just before the 1996 Lok Sabha elections. The antecedents of the Samata Party, like that of the Samajwadi Janata Party, go back to the Janata Party/Dal. The Haryana Vikas Party entered the electoral fray in 1996, under the leadership of Bansi Lal, the Congress chief minister of Haryana during the Emergency and a close associate of Sanjay Gandhi. Bhajan Lal, a Vishnoi, and Devi Lal and Bansi Lal, both Jats, have changed parties, perhaps more than once, but retained a sizeable group of personal followers in moving from one party to another. Bansi Lal was tainted by his association with the authoritarian excesses of the Emergency regime (1975–77), but was perceived to be an effective administrator. Devi Lal came under a cloud when chargesheeted by the CBI with regard to the hawala scandal and his son, Om Prakash Chautala's infamous regime as the JD chief minister from 1989–90, which was marked by the Meham electoral scandal and his uncalled for arbitrary ways while in power. Bhajan Lal gave the state a stable government, but his regime is perceived to be highly corrupt. The BJP, which has come to acquire a pervasive presence in the Hindi heartland, has not crossed into the Haryana borders in a significant way. The HVP in this election, however, entered into an alliance with the BJP. Ironically, the Samata Party in Haryana was not aligned with the BJP, though the party's Bihar unit was.

Though the issues of governmental performance—past and present—were very much evident in the Haryana campaign, an instantly popular issue that had evoked the greatest public response was the total prohibition promised by both the HVP and Samata Party. It seemed targetted positively at the women voters but it was also negatively directed at the Congress chief minister, whose son-in-law owned the largest group of distilleries in the state. There is an element of personalism in the Devi Lal-Chautala campaign, as the patriarch made an emotional appeal to the people to fulfil his last political ambition of seeing his eldest son rule Haryana again.[28]

The Jats, who form 30 per cent of the state's population, are a dominant landowning caste with a fair measure of education among them. According to a close observer of the campaign:

> Conscious of the fact that the split in the Jat votes will go in the chief minister's favour, Chautala, like Bhajan Lal is going all out to woo the other castes, though both are claiming that the elections will be won on the issues of crime and corruption. While Chautala is targetting the Backward Castes, promising to give plots to those who are economically backward, Bhajan Lal has been touring the state addressing Brahmin, Rajput, Kashyap and Punjabi sammelans.[29]

Bansi Lal perhaps carried an aura of wider appeal to Hindu identity because of the HVP's alliance with the BJP. The HVP-BJP alliance won and formed the government following the elections.

Akali Dal Campaign

Contrary to the usually fractious nature of the Shiromani Akali Dal with often as many as half a dozen splinters, the party entered the parliamentary election fray in 1996, with all factions of the Akali parivar, except the secessionist Simranjit Singh Mann group, united under the moderate leadership of Prakash Singh Badal, the former Akali chief minister of Punjab. The Mann group had won the previous Lok Sabha elections and all Akali factions had boycotted the last assembly polls won by the Congress, whose regime is credited with restoring peace in the militancy-infested state. The United Badal Akalis were this time campaigning in alliance with the BSP (a rather new party that had considerably cut into the sizeable scheduled-caste segments of the Congress support-base) and the BJP (that thrives on the urban Hindu vote). The Badal Akali's ties with both these parties were not compatible with the image and ideology of the party. For, traditionally, Akalis have been a party mainly of the prosperous Jat peasants and farmers and they have been advocates for a special status for the Sikhs and for a federal structure with greater state autonomy. The main campaign planks of the Akalis were corruption and human-rights violations during the Congress regime, and a better deal for farmers; even Mann was discreet in his electioneering, 'driving through the villages, talking of issues that have never dominated the election scene in Punjab.' The Congress campaign took credit for its role in restoring peace to Punjab and blamed the Akalis for religious communalism and supporting the terrorists.[30]

Asom Gana Parishad Campaign

Originating in the anti-foreigners (mainly Bangladeshi and Nepali) and anti-migrant (from other Indian states) movement that gathered momentum in the late 1970s and early 1980s and that engulfed the state through direct action, protest and terrorism (verging on separatism), the AGP was an instant success in the 1985 elections that dislodged the Congress. The elections and the peace accord with the centre (1985) restored democratic processes in the state, but the AGP regime was plagued by the ULFA terrorists and factionalism and splits in the ruling party. In the election that followed in 1991, the AGP government was replaced by the Congress, and its parliamentary contingent also suffered in the hands of the latter.

This time round, the AGP-led Left alliance, bickerings notwithstanding, emerged as a formidable challenge to the Congress which bore the blame for the lack of full implementation of the Assam accord and death on the saddle of chief minister, Hitendra Saikia, though in the penultimate phase of the campaign. Comments an observer:

> Things look brighter for the Left alliance this time since the AGP has decided to underplay the problem of illegal Bangladeshi migration into the state. The party manifesto talks of national unity, peace and communal harmony. This had come as a relief to the CPI(M), which was concerned that the hardline stand on this issue could cost the Left Front the Muslim vote.[31]

The campaign of almost all parties seemed to be carried out by state leaders, except for CPI(M) leaders like Surjeet and Sitaram Yechuri who made frequent visits to the state.

Campaigning in Jammu and Kashmir

The belated but long campaign (polling being in the last phase) in the state, especially in the valley, was carried out in the midst of tight security but rare transparency. The concern initially focussed more on whether polling could be held at all and whether the people would participate, rather than on the prospective winners. The dominant regional party, the National Conference, declared its non-participation in the elections unless the pre-1953 situation was conceded by the centre for the state.

But several militant-turned anti-insurgency groups came forward for talks with the government and joined the electoral fray. Three distinct anti-insurgency groups were reportedly active, the leading one among them being the Awami League of Kukka Parray that fielded candidates in all the three parliamentary constituencies in the valley. The Pandits, who migrated to other parts of India during the seven-year militancy in the state; held 96,000 votes in the three constituencies and is a reflection of the tragic dimension of the polls in the state. Their votes could be split among the Awami League, BJP and Congress. Other parties in the fray included the JD, CPI, Panthers Party and BSP.[32] A successful parliamentary election earlier had paved the way for assembly elections in the state under the extended president's/governor's rule since the National Conference government headed by Dr Farooq Abdullah was dismissed by New Delhi following the intensification of militancy in the state in the wake of a change of guard in New Delhi and Srinagar in 1989.

Aggregation

Before concluding this chapter, we take an integrated view of electoral alliances among parties in the 1996 elections, and of the relative standing of parties and fronts in relation to the final outcome. Table 5.1 shows the patterns of electoral alliances among the all-India parties and those between national and regional or state parties. The Congress and the BJP were more isolated than the Janata Dal and the communist parties, though the ones with relative isolation were also the biggest two parties of the system. Broadly, the configuration yielded three major groupings, leaving aside limited alliances among the BSP and Akali Dal (Badal) in Punjab, the BSP and JD in Madhya Pradesh, the communists with the AGP in Assam and the TDP (Naidu) in Andhra Pradesh, the JD and TDP (Parvathi) in Andhra Pradesh.

TABLE 5.1
Party Alliances in the 1996 Elections

Party	*Allies*	*State*
Congress	AIADMK	Tamil Nadu
BJP	Samata Party	Bihar, but not Haryana
	HVP	Haryana
	Shiv Sena	Maharashtra
Janata Dal	Samajwadi Party	Uttar Pradesh
	Left parties	National, but not AP
BSP	Akali Dal (Badal)	Punjab
	JD	Madhya Pradesh
Indira Congress	DMK (likely)	Tamil Nadu
Left parties	AGP	Assam

Source: Yubraj Ghimire, 'Alliances: Principles Be Damned', *Outlook*, 10 April 1996: 19.

The conventional Right, Centre, Left, ideological labels have already broken down. There are difficulties in continuing to treat the Congress and JD as centrist parties as such, though the right-wing BJP and left-wing communists present less of such problems of characterisation. The centrist tenors of the Congress and JD on many issues continue, but the Congress has significantly moved to the Right on the issue of economic liberalisation. The economic policies of the communist parties today are the only reminders of the Nehru-Indira era. The JD harks back to the importance of kisans and the rural bias in the Gandhian ideology. The communists have become more socially democratised than in the past, but retain their pro-working class ethos. The BJP's swadeshi has a strong pro-middle class bias and its adherence to Hindutva is more dogmatic, but, not lacking in pragmatic secularism. Even regional parties in 1996, were less aggressively oriented towards the federal arrangement in the 1950 Constitution than they were, for instance, in the 1980s. The manifestos of some parties in that decade and the memoranda and submissions of regional parties and state governments to the Sarkaria Commission on Centre-State

Relations (contained in volume 2 of its report) were much more autonomist than the manifestos of parties and fronts in 1996.

An assessment of the relative positions of the Congress, BJP and NF-LF through three phases—pre-campaign, campaign and post-campaign—by Prannoy Roy and Dorab Sopariwala show fairly differentiated patterns. The Congress(I) was at pains to negotiate with the others but found few parties—it could ally within the first phase. The position of the BJP was more or less similar in this phase. The NF-LF, despite their failures in maintaining alliances in the past ended up having coalitions with the largest assortment of parties. In the second phase, during the campaign, the Congress was handicapped in their lacking charismatic vote-getters, whereas the BJP was on a strong innings with Vajpayee (and we may add Advani) and the party (and we may add RSS) cadres. With an array of charismatic regional leaders, the National Front in their assessment was on the strongest ground. In the post-election coalition building for the formation of the government, the Congress was seen by them to be in the strongest position, as it needed only 180 seats more from the others to take it to the majority position. The BJP was rated the weakest, and the NF-LF was also considered weak in this regard, riddled as it was with numbers and internal differences. As it turned out, the Congress did not stake a claim to form a government, the BJP made a government but it fell in the motion of confidence, and a new coalition calling itself the UF took over.

Since 1971, all parliamentary elections until the 1989 one were dominated by overriding national issues and some sort of electoral wave across the country. Those were plebiscitary elections with single symbolic issues encompassing anti-establishment negative votes. In 1971, it was Indira Gandhi's electoral plank of *garibi hatao* that cast aside the old-guard Congress party bosses. In 1977, it was the anti-Emergency plebiscite that won an electoral landslide for the Janata Party. In 1980, it was Indira Gandhi's promise of a 'government that works' and her directing attention to the continuous factional feuding and anti-Indira obsession as the only agenda of the

TABLE 5.2
Relative Position of Parties in Phases, 1996 Elections

Parties	*Phase I* *Pre-campaign* (March 20–April 6)	*Phase II* *Campaign* (*April 7–May 7*)	*Phase III* *Post-election* (*May 8–May 15*)
Congress(I)	Strong. Good at negotiations, but few want to ally.	Weakest. Poor vote-getter, tends to make little head-way during a campaign	Strongest. Needs only 180 seats, which can be transformed into a majority.
BJP	Strong. Good at the give-and-take of forming alliances but seldom used.	Strongest. Vajpayee and BJP cadre are their best vote-getters	Weakest. Unlikely to win support from other parties, need to get a majority on their own (with pre-election allies).
NF-LF	Weak. The NF is perceived to have an abysmal record of forming alliances, but, in fact, has had the most alliances.	Strongest. An array of charismatic campaigners. The NF gains the most during the campaign period.	Weakest. Riddled with inner party dissension and too many leaders who want to be prime minister.

Source: Prannoy Roy and Dorab Sopariwala, 'Cover Story: Political Alliances', *India Today*, 15 April 1996: 37.

Note: The 'NF-LF' in the Table is inaccurate as the National Front had been practically defunct after the fall of the V.P. Singh government and never really revived in the run-up to the 1996 polls. Even the Left Front at the national level is a misnomer, though less so than the National Front. The only notable fronting around election time was the rapprochement between the Janata Dal and Samajwadi Party in Uttar Pradesh with active goading from the Left parties.

Janata government that brought her back to power. In 1984, it was the 'sympathy vote' for an orphaned young premier and a national revulsion to terrorism that took Indira Gandhi's life and posed a threat to national unity. Beginning with 1989, the patterns of electoral response became increasingly regionalised and segmented. The pattern remained unchanged in the mid-term polls of 1991. In 1996, there was no departure from this pattern either. To quote the impressions of an observer of the 1996 campaign:

> No national issues dominate this poll. There is no nationwide wave for or against any political combine. Yet, there are mini-waves at the local level which are dominated by local issues as in the case of Tamil Nadu, Bihar, West Bengal, or Madhya Pradesh. The absence of major issues have led to a greater campaigning on lines of caste and community. Everybody, including the politicians involved in the campaign believes that polls will result in a hung parliament.[33]

This is an index of the growing democratisation of Asia's, perhaps the world's, most complex tradition where sociological and ideological matrices of politics of the yesteryears are in decline and regeneration. Castes and communities today stand radically altered in their constitutive and interactional ingredients and their political preferences. Economic liberalisation, Mandal, and mandir have also transformed the ideational framework of politics, slowly and imperceptibly earlier, but, with a rush since 1989. The Nehruvian consensus is all but gone, leaving India rudderless on an uncharted course to search for a new consensus for a more federal governance. Stability of the parliamentary government is also critically dependent on this quest.

Notes

1. Lloyd Rudolph and Susanne H. Rudolf, *In Pursuit of Lakshmi*, 1987: 7.
2. *Ibid.*

3. *The Times of India*, 14 and 17 March 1996: 9 and 5, respectively.
4. *The Hindu*, 21 March 1996: 1 and *The Times of India*, 2 April 1992: 5.
5. The Election Commission, *Stat. Report on Gen. Elections, 1996*, *The Eleventh Lok Sabha,* vol. 1: 92.
6. *The Times of India*, 17 March 1996: 9.
7. *The Hindu*, 30 March 1996: 3.
8. *The Hindu*, 7 March 1996: 4.
9. *The Times of India*, 25 March 1996: 1.
10. *The Hindu*, 25 March 1996: 3.
11. *The Times of India*, 1 April 1996: 1.
12. *The Hindu*, 29 March 1996: 7.
13. *Outlook*, 24 April 1996: 38.
14. *The Hindu*, 6 April 1996: 5.
15. *The Times of India*, 19 March 1996: 7.
16. *Outlook*, 1 May 1996: 5.
17. *India Today*, 19 March 1996: 51.
18. *Outlook*, 3 April 1996: 18–19 and 24 April 1996: 37–38.
19. *India Today*, 15 May 1996: 87.
20. *India Today*, 15 April 1996: 60–61.
21. *Outlook*, 24 April 1996: 25, 28.
22. *Ibid*: 43.
23. *The Hindu*, 19 April 1996: 9.
24. *India Today*, 15 May 1996: 65–67.
25. *Ibid*: 66.
26. *Ibid*: 62–65.
27. *India Today*, 15 April and 15 May 1996: 44–46 and 82–83 respectively.
28. *India Today*, 15 April and 15 May 1996: 49–53 and 69–70 respectively.
29. *India Today*, 15 April 1996: 50.
30. *India Today*, 15 April and 15 May 1996: 58–60 and 98–100 respectively.
31. *Outlook*, 24 April 1996: 37.
32. *Ibid*: 56.
33. Padmanand Jha, 'Cover Story: An Election Without an Issue', *Outlook*, 1 May 1996: 4.

CHAPTER SIX

The Mid-Term Polls 1998

The Backdrop

The 1998 Lok Sabha election was the second mid-term poll since 1989. It will go down in history as an indicator of the continuing governmental instability that has become endemic since the 1990s. Since then, coalitional and/or minority governments have become the order of the day. These elections were preceded by six prime ministerial changes, five of which were caused by the premature fall of governments on account of unstable coalitions. Three Lok Sabhas in nine years with only one completing its full term formed the backdrop of the 1998 polls.

The immediate cause of the fall of the United Front government, headed by I.K. Gujral, was the withdrawal of outside support by the Congress(I) to the government on the issue of the indictment of the DMK by the Jain Commission's interim report on the assassination of Rajiv Gandhi. The Congress(I) carried through its threat of their withdrawing from the *legislative* coalition with the United Front if the prime minister did not remove the DMK ministers from the cabinet. In retrospect, it appears that but for the action of the Congress(I) the government may well have survived. The Congress(I) seemed to be using a double-edged sword: its demand would drive a wedge into the cohesion of the United Front for one, or else it would provide an opening for an alternative government in the existing House led by it, failing which the country would be forced to go to the polls on an emotive issue which may turn the electoral tide in its favour. The election was forced on an unwilling political class and a reluctant electorate by the Congress(I) which happened to be in the grey zone of the government-opposition divide, i.e. supporting the government without joining the cabinet. Gujral refused to play the Congress(I) game. He, instead, bowed out without recommending the dissolution of the House to the president as some United Front constituents were opposed to the idea. President K.R. Narayanan also initially appeared averse to an immediate dissolution, presumably because the United Front government represented a wide, federal coalition that had performed reasonably well, notwithstanding policy and personal differences within the Front. The core steering committee of the Front under the chairmanship of the prime minister and convenorship of the Andhra Pradesh TDP chief minister, Chandrababu Naidu, emerged as the main arena for reconciliation of inter-party differences. The president first explored the possibilities of an alternative government by one of the three major party fronts headed respectively by the Congress(I), the Janata Dal and the BJP. He found all the leading parties keen to form a government but unable to convince him about their mustering a majority. He, therefore, secured the dissolution of the House from the caretaker Gujral government and ordered fresh elections. The presidential proclamation added, 'the people of India need a reprieve from political instability.' In hindsight, this would appear to have been wishful thinking.

The political landscape on the eve of the 1998 elections had been laid out in the early 1990s and had hardly changed towards the end of the decade. The principal contours of this scenario were (1) the decline of the Congress predominance in 1989, (2) the 'Mandalisation' of politics in the wake of the implementation of the Mandal Commission Report by the National Front government headed by V.P. Singh in 1990, (3) the Ram-Janmabhoomi-Babri-Masjid movement spearheaded by the BJP and the Sangh Parivar culminating in the demolition of the Babri Masjid in December 1992, (4) the phenomenal rise of regional parties through the 1980s–1990s and the fragmentation of all-India parties, (5) economic liberalisation stepped up by the Rao-Manmohan Singh team during the Congress(I) administration in 1991, and (6) some evidence of the regeneration of political institutions expressed through a growing accent on federalisation, activism of the judiciary, the Election Commission and the new social movements and the NGOs. All these factors together have transformed the Indian political scene beyond recognition.

In the short-range view, however, the 1998 mid-term polls were held in the context of continuities in the decade in question rather than in change. The continuities were particularly evident in party politics and unstable coalition and minority governments. In view of this, the president's hope for respite from governmental instability appeared to be far-fetched.

The 1998 elections found the party system as much fragmented and polarised as the previous elections in the 1990s. The complex pattern of inter-party alliances in 1998, continued to be as varied as a patchwork quilt at the centre and state levels as at the beginning of the decade. Three major party fronts encountered one other in the electoral fray:

1. The United Front comprising the Janata Dal, TDP, CPI, CPI(M), AGP, HLDR, BSP (allied only in Haryana), DMK, TMC, Samajwadi Party, Left Front in West Bengal and Left Democratic Front in Kerala;
2. The Congress alliance consisting of the UMF in Assam, RJD in Bihar, RJP in Gujarat, JMM in Bihar, RPI and Samajwadi Party (allied in Maharashtra), BSP and CPI (allied only in Punjab), BKPP in Uttar Pradesh, and SFB and Jharkhand Party in West Bengal; and
3. The BJP alliance including the Shiv Sena, Samata Party, Haryana Vikas Party, Lok Shakti, Biju Janata Dal, Shiromani Akali Dal (B), AIADMK, MDMK, Janata Party, PMK, Rajiv Tamil Nadu Congress, BSP(J), West Bengal Trinamool Congress and BSP (allied only in Punjab).

These pre-poll alliances underwent some transformation after the electoral outcome. In the aftermath of the polls, the main beneficiary of the shift in the allegiances of parties was the BJP alliance. Its post-poll allies were the TDP (Naidu), National Conference, HLD(R), and Arunachal Congress. In the final tally after the realignments in the parliament, the BJP alliance came to comprise 17 parties, the United Front after the desertions were left with eight parties, and the Congress(I) and its allies consisted of seven parties. Apart from these configurations, there were eight unattached parties plus five independents, four of whom defected to the post-poll alliance with the BJP.

A notable feature of the elections in the 1990s, is the blurring of the government-opposition demarcation. In the era of Congress dominance, it was commonplace to bemoan the lack of vigour of the opposition. This theme was so recurrent that inter-party relations came to be characterised by an obsession with 'anti-Congressism'. This was the typical opposition strategy to consolidate the anti-Congress vote as far as possible in a non-Congress alliance of parties. The major landmarks of this trend were witnessed in 1971, 1977 and 1989. The strategy miserably failed in 1971, when the grand alliance of the Bharatiya Jan Sangh, Bharatiya Lok Dal, Socialists, Swatantra Party and others came to naught in the face of the landslide victory of Indira Gandhi in the aftermath of the Congress split in 1969 and the mid-term polls that followed. However, the consolidation of the non-Congress and non-communist opposition into the Janata Party in the shadow of the Emergency and during parliamentary elections in 1977 was a resounding success. The Congress was dislodged from New Delhi for the first time, since its defeat in half of the states of the union in 1967. Non-Congressism again peaked in 1989, when the National Front led by the Janata Dal and comprising some regional parties and the Left Front defeated the Congress(I) and ushered in the era of a multi-party system and coalition and minority governments at the centre.

Over the 1980s and 1990s, as Congress dominance was gradually eroded, the earlier non-Congressism was replaced by non-BJPism. In other words, the 'Congress versus the rest' was replaced by 'BJP versus the rest'. This was in response to the gradually increasing electoral success of the BJP, although it had always fallen short of the majority mark. Particularly in the wake of the Ayodhya movement, the non-Congress and the non-BJP parties feared that the Hindu nationalist party might emerge as another dominant party in the trail of the Congress decline.

By the 1990s, the recurrent theme of party political processes had become the weakness of the government. This is symptomatic of the blurring of boundaries between governing and oppositional parties. One indicator of this trend is what has come to be called 'outside' support to the government by some parties from the parliamentary floor without joining the cabinet. Thus the *executive* and *legislative* coalitions do not always coincide. Practically all governments in the 1980s have collapsed on account of this factor: the National Front government following the withdrawal of support by the BJP in 1990, the SJP (Chandrashekhar) government by a similar act of the Congress(I) in 1991, and the United Front governments led by Deve Gowda and Gujral again, owing to the Congress(I) pulling the rug from under their feet in 1996 and 1997, respectively. Another indicator of the blurring of the government-opposition divide was the frequent change of governments which resulted in the turning of tables among parties. So, the parties in power today become the opposition parties of tomorrow.

Ideologically, the Indian party system would appear to have become more 'integrated', despite persisting multi-polarities. The sharp ideological cleavages have considerably narrowed since the 1990s, owing to the shifting alliances among parties. Thus, the *pariah* status of the communists, the Congress and the BJP at different points in time have become a thing of the past. Indeed, the communists along with the Janata Dal, the BJP and the Congress(I) have become three pivotal groups of parties around which smaller parties have tended to cluster in government-formation and opposition. The three pivots have moved closer without becoming indistinguishable. These parties have been forced to shed their more radical ideological positions and become moderate. This moderation would not have easily come about without the politics of coalition and minority governments. In these governments, the 'nationalist' BJP and 'globalist' Congress(I) rub shoulders with regional and parochial parties. The Congress(I) has extended support from the parliamentary floor to governments in which communists have shared power with the Janata Dal and regional parties, and so on. Not that ideologies do not matter at all. The point is that they have tended to converge considerably. The secular-communal divide, the regional-national cleavages and the swadeshi-globalism divide are still very much the issues on which alliances are made or unmade. However, despite surface turbulence and conflicts, a certain degree of stability in economic and secular policies at the centre has come to pass, which may be largely attributed to the balancing act of coalitional/minority governance.

Inter-Party Alliances

After its losing dominance, the Congress Party's efforts to forge a winning coalition suffered from two major eroding factors. First, its leaders could not easily adjust themselves to the altered electoral scenario. They still appeared to suffer from delusions of grandeur and preferred to contest alone in the hope of their meeting with better electoral prospects. This was, however, not to be. This was—and this brings us to the second point—because of the major electoral realignment that had taken place in 1989 and after. The social coalition behind the Congress dominance was built on a disproportionately larger support for the party among the important minorities and disadvantaged sections of the population such as the upper castes, Muslims, Sikhs, SCs, STs, all over India. In the recent decades, these loyalties have tended to shift to other parties. The OBC vote bloc had in fact been largely lost by the Congress(I) even earlier, especially since the formation of the Janata Party in 1977 and its various reincarnations ever since. The Muslim vote-bank had also moved away from the party owing to the Emergency excesses and on account of a covert understanding of the Congress(I) with the BJP in the 1980s during the Indira Gandhi, Rajiv Gandhi and Rao regimes. The Janata parivar parties had been the main beneficiaries of this electoral shift in the Muslim vote. The Dalit vote bloc became disillusioned with both the Congress(I) and the JD and came to be mainly mobilised by the BSP. Likewise, the upper-caste vote was lost both by the Congress(I) and the Janata Dal to the BJP as the main advocate of the Hindu interests with Bania-Brahmin overtones. In the post-Blue Star Operation phase in Punjab, the Congress(I) came to be sandwiched between the Akali Dal and the BJP as the sheet anchor of the Sikhs and the Hindus. Moreover, with the formation of regional parties in non-Hindi linguistic provinces such as Andhra Pradesh and Assam, the traditional Congress(I) vote came to be divided between the regional parties and the Congress(I) party.

Moreover, splits in the ranks of its adversaries such as the Janata Dal in Bihar and the BJP in Gujarat brought some windfall gains for the Congress(I) in terms of new allies. The RJD formed by Laloo Yadav and the RJP formed by Shankarsinh Vaghela in fact ruled in the two states with the outside support of the Congress(I). Besides, owing to local circumstances, the Congress(I) also found it feasible to forge limited alliances with the Republican Party and Samajwadi Party in Maharashtra, the BSP and CPI in Punjab, the BKPP in Uttar Pradesh, the United Minority Front in Assam and factions of the Jharkhand Party in Bihar and West Bengal.

In the wake of the decline of the Congress(I), a coalitional possibility had first appeared in the Janata Party in 1977 as an alternative and which was a combination of major non-Congress and non-communist political formations. But a significant limitation of the Janata Party, later Janata Dal, was that its base was restricted to north India, especially in the Hindi-speaking states, and of course, Karnataka, Orissa and Gujarat. This limitation was partly compensated by the Janata Dal's alliances with the Left Front parties in West Bengal and Kerala and with the major regional parties from the non-Hindi mainland, such as the TDP in Andhra, AGP in Assam and DMK in Tamil Nadu. Together, these parties in the National Front came to have a fairly all-India spread. In terms of voting blocs, the National Front parties were also able to count on the middle castes in a major part of the country as also the middle classes and working classes in the states where the Left Front parties dominated. However, the communist parties lent support to the National Front government only from the outside without joining the cabinet. When the National Front transformed itself into the United Front in 1996, the communists moved closer to it, with the CPI's joining the cabinet but the CPI(M) still only joining the coordination committee of the Front. However, the National Front and the United Front governments could not achieve a majority and were forced to depend on the legislative coalitions with parties from outside the coalitions. The National Front had to lean on the external support of the BJP and the Congress(I) and the United Front had to count on similar outside support from the Congress(I). Consecutive elections in 1989 and 1991, and 1996 and 1998, offered an opportunity to the National and United Fronts to govern and to make repeated electoral campaigns to be voted in the majority. The efforts came to naught. Even though it gained some new allies on the way in this period such as the TMC in Tamil Nadu, the BSP and HLDR in Haryana, it did not prove to be of much help. Internal fragmentation in the leading party of the coalition, the Janata Dal, (e.g., splits which produced the Samajwadi Party in Uttar Pradesh, the RJD in Bihar, the BJD in Orissa), in addition to external competition from the BJP and Congress(I) probably contributed to its failure.

A notable feature of recent elections in India has been the rather swift electoral volatility. This is indicated by the tendency of the electoral pendulum to swing from one side to the other in a short span of time. For example, on the eve of the 1998 Lok Sabha mid-term polls, there appeared to be in evidence a major electoral realignment towards the BJP, which first took place among the political class and, subsequently, among the electorate to a certain extent. Compared to its lot after the 1996 Lok Sabha elections, the BJP found it considerably easier to line up an impressive array of allies practically in all regions of the country. Its previous alliances included the Shiv Sena (which headed a coalition government with the BJP in Maharashtra), Samata Party (in alliance with the BJP in Bihar since 1996), Loktantrik Congress (a breakaway Congress group that had joined the BJP government in Uttar Pradesh), Haryana Vikas Party (which headed a coalition government with the BJP in Haryana), and Akali Dal (which headed a coalition government with the BJP in Punjab). Among its new alliances the first major success was the understanding with the AIADMK in Tamil Nadu. Beginning with Jayalalitha's (AIADMK) decision to snap ties with the Congress and align itself with the BJP, there followed in quick succession other allies such as the Trinamool Congress in West Bengal, Biju Janata Dal in Orissa, Akali Dal in Punjab and Lok Shakti in Karnataka. All these new allies did not jump on the BJP bandwagon at once, for, they initially appeared to be hesitant to join hands with a party that had in the past been a political untouchable. Some of them in the beginning kept their options open for an alliance with the Congress or with the United Front. Hectic negotiations continued for weeks before they finally threw in their lot with the BJP.

A number of factors contributed to the suspense of the denouement of the BJP's allies as there was still feverish negotiation by the BJP with other parties. Given the options between the Congress(I) and the Gujral government, adjustments with the Congress or United Front did not appear too attractive in the immediate wake of the fall of the Gujral government. The farcical goings-on within the Congress(I) where Sitaram Kesari held the lease of the party presidency and Sonia Gandhi maintained an enigmatic and ambivalent stance towards assuming an active role in the party, created some apprehensions. In fact, some of the new BJP allies were new political formations that had split from the Congress(I) in rebellion against Kesari and the state Congress leaderships in some states, e.g., Trinamool Congress formed by Mamata Banerjee. Ms Banerjee, in fact, let it be known that, at least initially, if Sonia Gandhi took active interest in the Congress, she should very well like to stay within the party. She had, indeed, a meeting with Sonia Gandhi hoping that the latter's interventions would redress her grievances against Kesari and the West Bengal Pradesh Congress president. However, Sonia Gandhi remained non-committal, and Mamata Banerjee's fate was sealed within the Congress. Thus, in view of her incompatibility with the Congress as well as with the CPI(M) in West Bengal, she had no other option but to align with the BJP. Walking out of the Congress, she held a huge mass rally in Kolkata, separate from and simultaneous with an AICC session there, that demonstrated her personal popularity independent of the Congress. But this was not comprehensive enough to dislodge the ruling Left Front in the state. So, her considerable following in the state would have some manoeuvrability in a national coalition in a mutually advantageous relationship. The BJP welcomed her with open arms and after some initial hesitation she finally joined hands with this national party on her own terms.

Jayalalitha's decision to break away from the Congress(I) was also related to strains within Congress and Tamil Nadu politics. With the DMK in power in the state and the majority of local Congressmen deserting the parent party to form the TMC on the eve of the 1996 Lok Sabha elections, there were compelling reasons for her to look for other allies. Even the Congress party leadership at the centre did not appear to be in a good shape to continue to be a useful national ally. Moreover, she was embroiled in corruption charges and if perchance the BJP alliance came to power, it could be a possible escape route to use through a politics of pressure.

The Samata Party's national leadership opposed the BJP's alliance with Jayalalitha mainly on the grounds of her alleged involvement in corruption cases. The BJP leadership, however, asserted that it would not consult its previous allies on new alliances as at that moment it was mainly concerned with making electoral adjustments, and would leave the issue of a common minimum programme for the second stage after the elections.

Moreover, the Bihar state unit of the BJP opined that there was a difference between Laloo Yadav and Jayalalitha in that the entire RJD government in Bihar was involved in looting the state treasury, whereas the Tamil Nadu leader was facing some personal charges of corruption as the former chief minister of the state.

The JD national leadership had incurred the displeasure of Rama Krishna Hegde and Naveen Patnaik. Even though Hegde had once been a Congressman and Naveen's father, Biju Patnaik, was also in the Congress at one time, the bulk of their lives had been spent in the Janata Dal. Hence, the only feasible way open to them was to float regional outfits and align with a national party like the BJP. The only hurdle was the BJP's Hindu, communal overtones. Even this problem had been at least partly mitigated by the BJP's short stint in power in 1996, and its alliance with the Samata Party on the basis of the latter's reservations about the BJP's more extremist agenda. During the fateful two weeks in power in May that year, the BJP government had shown considerable moderation and also persuaded its ruling ally, the Shiv Sena in Maharashtra, to reactivate the Sri Krishna Commission to inquire into the Mumbai riots which the Shiv Sena chief minister had wound up earlier.

The BJP's alliance with the Akali Dal in Punjab had already been forged in the previous assembly elections, following which they had formed a coalition government. Thus, it meant only an extension of the political arrangement in the state to the national level.

A close look at these earlier and recent alliances forged by the BJP make it clear that they helped to compensate for two major deficiencies in its support-base. First, the BJP had traditionally been weak beyond the Hindi heartland, and second, it had also been a predominantly upper-caste political formation. The alliances with Jayalalitha, Mamata, Hegde, Naveen and the Akali Dal gave it a foothold in the non-Hindi-speaking states of the south, east, north-west and west lending it an all-India presence. In some of these areas, such as Karnataka, the BJP had already gained some electoral dividends in the previous elections.

Its alliances with the Samata Party and Shiv Sena brought within its fold the support of politically significant middle castes in Bihar, Uttar Pradesh and Maharashtra. The BJP itself had in the recent past been trying to win over the OBC vote blocs by its new strategy which it called 'social engineering', a strategy mainly formulated by K.N. Govindacharya, which aimed at making special appeals to the OBCs and Dalits. Some of the prominent mascots of this strategy were Kalyan Singh, then chief minister of U.P., and Uma Bharati a union minister of the same, both belonging to the OBC Lodh caste. Moreover, some of the new allies had the added advantage of enjoying the goodwill of the Muslim minority. We could particularly mention in this context George Fernandes, Mamata Banerjee and Rama Krishna Hegde. Even after their joining the BJP alliance, these leaders have been cautious in maintaining their rapport with the Muslim voters in their respective regions. Indeed, the BJP itself in the recent years, had appeared very keen to build bridges with the major minority communities.

Candidate Selection

The formal procedure of candidate selection by political parties for 1998, especially national parties, may be sampled by case studies of the BJP and the Indian National Congress, the two largest single parties, and of the Left Front in West Bengal which has enjoyed an uninterrupted stint since 1977. Developments in some other parties are also covered in brief. The process followed in the largest two parties was more or less similar. The state units of the parties prepared their panels of candidates for the seats, as far as they were unanimous in their choice, and forwarded their recommendations to the Central Election Committee of the party concerned, for final approval. Where unanimity was not possible, more than one candidate was recommended, leaving the final decision to the central leadership. The BJP Central Election Committee met from 10 to 12 January and then again from 27 to 28 January to finalise the list after scrutinising the candidates statewise on the basis of the panels received from the state units. Barring protest against one sitting MP from Karnal (Haryana) at the national headquarters of the party in Delhi for his neglect of the constituents and involvement in illicit liquor trade,[1] there were no major controversies over other seats. On key constituencies, senior party leaders such as Vajpayee and Advani in consultation with senior RSS leaders were reportedly given the final say.[2] The composition of the state election committees in some states was keenly contested. For example, in Madhya Pradesh, the election committee originally turned out to have a majority for the Patwa-Thakre group, leaving the Uma Bharati faction disgruntled. The state party president, Nand Kumar Sai, subsequently expanded the committee to accommodate some of his supporters. In Delhi, the 16 district BJP presidents comprised the state election committee.[3] However, with the central party having already adopted a broad policy of renominating the sitting Lok Sabha members,[4] the choice of the Pradesh Election Committees was rather constrained. In a way, so was the Central Election Committee, except where the top party leaders decided to intervene.[5]

With the spate of new entrants into the party on the eve of elections, the BJP faced some controversy over the granting of tickets. The longstanding members of the party expressed concern and criticism about nominations that went to the new individuals and groups.[6] While the party leadership clarified that the new members had not laid down any pre-conditions,[7] it is understandable that the central party leadership must have had to use persuasion with the old-timers to help accommodate the fair-weather friends who scrambled to the BJP in the months preceding the election. The BJP leadership was also piqued over their Akali allies offering a walkover to Gujral in Jullundhar. A party spokesman said, 'the BJP was free to field its own candidates against Gujral.'[8]

The selection of candidates in the Congress(I) in 1998, appeared to have diverged from the past tradition in the party with a top-heavy decision-making process in the Indira-Rajiv period. The party organisation under Rao, at least, in the initial years of his tenure, and later, after his departure under Kesari, came to provide an opening for a more collective leadership. By the time Rao was forced to lay down his office on charges of corruption, he too had established a tight control over the party. In 1998, the party tended to have a more collective leadership under Kesari's presidentship. But with Sonia Gandhi's belated decision to campaign for the party which was announced on 30 December, No. 10 Janpath, her residence, which had always been a dormant centre of power, became a more active, indeed dominant, influence in the party for Kesari to reckon with. Nonetheless, Sonia Gandhi made it clear that she would neither contest a Lok Sabha seat nor seek prime ministership. She also indicated to Kesari and other party leaders that she did not want to get actively involved during the selection of party candidates. However, dissatisfied groups and individuals started lobbying for her support, and in a few cases she seemed to have conveyed her pleasure as well as displeasure to the party president at accommodating those who actively sought her intervention. The gates of her residence were thrown open for Congress delegations that kept pouring in from far and wide. She, thus, acted as an appellate authority over the party president and regular party organs. The normal nomination process used by the Congress consisted of recommendations from the Pradesh Congress Committees, which was first scrutinised by an AICC screening committee for each state and comprised a CWC member, the AICC general secretary in charge of the state and his joint secretary, besides the PCC president and the CLP leader. The scrutinised panels thus processed were finally referred to the Central Election Committee. The CWC itself became a central election committee for this purpose. The finalisation of the list was reportedly delayed, creating anxieties about sufficient time for the selected candidates to do the electioneering, particularly in view of the reduction of the campaign period by the Election Commission to two weeks.

The panel of candidates recommended by the Maharashtra Pradesh Congress Committee to the CEC included the rebels such as Praful Patel and Dutta Raghobji who were among the

40 MPs who had threatened to join the BJP when Kesari decided to withdraw Congress support to the Gujral government. This was part of the reconciliation initiated by the Maharashtra strongman, Sharad Pawar, and the national party president, especially in the wake of the election-eve desertion from the party of Suresh Kalmadi, Anadicharen Sahu, Mohan Belkar and Gopal Pandel, some of who joined the BJP and some like Kalmadi who floated a separate party largely with the support of the municipal corporators in Pune. The threat of punishment to the rebels by the Disciplinary Action Committee headed by Vijaya Bhaskar Reddy was thus played down in the interest of party unity. Similarly, the Orissa chief minister, J.B. Patnaik, was instrumental in including the names of P.V. Narasimha Rao from Berhampur and Pinaki Mishra from Puri. Mishra was also one of the 40 rebels who had resisted Kesari's move to undermine the UF government just before the elections. Rao's candidature passed muster in the Orissa Pradesh Congress Committee list, but was finally dropped by the central leadership on account of the corruption cases against him. His detractors in the party pointed out that the party should not adopt double standards, however high an office one may have held in the past. They also cited Rao's own decision as party president in 1996, to deny tickets to the hawala-scam-tainted ministers.

Early announcement of some candidates—three from Delhi, two from Punjab, and one from Madhya Pradesh (Arjun Singh, Hoshangabad)—by the Congress president even before the CEC had met brought a volley of protests from the Congress members, which included an expression of mild displeasure from Sonia Gandhi. The plea that these candidates were either CWC members whose names were the only ones recommended by the respective PCCs or were announced in the presence of the Punjab CLP leader and Manmohan Singh did not cut much ice.[9] A Delhi MLA and Pradesh Congress leader went to the press demanding reconsideration of the announced candidates who were standing from Chandni Chowk and New Delhi and also suggested that the seven Lok Sabha tickets in Delhi should be balanced in terms of a nomination each to a Muslim, a Sikh, a Brahmin, and a backward caste.[10]

The Left Front in West Bengal displayed remarkable consensus as well as speed in announcing its entire panel of 42 Lok Sabha candidates in the state, except in Kolkata Northwest which had been left for the Janata Dal in 1996, even though the Janata Dal had not yet contacted the Front in this regard in 1998. In case of the Janata Dal's opting out, the seat would go to the Forward Bloc which had been contesting it before 1996. Out of the 31 nominees from the CPI(M), 18 were sitting MPs. Performance was said to be the criteria for denying renomination. However, the Jalpaiguri MP was withdrawn to accommodate a woman candidate for the first time. The CPI and RSP fielded all their sitting MPs, three and four, respectively. The Forward Bloc with three seats also renominated the previous candidates, except in Barasat which fell vacant following Chitta Basu's death. The Left Front put up the veteran Prasanta Sur, the former mayor, against the Trinamool Congress leader, Mamata Banerjee. The Front also fielded two serving mayors of the twin cities of Kolkata and Howrah. The consideration in their fielding strong candidates was obviously aimed at capitalising on the split between the Congress and Trinamool Congress in the state. All the parties of the Front announced the entire list in one go and at a joint press conference in Kolkata on 6 January 1998.[11]

The Janata Dal after successive chain-splintering became virtually confined to Karnataka. The procedure for candidate selection adopted in the state included recommendations from the grass roots by legislators, zila panchayat presidents belonging to the party along with district party presidents and by senior, state party leaders in Bangalore during the second week of January to finalise the panel.[12] The Rajasthan Janata Dal unit announced their list of 10 candidates in Jaipur, adding: 'These are our candidates unless someone decides not to contest.' Out of a total of 25 Lok Sabha seats in the state, the party decided to contest only ten.[13]

A broad comparison of the turnover of candidates fielded by parties reveals that in 1998, the BJP and the two major communist parties were more inclined to renominate their candidates, especially those who happened to be sitting MPs in the immediately dissolved Lok Sabha in the state under their rule (Table 6.1). This was particularly characteristic of the incumbent parties, whether national or state. Parties in the political wilderness were more likely to try fielding new candidates. The relatively larger number of new candidates in several national parties is deceptive inasmuch as it reflects a large number of constituencies where these parties were fielding their candidates for the first time in 1998, to spread out their national presence. In the BJP, this occurred because of the spate of new entrants in the party on the eve of elections. In the cases of new party formations such as the RJD, BJD and Trinamool Congress, the table shows that the entire list of candidates were being newly fielded. This is also deceptive in a different way, since the bulk of these party candidates were formerly with the JD in Bihar and Orissa or with the Congress in West Bengal.

TABLE 6.1
Selection of Candidates by Major Parties, 1998

Party	*Renominated*	*(%)*	*New*	*Total*
Andhra Pradesh (42 seats)				
TDP	23	(65.7)	12	35
Congress	22	(53.7)	19	41
BJP	7	(21.9)	25	32
Arunachal Pradesh (2 seats)				
INC	0		2	2
BJP	1		1	2
Assam (14 seats)				
INC	5	(41.7)	7	12
AGP	4	(40.0)	6	10
BJP	3	(21.4)	11	14
Bihar (54 seats)				
RJD (New Party)	—		38	38
BJP	22	(31.2)	10	32
Samata	10	(47.6)	11	21
INC	5	(25.0)	15	20

Party	*Renominated*	*(%)*	*New*	*Total*
CPI	6	(60.0)	7	13
CPI(M)	0		4	4
CPI(M-L)	5	(31.2)	11	16
JMM	3		3	6
JMM(M)	3		0	3
Goa (2 seats)				
INC	0		2	2
BJP			2	2
MGP/MAG	1		1	2
Gujarat (26 seats)				
INC	12	(48.0)	13	25
BJP	17	(65.4)	9	26
RJP (New Party)			20	20
Haryana (10 seats)				
HVP	2		2	4
BJP	5		1	6
HLDR			7	7
INC	2		7	9
Himachal Pradesh (4 seats)				
INC	3		1	4
BJP	2		2	4
Jammu and Kashmir (6 seats)				
INC	2		4	5
NC (did not contest '96)			6	6
BJP	3	(50.0)	3	6
Karnataka (28 seats)				
JD	14	(53.9)	12	26
INC	10	(62.5)	16	26
BJP	11	(64.7)	6	17
Kerala (20 seats)				
INC	5	(41.7)	7	12
CPI(M)	3	(37.5)	5	8
CPI	1		1	2
BJP	2	(13.3)	13	15
Madhya Pradesh (40 seats)				
INC	6		17	23
BJP	19		4	23

Party	*Renominated*	*(%)*	*New*	*Total*
Maharashtra (48 seats)				
SS	12	(54.5)	10	22
INC	15	(36.6)	26	41
BJP	16	(64.0)	9	25
RPI	2		2	4
Manipur (2 seats)				
MPP			1	1
INC	1		1	2
CPI			2	2
Meghalaya (2 seats)				
INC	1		1	2
BJP	1		1	2
CPI	1		1	2
UDP			2	2
Mizoram (1 seat)				
INC	1			1
MNF	1			1
BJP	1			1
Nagaland (1 seat)				
INC	1			1
Orissa (21 seats)				
INC	14	(66.7)	7	21
JD	3	(18.7)	13	16
BJP	5	(55.5)	4	9
Punjab (13 seats)				
SAD	4	(50.0)	4	8
SAD (M)	2		2	4
BJP			3	3
INC	4	(50.0)	4	8
Rajasthan (25 seats)				
INC	9	(36.0)	16	25
BJP	14	(56.0)	11	25
JD	2	(11.8)	15	17
Sikkim (1 seat)				
SDF	1			1
INC			1	1

Party	*Renominated*	*(%)*	*New*	*Total*
Tamil Nadu (39 seats)				
DMK	11	(64.7)	6	17
AIADMK	2	(9.1)	20	22
TMC(M)	17	(85.0)	3	20
INC	10	(28.6)	25	35
MDMK	1	(12.5)	7	8
BSP	0		10	10
SAP	1		3	4
Tripura (2 seats)				
CPI(M)	1		1	1
INC	0		2	2
BJP	2		0	2
Uttar Pradesh (85 seats)				
BJP	26	(31.7)	56	82
INC	13	(17.1)	63	76
BSP	12	(14.1)	72	85
JD	3	(13.6	19	22
CPI	2	(40.0)	3	5
CPI(M)	0		2	2
SP	28	(34.6)	53	81
West Bengal (42 seats)				
CPM	21	(65.6)	11	32
CPI	2		0	2
INC	6	(15.4)	33	39
BJP	1	(7.1)	13	14
BSP	1	(7.1)	13	14
SAP	0		1	1
RSP	4		0	4
FBL	2		1	3
FB(S)	0		1	1
WBTC (New Party)	0		29	29

Notes:

1. Based on comparison of candidates as reported by the Election Commission of India (1996 and 1998, vol. 3 of both).

2. The detailed results in 1996 from 17 constituencies in MP, from four in Kerala and from two in Karnataka were missing from the volume used here. For the lack of a base for comparison these constituencies were excluded altogether from this table.

An analysis of the success rates of renominated vis-a-vis newly fielded candidates carried out for major national and regional parties in bigger states, showed that the former performed considerably better in the BJP (39.03 per cent) and communist parties (35.13 per cent). Newly fielded candidates had also slightly better chances in the Congress (17.47 per cent) than the veterans (14.02 per cent). There was not much difference between the success rates of the two categories of candidates in the major regional (state) parties in more populous states (excluding those formed just prior to the 1998 elections): 18.09 per cent as against 19.09 per cent (see Table 6.2). The greater incidence of renominations as well as better success rates of more experienced parliamentarians in the BJP and communist parties may suggest a higher degree of institutionalisation of these major parties of the Right and the Left and a corresponding deinstitutionalisation of the centrist parties like the Congress and Janata Dal. The latter two in the recent decades have in fact, tended to move to the Right and to the Left on economic issues respectively, without absolutely moving away from the middle ground. Besides, both these centrist parties have recently suffered a series of fragmentations on regional lines. Moreover, the success of major regional parties in their bringing about a more or less balanced circulation of parliamentary elites may be, perhaps, partly attributed to the regional popularity of the satraps who were leading these state parties.

TABLE 6.2

Winning, Renominated and New Candidates in Major National and State Parties, 1998 Lok Sabha Polls

Party	*Renominated* (*N*=)	(%)	*New* (*N*=)	(%)
BJP	121	39.03	45	14.52
INC	61	14.02	76	17.47
CPI(M)/CPI	26	35.13	11	14.86
Major State Parties	36	18.09	38	19.09

Note: State Parties here included were TDP, AGP, Shiv Sena, SAD, DMK, AIADMK, Samajwadi Party.

An aspect of party nominations that has been causing increasing concern in recent years is what has popularly come to be called the criminalisation of politics. The information available with the Election Commission suggests that around 1,500 candidates with a criminal past contested the 1996 elections. Of these 40 were elected to the Lok Sabha and 700 were voted to various legislative assemblies. Most of them happened to be party candidates rather than independents. Alarmed by this trend the commission proposed to the government, a statutory bar that screens out convicts and extends beyond the provisions of the Representation of the People Act, 1951, to debar candidates involved in criminal cases of a serious penal nature such as murder, rape, corruption, etc. The legal opinion continues to be divided on the issue. A senior Supreme Court advocate, R.K. Jain, for example, holds that 'unless one is held guilty by the final court he cannot be deemed to be a convict.' The United Front government did not attempt to bring about a legislation to this effect, though the law minister, Ramakant D. Khalap, paid lip-service to the commission's recommendation saying, 'Whatever the Commission decides, it would be acceptable to the government.' The Supreme Court, on its part, has time and again suggested to the government to amend the penal and electoral laws to make them stringent enough to foreclose the entry of criminals into politics.[14] President K.R. Narayanan also told a television journalist in an interview that the entry of criminals can be prevented by law but even without such a legislation it was within the powers and responsibilities of political parties to see to it that persons with dubious antecedents are not selected as candidates.[15]

The problem is obviously more serious than what may appear from the foregoing. During the 1998 Lok Sabha elections, an eminent panel consisting of Justice Kuldip Singh, Madhav Godbole, C. Subramanium and Swami Agnivesh, after a careful scrutiny, identified as many as 72 Lok Sabha candidates facing serious criminal cases. This panel formulated six categories for identifying candidates unfit to run for office:

TABLE 6.3
Candidates with a Criminal Background in the 1998 Lok Sabha Elections

Description	*Number*
Category 1	
Those convicted of moral turpitude and offences listed in the RPA by a criminal court regardless of whether an appeal is pending with a higher court.	00
Category 2	
Persons chargesheeted by a judicial court in a criminal case.	34
Category 3	
Persons against whom there are prima facie findings by an investigating agency on the basis of which a chargesheet has been filed in a court.	39
Category 4	
Persons who have been absconding from law, although they may not have been chargesheeted.	3
Category 5	
Persons who are in jail under preventive law on economic and criminal grounds after approval by the advisory board.	1
Category 6	
Persons who have a long crime history and as such are considered anti-social and unfit to contest elections.	31

Source: *Outlook* (New Delhi), vol. IV, no. 7, 23 February 1998, pp. 10–11.
Note: Since some persons fall in more than one category used here, multiple counting has perhaps been made. That may be the reason why the total in this table exceeds 72.

It is evident from the table that the majority of criminals enter the electoral fray through the medium of national and state parties, including the two largest national parties. The BJP has the dubious distinction of fielding the largest number of criminals, followed—in this order—by the Samajwadi Party, Congress, BSP and RJD. Another alarming fact is that the bulk of the criminal candidates fall in categories 3, 2 and 6 which include persons already chargesheeted by a judicial court or by an investigating agency and those with a long history of crime.

TABLE 6.4
Candidates with a Criminal Background by Parties in the 1998 Lok Sabha Elections

Parties	*Criminal Candidates*
National Parties	
BJP	17
Congress	9
Janata Dal	1
BSP	6
Samata Party	2
State Parties	
Samajwadi Party	12
Jharkhand Mukti Morcha (S) and (M)	3
Shiv Sena	2
AIADMK	2
Registered (Unrecognised) Parties	
RJD	5
RJP	1
Rashtriya Haryana Lok Dal	1
Himachal Vikas Congress	1
Karnataka Vikas Party	1
Bihar Jana Congress	2
CPI(M-L)	1
Jantantrik BSP	1
BJP rebel	1
Independents	4

Source: *Outlook* (New Delhi), vol. IV, no. 7, 23 February 1998, pp. 12–13.
Note: Classification of parties according to the Election Commission's, *Statistical Report on General Elections, 1998, to the Twelfth Lok Sabha*, vol. 1, 1998, pp. 1–5. However, the RJP, Bihar Jana Congress, Jantantrik BSP and BJP rebels are not mentioned in the Report for some technical reasons.

Manifestos and Issues

The ideological spectrum of the Indian party system in the 1990s have presented broadly three major perspectives on Indian nationalism and strategies of economic development. The two largest parties present a more or less centralised model with some internal variations, whereas the third approach lies somewhere in between. The traditionally dominant Congress emphasis has been on the pluralist and composite Indian culture with an accent on a multi-class and multi-ethnic formally secularist version of Indian nationalism combined with a state-led strategy of economic (industrial) development during the post-colonial era and one of economic liberalisation since 1991. The ascendant BJP's version of a so-called cultural nationalism with an emphasis on Hindutva has flaunted the concept of a 'One Nation, One People, and One Culture'. Its approach to economic development had been traditionally anti-statist but has been gradually discovering a facilitating role for the state by promoting a mildly protectionist swadeshi pattern of economic development. The 1998 BJP manifesto appears to make some concessions to India's pluralist civilisational heritage by affirming its commitment to 'common living and common and shared values, beliefs, customs, struggles, joy and sorrow as well as symbols of high degree of unity without uniformity'.[16] The third conception is offered by the National Front/United Front of Left and regional parties initially led by the Janata Dal but gradually marked by the growing influence of the socially democratised communist parties. There is a loose confederal United Front, which advocates the most pluralist and regionally diverse notion of Indian nationalism coupled with a strategy of economic development which still harks back to the statist Nehruvian Indian socialism with an accent on autonomous, regional centres of power.

The platforms of major political formations and their groupings in 1998, did not radically diverge from those of 1996, except in terms of a greater emphasis on the question of stability because of the premature collapse of at least three successive governments since the previous elections. Even the BJP manifesto did not radically differ from the past, though this party and its allies faced the electoral challenge with evident verve and vigour riding on the crest of a new optimism. The manifesto contained a repetition of such issues as the Ayodhya temple, common civil code and deletion of Article 370 on Kashmir which had been omitted from the presidential address to the joint session of the parliament prepared by the Vajpayee government in 1996. A slight change, however, was detected on the Ayodhya issue where a consensual approach was emphasised; it also did not mention Kashi and Mathura that continued to be high up on the VHP agenda. The rest of the major parties displayed a remarkable degree of consensus on Ayodhya with the Congress, United Front and the Left parties suggesting a strictly legal approach to the problem and a resolve to abide by the Supreme Court ruling as well as to ensure strict enforcement of the Places of Worship Act (1990). A similar gulf existed between the BJP and other parties on some other problems relating to the minorities. The BJP would wind up the Minority Commission and merge its jurisdictions with the Human Rights Commission. The Congress would create a separate ministry for minorities and increase the corpus of the Maulana Azad Educational Foundation. The United Front would do something similar by establishing a Minority Development Authority and make a separate budgetary allocation for minority education as well as increase aid to the Maulana Azad Educational Foundation to the tune of Rs 150 crores. Another issue that over the years has traversed an early contentious phase and now has become an area of all-party consensus, even though with varying emphasis, is the issue of Mandal reservations. Apparently, under the compulsions of electoral politics, all parties excepting the BJP, have come to endorse OBC reservations with as much tacit concensus as those endorsed for the SCs/STs unlike the Mandal reservations. While we are on the subject of inter-party agreement, we may as well add the issue of the extension of reservation for women beyond the panchayati raj level to the state legislatures and parliament, on which all parties were more or less in consensus in 1996. The only discordant note was struck by Mulayam Singh Yadav's Samajwadi Party and Laloo Prasad Yadav's Rashtriya Janata Dal which advocated separate quotas for OBC women within the overall women's reservation.

Another area of agreement among practically all parties was on a Lokpal legislation to deal with charges of corruption including those against the prime ministers and the chief ministers.

The 1998 election manifestos continued the trend of greater stress on federal issues and renegotiated centre-state relations that became a particularly salient issue in the 1980s and 1990s. Manifestos of all major national parties and groupings of parties such as the United Front and Left Front were remarkably similar in their approach to the federal question. All of them advocated greater consultation between the union and the states by a strengthening of inter-governmental agencies such as the IGC and the NDC besides their proposing a new federal deal assuring the states a greater fiscal allocation as well as transfer of centrally sponsored schemes to the states as far as possible. The BJP was more specific and promised a 33 per cent share to the states in the divisible tax revenue. The Congress and Janata Dal also promised to work towards the introduction of the value-added tax (VAT) system to replace the sales tax and to promote better inter-state commerce. Most parties also supported the creation of smaller states where there was an evidently sizeable demand for it. However, both the BJP and Congress took an ad hoc approach to the problem, whereas the Samata Party stood, 'for the setting up of States Reorganisation Commission to make recommendations on all demands for smaller states.'[17] The Left Front did not specifically mention the issue of creation of smaller states, but it proclaimed that its constituent parties 'have been in the forefront in championing the democratic aspirations of the people's diverse cultures and of languages in a federal set-up as a basis for strengthening Indian unity'.[18] It also went on to guarantee regional autonomy to Jammu and Ladakh regions in the state of Jammu and Kashmir and, its commitment to retain Article 370 of the Indian Constitution.

Besides, the socio-cultural and political issues discussed above, the question of economic liberalisation became one of the most important questions in the election manifestos since 1991, when the Rao-Manmohan Singh team introduced radical economic reforms even though the Congress election manifesto of the year had not made it an electoral issue. Since then, gradual liberalisation of the economy has more or less continued under all successive governments. Since these governments have been minority/coalition governments, in some of which even the Left parties participated, we may surmise that at least among the political class there appears to have emerged a broad consensus as to the necessity of these reforms. There has, however, always existed some degree of variation in the approach of various parties on this issue. This broad consensus with persisting differences in emphasis was evident in the 1998 manifestos as well. The Congress continued to be more forthright in its advocacy of economic reforms, whereas the Left parties were most critical of them. Other parties such as the BJP, Janata Dal and Samata Party took their positions somewhere in the middle. Comparing the 1998 manifestos with the earlier ones of the decade, we find that whereas the Congress declarations of economic reforms has over the years become somewhat less enthusiastic, the earlier more vocal critics have become more mellowed, without, however, welcoming the reforms with open arms. If anything, we feel a growing consensus in the political class in favour of a more cautious approach to economic reforms. The Congress manifesto promised to 'continue the process of industrial and trade liberalisation that it initiated in 1991'. It went on, however, to add that it would 'ensure that competition is free and fair. It would also ensure that Indian companies are given every support to compete effectively with foreign companies at home and abroad'.[19] It was almost reminiscent of the BJP's swadeshi without using the term. The Congress policy towards the public sector also indicated a mix of pragmatism and ideological posturing. In its view 'it is time to redefine fundamentally the role of the public sector given the growth of entrepreneurship in the country and the pressure on public expenditure from more essential social sectors like education and health'.[20] Where it supported a continued role for the public sector as in security and strategic industries, it promised to reorganise them on 'commercial lines' with 'adequate autonomy and accountability'. It also promised to more seriously implement recommendations of the Disinvestment Commission than the United Front government had done. Besides, it proposed to give this commission, a statutory status with greater professionalism and executive authority. It also promised to continue to provide necessary incentives to the small-scale industry which is regarded as 'the backbone of the Indian economy'.

The BJP manifesto appeared to be equally critical of both the Nehruvian socialism and economic liberalisation of the 1990s. Perhaps, the most notable advocacy of the swadeshi approach to economic development was to be found in the BJP manifesto. However, compared to its earlier advocacy of swadeshi, the BJP was now seeking to reconcile swadeshi with what it called 'full liberalisation and calibrated globalisation', but this full liberalisation was mainly internal in its scope, for, it went on to add that 'the greater the liberalisation, the more demanding was the involvement of the government to protect national industry and employment'.[21] The swadeshi was simply defined as 'India First' and 'India shall be built by Indians'. It went on to say: 'national development will largely depend upon national effort and national capital and savings. Even after the so-called reforms, the share of FDI in national investment is less than two per cent, i.e. out of the total national investment of over Rs 12,30,000 crore, FDI amounted to only Rs 18,500 crore during the year 1991–96'.[22] It, however, visualised a 'crucial' role for foreign capital in sectors like infrastructure.

Both the United Front and Left Front—the two partly overlapped, as the former included the latter—in their manifestos were squarely critical of the economic reforms package introduced since 1991. The new United Front document was Janus-faced because on the one hand, it referred back to its common minimum programme of June 1996 which had welcomed foreign investments in the infrastructure sector, and on the other, verbalised anti-reform sentiments. It set greater store on the implementation of land reforms which, it was hoped, would result in increased productivity and distribution that in turn would expand the purchasing power of the people. It did not even mention the economic reforms. Its emphasis was more on social justice than growth with a focus on three primary objectives—foodgrain in every home, health for all, and schooling for every child.[23] This clearly showed the influence of the Left Front on the new manifesto of the United Front. The Left Front manifesto itself went on to assert:

> The policies ushered in the name of economic reforms since 1991 have only worsened the situation. Liberalisation has meant a bonanza for the big business houses, landlords, financial speculators and big traders who make super-profits and accumulate huge incomes. Under the IMF-World Bank dictated model, the priorities for India's economic growth are determined not in the interests of the Indian people but for a narrow affluent section at home and foreign capitalists.[24]

India's foreign policy has displayed a remarkable degree of continuity since independence. This continuity is particularly notable in the context of some basic changes in the international scenario in the last decade, e.g., the formal end of the Cold War and the disintegration of the Soviet bloc. The election manifestos of 1998 were replete with premises and assumptions underlying Indian foreign policy formulated after independence. The BJP manifesto was critical of 'a renewed tendency by some big powers to dominate and to impose conditionalities to advance their political and economic interest even if it is detrimental to others'.[25] The Congress manifesto paid glowing tributes to 'the foresight and wisdom of Jawaharlal Nehru that the foreign policy framework crafted by him remains intact in its basics and fundamentals'.[26] The Janata Dal manifesto remarked that 'despite major changes in world politics, non-alignment remains the right policy for India', which is 'directed to the promotion of peace, freedom, disarmament and just and equitable world order'.[27] All manifestos went on to emphasise the importance of improving diplomatic and economic relations with the neighbours, especially within the framework of SAARC and SAFTA, South-South cooperation and with the great powers and trading blocs in the world. Both the BJP and Congress manifestos underlined India's 'long and traditional' (BJP) and 'special' (Congress) relationships with Russia and emphasised improving Indo-US relations based on 'mutual respect, shared values and congruence of interests' (BJP). The Congress manifesto noted that the USA had emerged as 'India's largest trade and investment partner' and promised to give 'a new momentum to Indo-US economic, commercial, scientific and technological relations'. The manifesto of the Left went on to deplore 'the new world situation where the United States and its western allies seek to dominate the world'. It highlighted its opinion that it was 'imperative that India's foreign policy continued with its basic orientation embodied in the non-aligned policy'.[28] It also called for cancellation of Indo-US military cooperation and removal of the US nuclear base in Diego Garcia in the Indian Ocean. All manifestos supported India's resistance to western pressure to sign the NPT and CTBT. Most manifestos also demanded a permanent seat for India in the UN Security Council. Moreover, the BJP manifesto promised to establish a National Security Council as a continuous advisory agency of the government to develop a wholistic view on India's defence and security. The Janata Dal manifesto promised to appoint a Foreign Policy Advisory Council for periodic review of India's external relations. This would consist of the prime minister, the external affairs minister, defence minister, finance minister, commerce minister, home minister and experts on foreign policy, defence and science and technology.

The Campaign

The electoral campaign in 1998, revealed the growing regionalisation of Indian politics as well as the continuing relevance though not efficacy of nationwide mobilisation. The three major political formations mounted three patterns of campaigns suited to their specific alliance patterns and leadership resources. The BJP campaign was most upbeat to begin with, as also more nationwide in terms of its potential appeal. Its two star campaigners—Atal Behari Vajpayee and L.K. Advani—enjoyed a nationwide image and presence supplemented by their regional satraps, notably Jayalalitha in Tamil Nadu, Mamata Banerjee in West Bengal, R.K. Hegde in Karnataka, George Fernandes in western India, Nitish Kumar in Bihar and Naveen Patnaik in Orissa. Initially, the BJP campaign suffered on account of the hesitation of some of its regional allies to mount a joint campaign because of their reservations about their being seen to move too closely with the Hindu, communal BJP. This was particularly evident in Mamata Banerjee's fear of losing her considerable appeal to the Muslim voters in West Bengal. A similar precaution was taken by the Samata Party leaders who openly voiced their opposition to the BJP's alliance with AIADMK in the context of its leader facing prosecution on charges of corruption. Even the Samata Party's own alliance with the BJP was not entirely unproblematic. For example, George Fernandes took pains to clarify in the course of the campaign that he condemned the demolition of the Babri Masjid in Ayodhya, but he could not justify the on-going Hindu-Muslim tension nor his party's alliance with a communal party. He made reference to his own socialist past and the BJP's keenness for a democratic reconciliation.[29]

The BJP alliance took the lead in its nominating Vajpayee as the prime ministerial candidate, presumably to capitalise on his liberal outlook and national image. The strategy of the BJP alliance to project Vajpayee as its leader right through the campaign did benefit it, as an opinion poll showed that Vajpayee was ahead of all other prime ministerial figures included in the survey, followed by Sonia Gandhi. In a first-hand observation conveyed to us by an investigator from the field it was found that in Tamil Nadu, Vajpayee's face was almost as visible in election posters and billboards as those of the top two regional leaders. None of the other political combinations could project a prime minister in the waiting. The Congress party initially entered the campaign under its president, Sitaram Kesari's leadership, whose lacklustre image further suffered under criticism from the usual voices within the organisation which requested Mrs Sonia Gandhi to come forward to lead the party to which she remained impervious in the early phase of the campaign.

The Congress campaign initially presented the spectacle of a sinking ship in stormy waters. Sonia Gandhi's abrupt decision to make herself available for campaigning brought about a palpable change in the scenario. It gave a shot in the arm to the Congress organisation and drew huge crowds in most places where she addressed mass meetings. Accompanied by her daughter, Priyanka Gandhi, son-in-law, Robert Vadhera and son, Rahul Gandhi, she turned out to be an object of considerable curiosity to the people. Crowds thronged and lustily cheered her presence. She spoke from brief, prepared speeches haltingly read out in Hindi. She kicked off her campaign from Sriperambudoor in Tamil Nadu, the site of her husband's assassination seven years ago, where she initially spoke in Tamil and subsequently slipped into Hindi. By the end of the campaign she had visited all the major states of the union. The main burden of her speeches consisted of emotionally surcharged references to her association with the Nehru-Gandhi family, her bereavements, her identification with the masses, the ability of the Congress to address the problems of the nation and the failings of other parties and combinations. She initially avoided personal attacks but mostly decried Hindu communalism and the damage it had done to the Indian nation. She also offered apologies on behalf of her party for Operation Blue Star in Punjab and the failure of the Congress government at the centre to protect the Babri Masjid in Ayodhya. She also dared the government to come out with any definite information on the Bofors scandal. Ironically, the Jain Commission Report which had been the issue on which the Congress brought down the United Front government was not made an issue in the Congress campaign at all. As the Congress campaign heated up, Sonia Gandhi became increasingly more aggressive, calling Vajpayee a liar in a frontal attack on him for his charge about Rajiv Gandhi's involvement in the Bofors scandal. Vajpayee's anguished response was: 'I have never lied; even Nehru and Indira could never say that of me.'[30]

The impact of Sonia Gandhi's campaign on the election was generally discounted by her opponents. While the reactions of Mulayam Singh Yadav and Laloo Prasad Yadav were somewhat restrained, the BJP and communist parties were most dismissive. Jyoti Basu, for example, opined: 'Sonia Gandhi is a housewife who has been pushed into political campaigning by a bankrupt Congress party.'[31] The comments in the press were divided on whether her evident popularity would be translated into votes without a well-organised party organisation in place. According to an opinion poll commissioned by *The Pioneer* and conducted in eight Lok Sabha constituencies in the first week of January, her campaign had improved Congress prospects by at least four per cent though it was insufficient to fully make up for the negative swing the party was facing in comparison to its previous performance.[32] Between 11 January and 26 February, Sonia Gandhi had visited 30 places more or less evenly spread out throughout the country (17 states and the union territory of Chandigarh), occasionally making her appearances in as many as seven cities or towns in a single day. Her campaign trail thus indiscriminately covered most states, irrespective of evidence of appreciable Congress(I) electoral support or its absence. Of the total 142 constituencies visited by her, 61 were held by Congress(I), 56 by BJP, 22 by United Front parties, one by BSP, one by MIM, and one by a non-party independent. Ten each of these constituencies were reserved for SCs and STs.[33]

The UF had at least three past prime ministers in V.P. Singh, H.D. Deve Gowda and I.K. Gujral within its fold, to say nothing of other aspirants such as Jyoti Basu, Mulayam Singh Yadav and Laloo Prasad Yadav. Indeed, Jyoti Basu could have become the prime minister in 1996 itself, but for his party's reluctance to join a coalition government in which it was not a dominant partner. The Front, however, could not project any of them officially as its prime ministerial mascot for the obvious reason that it had to contain the internal contradictions and personality clashes until after the election.

The United Front campaign appeared to be least orchestrated, except for the launching of their joint campaign from a common platform in Hyderabad where almost all major Front leaders appeared and addressed a mass rally. Thereafter, the constituents of the Front proceeded to concentrate on their respective areas of regional influence. V.P. Singh by and large shunned active campaigning, and donned the mantle of an elder statesman. This was reminiscent of JP's role in the 1977 campaign without, however, the Gandhian socialist patriarch's manoeuvrability with the leaders and huge popularity with the masses. The leader who mandalised Indian politics in a veritable earthquake in the early 1990s, was apparently avoided by the Mandal satraps in Bihar, U.P. and Madhya Pradesh. Gujral, the incumbent prime minister appeared to be beleaguered in the Jullundhar parliamentary constituency where the ideologue without mass following was desperately trying to win with the controversial support of the Akalis which was resented by the other parties of the United Front. Among the United Front campaigners who tried to project national profiles were Chandrababu Naidu, Deve Gowda, and Ram Vilas Paswan. Even Jyoti Basu mainly limited himself to West Bengal, the Samajwadi Party leader, Mulayam Singh Yadav sought to strike a national posture beyond Uttar Pradesh, but his alliance with the Congress and Republican Party of India in Maharashtra did not meet with spectacular success; it also made his loyalty to the United Front appear suspect.

Regional parties were less divided and strained by the compulsion to project a national profile. They concentrated their campaign resources and appeals to their respective pockets of influence. They harped primarily on issues and concerns closer to the people in the regions. This feature broadly characterised the campaign by state parties in Orissa, Bihar, Punjab, Gujarat and Tamil Nadu. The women's turnout at Laloo-Rabri rallies in Bihar was reported to be 'the most striking feature of the 1998' campaign by one observer.[34]

Chandan Mitra draws attention to a palpable north-south contrast in the styles of campaigning in 1998 as also earlier. The campaign south of the Vindhayas has always been more colourful and enthusiastic than in the north. To quote him:

> At election time, Tamil Nadu as well as Andhra Pradesh reverberate to loud parodies of popular film music through the daylight hours, rather till 10 p.m. Most parties also popularise election symbols through especially recorded songs extolling their virtues. ... Compared to vibrant, colourful, cacophonic Tamil Nadu, neighbouring Andhra Pradesh would appear quite staid. But by current north Indian standards, even that is remarkably vivacious. First, the ruling TDP's chosen colour, blinding yellow, is loud enough. Then, the TDP makes full use of its bicycle symbol by routinely taking out cycle yatras.[35]

Both in the south and north electioneering was marked by vivid, visual symbols accompanied by the loud blaring of adapted versions of film songs. Those with long memories may testify that in earlier decades, folk limericks were more in use. The 1998 polls will probably be remarkable in electoral history as the year in which all the major parties vied with each other for the services of film stars from both Hindi films and regional ones.

The campaigns in the 1990s also marked a watershed in the liberal use of the electronic mass media as well as of helicopters and planes. The Election Commission worked out the apportionment of radio and TV time among recognised political parties on the official media. A private TV channel, the STAR, introduced a round-the-clock news channel on the eve of the 1998 polls besides, and a morning to night coverage of a day in the lives of star campaigners of all the major political parties. Moreover, parties, at least the major ones bought advertising space in national and regional newspapers. A few more resourceful ones for the first time opened a website on the internet, e.g., the BJP and INC.

Despite this extent of mechanisation of electioneering, the traditional ways of campaigning were not dispensed with. Political formations put no less emphasis on the organisation of mass rallies in metropolises which were addressed by leaders who had greater visibility and public appeal. According to one reckoning:

> On average, Vajpayee alone addressed meetings in five constituencies each day for 45 days. This adds up to a whopping 225, give or take 10. BJP president Lal Krishna Advani covered an almost the same number. The Congress sole show-piece, Sonia Gandhi, escorted by junior claimants to the dynasty's inheritance, would be ending up with around 150. Such extensive coverage by top leaders of political parties never happened before the age of the chartered plane and the ubiquitous chopper arrived.[36]

It would thus appear that the campaign input by national leaders in 1998 was by no means meagre. Although the regional streams in the campaign still prevailed over large areas and left the mandate fragmented, this was not for the lack of efforts on the part of the national leaders. However, some party reforms that may influence the thrust of voters' alignments must be considered, such as the holding of a national leadership convention within important national parties to elect the leaders before every general election. This would enable the national parties, as in Canada, to elect their leaders prior to the polls in the glare of nationwide publicity and introduce in the voting behaviour of the people a nationally aggregative process.

As in earlier elections, in 1998 as well, the typical method of campaigning by direct mass contact remained unchanged. Cavalcades of cars on their way from the airstrip to the venue of a rally would make brief stops for the contestants to address the crowds and then move on. In urban areas, the candidates often undertook padayatras ending with nukkad and neighbourhood meetings. Posters, billboards and leaflets were liberally used, whereas election manifestos were limited to party offices and given out to interested journalists and academicians. Rathyatras, a major contribution of the BJP and emulated by regional leaders like N.T. Rama Rao (Chaitanya Ratham) and

Laloo Prasad Yadav (Garib Rath) were more a feature of the 1980s than the 1990s.

Another aspect of campaigning in the last two decades has been the security staff surrounding the VIPs. Indeed, the security paraphernalia has become a regular part of any VIP entourage at public cost. This has naturally added to the cost of campaigning both for the government and the parties. To quote Chandan Mitra, 'Despite television and the growing familiarity of the electorate with its leaders, the urge to see them in person has actually grown. Moreover, not visiting a particular constituency is usually seen as the leadership's tacit acceptance of the local candidate's weakness.'[37]

As in recent, previous elections, the 1998 campaign continued to be overseen and monitored by the Election Commission. Even after T.N. Seshan's departure from the Nirvachan Sadan, his successors maintained an activist, albeit a slightly restrained, profile of the commission to which free, fair and peaceful conduct of the polls may be attributed. Having tamed the parties in holding organisational elections according to their constitutions, the commission maintained a close surveillance over the campaign and the conduct of polls with the help of over 1,800 observers sent out to the fields.[38] This presumably explains fewer countermands and repolls ordered by the commission in 1998 than in 1996.

The commission tried to improve the administration of elections in several ways. First, it required candidates to maintain a register in the prescribed format which was to be made available for inspection to the concerned election authorities in the field once in three days instead of on a day-to-day basis as in the last election. The candidates were obliged to furnish details of the expenditure incurred by the:

1. political party which had fielded them;
2. any other party supporting them;
3. any other organisation supporting them; and
4. any individuals supporting them.

This step of the commission followed the Supreme Court directive in the Common Cause Case, 1996.[39]

Second, pending consideration by a parliamentary committee on electoral reforms, the commission proceeded to work out a scheme for limited state funding to parties during elections for use of government-owned electronic media for their campaigns. Under this scheme, finalised in consultation with political parties, seven national parties and 34 state parties recognised under the Election Symbols Order, 1968, were allowed a total time of 61 hours each on the Doordarshan and All India Radio networks nationally or regionally. Time vouchers were made available in denominations of five and ten minutes each and parties were free to combine them if they so desired. The actual date and time of the telecasts and broadcasts were decided by the Prasar Bharati Corporation in consultation with the Election Commission. The Commission also convened a meeting of representatives of television channels, major independent producers as well as the Prasar Bharati Corporation officers to facilitate a consensus on the issues of fair and balanced coverage of campaigns and other election-related news items, current affairs programmes, etc.[40] This facility, however, could not be made available to the RJD, the RJP and Trinamool Congress on account of their being formed late when they split from the JD, BJP and Congress, respectively. They could not thus join the category of recognised political parties.[41]

Third, the commission promptly acted on complaints of the use of government guest houses, Pradesh Bhawans, railway guest houses and of government machinery by the parties in power for purposes of campaigning in violation of the electoral code of conduct. The governments of Bihar and Punjab made specific requests for their being allowed to use state-government aircraft by the chief ministers during the campaign, either on hire as in the case of Bihar or on the grounds of security in the case of the latter. The commission, however, strongly advised them to hire private aircraft for the purpose.[42]

Similarly, the commission pulled up the Gujarat government for the 'extraordinary haste' in finalising deals in the power sector and advised it to keep them on hold till the completion of the election process on 15 March. Action was also initiated against governments of Bihar and Mizoram for their removing senior officials from poll-related duties.[43] The commission also prohibited distribution of sarees, dhotis and blankets under the social-security scheme of the labour department. The government's argument that the suspension of the scheme may result in the lapse of the budgetary allocations for 1997–98, was overruled by the commission.[44] The apprehension of possible violation of the code of conduct prompted the prime minister, I.K. Gujral, to postpone the launching of the second phase of the Rs 587 crore water-supply scheme for 96 villages in Rajasthan.[45]

Fourth, the commission also took the initiative to control defacement of public and private property by the use of posters, wall graffiti, hoardings, etc. It instructed the chief electoral officer of Delhi and the chief secretaries of all states and union territories to take steps to ensure a cleaner campaign by parties and candidates.[46]

Fifth, at least two decisions of the Election Commission in the context of the conduct of polls proved to be somewhat controversial. The first related to the shortening of the campaign period to 14 days from the rather long poll schedule of 20 days in four phases. The second was the ban on publication of pre-election polls from 14 February to 28 February and a similar restriction on publication of exit-polls from 16 February for a thirteen-day period, until the completion of the voting in all parts of the country, to preclude undue influence on voters, if any, by the opinion polls. While the political parties generally supported this move, the media and the legal fraternity were up in arms and even challenged the move in a court of law. The commission enforced this ban under Clause 2 of Section 126 of the Representation of the People Act, which prohibits 'display to the public any election matter by means of cinematography, television or any similar apparatus' during the '48 hours ending with the hour fixed for conclusion of the poll'.[47]

The commission's move was supported by the Press Council of India, an independent agency constituted under an Act of the parliament. The chairman of the council, Justice P.B. Sawant justified the ban citing similar restrictions in the USA, Canada,

France, Luxembourg, Netherlands, Spain, Portugal and Poland. He opined that the possible influence of the polls on voting behaviour was tantamount to influencing the electorate by money or muscle power.[48]

Sixth, the Election Commission could reasonably take credit for their having commendably conducted the 1998 polls as also the previous recent ones such that the nation's worst fears about violence did not, by and large, materialise. A joint strategy by the centre and the Election Commission and cooperation by the state governments facilitated the strategic deployment of para-military forces in hypersensitive and vulnerable areas. Yet, 26 deaths were reported in the first phase of polling, though widespread incidents were generally limited to Bihar, Uttar Pradesh and Andhra Pradesh. The second phase was more satisfactory with six deaths—four in Bihar and one each in Orissa and West Bengal—though not all these incidents were poll-related. The third phase mercifully witnessed even fewer incidents of violence and which were non-fatal.[49]

Conclusion

While the outcome of the 1998—and the previous—elections will be analysed together in the following chapter, we pull together here some analytical strands pertaining to these elections by way of concluding this chapter. The party system thrown up by these electoral churnings underline the continuing predicament of a hung parliament that began in 1989. These elections represent the efforts of a fragmented society to come to terms with the task of governance in an era where old answers to many problems have ceased to be relevant. The statist image of India under Nehru and Indira Gandhi has yielded to a considerably liberalised economy. The largest single party today —the BJP—seeks to balance the secularist nationalism by a 'cultural' nationalism more firmly rooted in the Indian tradition that espouses 'positive secularism' in place of 'minorityism'. A major national party until the other day—the Janata Dal—that 'mandalised' the electorate in search of the elusive OBC majority stands practically decimated today. Thus, while the dominance of the only truly all-India party—the Congress—was eroded by the late 1980s, neither the Hindutva majority nor the Mandal majority could take its place. The long-term dream of the left wing to extend their electoral base to the Hindi heartland either on their own or piggy-back on the Janata Dal or Congress, came to naught. Instead, the mushrooming of regional parties and continuing fragmentation of national parties, including the Congress and the BJP, portend the continuance of coalition and/or minority governments without their evolving a set of ground rules and culture of stable and purposive politics of coalition governments. This is the most serious crisis of the Indian party system since the Republic was born in the turmoil of partition in the wake of the retreat of British imperialism on its own terms. The 1990s, in particular, have revealed a serious crisis of political institutions and the developmental State to an extent that the very practice of parliamentary government at the centre and in some states, and the nascent welfare state as visualised in the chapter on the Directive Principles of State Policy in the Constitution has become well nigh beyond the pale of practical politics owing to the quick turnover of governments. It has been a decade of a surfeit of elections without parliamentary governance, though not without an opening for a greater federalisation of India's parliamentary-federal system that had previously worked predominantly as a parliamentary system.

Notes

1. *The Hindustan Times*, 8 January 1998.
2. *The Hindu*, 3 January 1998.
3. *The Indian Express*, 6 January 1998.
4. *The Hindu*, 3 January 1998 and *The Hindustan Times*, 8 January 1998.
5. *The Hindu*, 3 January 1998.
6. *The Hindustan Times*, 8 January 1998; *The Hindu*, 8 January 1998.
7. *The Hindustan Times*, 8 January 1998.

8. *Ibid.*
9. *The Hindu*, 3 January 1998; *The Indian Express*, 4 January 1998; *The Times of India*, 6 January 1998.
10. *The Hindustan Times*, 8 January 1998.
11. *The Hindustan Times*, and *The Pioneer*, both 7 January 1998.
12. *The Hindu*, 4 January 1998.
13. *The Indian Express*, 6 January 1998.
14. *The Hindu*, 5 January 1998.
15. *The Hindustan Times*, 8 January 1998.
16. BJP, 1998, *Election Manifesto 1998*: 4.
17. Samata Party, 1998, *Manifesto 1998*: 6–7.
18. Left Front, 1998, *Manifesto of the Left Parties for Lok Sabha Elections 1998*: 6.
19. Indian National Congress, 1998, *Election Manifesto, General Elections, Lok Sabha 1998*: 50.
20. *Ibid*: 49.
21. BJP, 1998, *Election Manifesto 1998*: 11.
22. *Ibid*: 10.
23. *The Hindustan Times*, New Delhi, 1 February 1998: 12.
24. Left Front, 1998, *Manifesto of the Left Parties for Lok Sabha Election 1998*: 8.
25. BJP, 1998, *Election Manifesto 1998*: 29.
26. INC, 1998, *Election Manifesto, General Elections, Lok Sabha 1998*: 54.
27. JD, 1998, *Power to Grassroots for Change with Stability: Janata Dal Manifesto, Lok Sabha Elections 1998*: 17.
28. Left Front, 1998, *Manifesto of the Left Parties for Lok Sabha Election 1998*: 7.
29. *The Times of India*, 9 February 1998.
30. *India Decides: Issues—Poll '98*, compiled by a Private T.V. channel, mimeographed.
31. *Ibid.*
32. *The Pioneer*, 25 January 1998.
33. *Indian Decides: Issue—Poll '98*, compiled by a private T.V. channel, mimeographed.
34. *The Pioneer*, 28 February 1998.
35. *The Pioneer*, 28 February 1998.
36. Chandan Mitra *The Pioneer*, 1 March 1998.
37. *The Pioneer*, 1 March 1998.
38. The figure is taken from *The Pioneer*, 22 February 1998.

39. *The Times of India*, 24 January 1998.
40. No. ECI/Press Note/05, 15 January 1998.
41. *The Pioneer*, 21 January 1998.
42. *The Hindustan Times*, 7 and 17 January 1998.
43. *The Hindu*, 1 January 1998.
44. *The Hindustan Times*, 24 January 1998.
45. *The Hindu*, 1 January 1998.
46. No. ECI/Press Note/98/05, 8 January 1999.
47. *The Times of India*, 22 January 1998.
48. *The Hindu*, 14 January 1998.
49. *The Hindu*, 12 February 1998; *The Times of India*, 17 February 1998 and 23 February 1998; *The Pioneer*, 2 March 1998.

CHAPTER SEVEN

From Elections to Elections: 1998

Unstable Coalition Governments

The Lok Sabha elections in 1996 and 1998—the former a regular one and the latter a mid-term exercise—were no remedies either, for the bout of governmental instability that began with the 1989 regular polls. Prior to 1989, the eight national elections since 1951–52 had produced one-party majority governments mostly led by the Congress that were remarkably stable, barring the Janata Party government that fell prematurely owing to insufficient parliamentary support. There were six prime ministers in the first four decades, whereas in the last decade alone there have been as many as eight. The average span of the PMs in the first phase was over six years, ranging between 16 years (Nehru) and five months (Charan Singh). In comparison, during the phase of unstable coalition and/or minority governments the average span was 17 months, ranging between five years (Rao) and 13 days (Vajpayee, the first term).

The coalition/minority governments that sprang from hung parliaments since 1989 have been broadly of four types. The new era began with the Janata Dal-led National Front, consisting, in addition, mainly of regional parties such as the DMK, Telugu

Desam, Asom Gana Parishad, etc, in the cabinet coalition. This minority coalition was propped up by 'external' support from the parliamentary floor by the Left parties and the Hindu-right BJP without their joining the government. Led by a Janata Dal leader with a Congress past (V.P. Singh), the policy frame of this government was essentially centrist with rural populist and economic nationalist rhetorics. The two major policy issues that rocked its boat related to the Mandal reservations and the Ram Mandir dispute in Ayodhya. The former was sparked off by a personality clash between the prime minister and his deputy prime minister, Devi Lal. The latter was because the rathayatra from Somanath to Ayodhya of the BJP was halted, with the arrest of L.K. Advani under the orders of the United Front government in New Delhi and the Janata Dal government, led by Laloo Prasad Yadav, in Bihar. On the latter issue, the BJP withdrew its parliamentary support abruptly, resulting in the fall of the NF government barely eleven months after its formation.

This was followed by right-centrist Congress(I) regimes led by Chandrashekhar of the Samajwadi Janata Party (a Janata Dal splinter) for four months (plus three months as a caretaker government) and the Congress government formed after the 1991 Lok Sabha election and led by P.V. Narasimha Rao that somehow completed its full term by means fair and foul. Both these were minority governments, the former supported by the Congress(I) from the parliamentary floor and the latter by the wide spectrum of opposition majority on issue-based contingent backing. The Rao regime managed to accelerate major economic reforms aimed at economic liberalisation and capitalist structural adjustment at the cost of political (democratic socialist) liberalism, with the support of a broad assortment of right-centrist parties but opposed by the left-wing minority. Approximately around the middle of its term the Rao government fabricated a majority for the Congress(I) through support from elections in Punjab and desertion from the ranks of other parties in the parliament. It survived three confidence votes in the Lok Sabha, of which the one in 1993 led to the infamous JMM bribery case that went up to the Supreme Court [P.V. Narasimha Rao vs. the State (CBI/SPE) 1998].

The left-centrist national parties and their regional allies in the National Front regrouped into the United Front after the 1996 Lok Sabha elections and forged a post-poll common minimum programme premised on federalism and economic nationalism tempered by economic liberalisation. The 14-party United Front ruled between the Lok Sabha elections of 1996 and 1998 with its two minority governments—one headed by H.D. Deve Gowda and one by I.K. Gujral, both from the Janata Dal, but, who were in the Congress earlier—propped up by the external support of the Indian National Congress from the parliamentary floor. The term of the first government lasted 10 months and the second 18 months, because of the withdrawal of Congress(I) support in both instances. The United Front first bought peace by sacrificing Deve Gowda as a scapegoat for his alleged insensitivities to the Congress(I) and replaced him with Gujral, who turned out to be more attuned to what he called the imperative of developing a 'coalition culture'. When the Congress(I) failed in forming a minority government of its own, it acquiesced to its extending outside support to the Gujral government. However, on the release of the Jain Commission interim report on Rajiv Gandhi's assassination, the Congress(I) demanded the expulsion of the DMK ministers in the union government. The issue arose because of the indictment of the DMK government in Tamil Nadu in the Sriperumbudoor bomb blast that killed the Congress(I) prime ministerial candidate in the midst of an electoral campaign in 1991. The Gujral government and the United Front stood their ground this time and preferred to be toppled by the Congress(I). The country was forced to go to the polls again in 1998.

The fourth type of coalition/minority government to have been formed during this phase was the right-centrist BJP-led government in alliance with some of the important regional parties which either directly joined the government or extended support from the parliamentary floor. In 1996, the abortive 13-day government headed by Vajpayee, augured ill for the prospects of the BJP, but, changed favourably when the BJP regained power in a coalition government after the 1998 elections. It ruled for 13 months until its largest ally, Jayalalitha's AIADMK, pulled the rug from under its feet and precipitated in 1999, mid-term polls. This was the first government in independent India headed by a prime minister with a non-Congress past. This was also the first government in which the Hindu-right forces predominated, even though in coalition with regional leaders, including the Samata Party leaders with socialist antecedents. In some ways the Janata Party government in the late 1970s could be compared with this government inasmuch as the previously Jan Sangh elements (now BJP) were also the largest constituent on that occasion too, but then the Janata prime minister, Moraji Desai, was a former Congressman and the Janata Party regime was at least formally a one-party government (with an absolute majority in the Lok Sabha). As with the Jan Sangh constituent of the Janata Party government, the BJP-led coalition also contributed to the process of liberalisation and constitutionalisation of the Hindu-right forces. The National Agenda for Governance that was put together after the election by over a dozen parties in the pre-poll alliance with the BJP relied more, in addition to policy preferences of other partners, on the president's address prepared by the Vajpayee government for the opening session of the parliament in May 1996, than on the BJP's 1998 election manifesto. The presidential address had skirted contentious issues such as the repeal of Article 370 relating to Jammu and Kashmir, Common Civil Code for all Indian religious communities and the construction of a Ram temple at Ayodhya. The national agenda also professed commitment to genuine federalism and economic nationalism defined in terms of the swadeshi.

Analysing the Electoral Outcomes

This chapter seeks to present a comparative analysis of the electoral outcomes in terms of the performance of various parties in 1996 and in 1998. While both the elections produced hung parliaments without any single-party majority, there were notable internal variations between the two parliaments. The previous section has already given a hint regarding the first difference. The eleventh Lok Sabha elected in 1996, formed left-centrist cabinet coalitions, whereas the twelfth Lok Sabha in 1998 propped up a right-centrist cabinet coalition in which the Hindu and the Sikh right-wing parties joined hands. Moreover, between the two elections, national and state parties suffered an overall decline, while registered (unrecognised) parties, many of them flash formations, increased their percentage of votes from 3.29 to 10.87 and seats from 0.38 to 5.63 per cent (See Table 7.1, Notes).

Table 7.1 also shows that the only parties to have gained in gross terms between the two elections were the BJP and BSP. The former increased its percentage of votes from 20.29 to 25.59 and seats from 34.18 to 46.91. The latter, which was a state party in 1996, rose to the status of a national party. Of the two main communist parties, the CPI(M) continues to be an appreciable political force in West Bengal and Kerala, and has kept its position intact between the two elections. The CPI(M) is an important party in Tripura though it has suffered a slide. The CPI had previously been less regionally concentrated than the CPI(M) but more widely spread out in a number of states. In 1998, it retained its performance of 1996 in Andhra Pradesh, Kerala, Meghalaya, Tamil Nadu and West Bengal. It improved its position in Manipur and Punjab, but, declined in Bihar as a result of its being squeezed in between the RJD and BJP-Samata Party. These election results also underline a long-term trend of the failure of left-wing parties to expand their support-base from their original pockets of influence, beyond West Bengal, Kerala and Tripura.

The Janata Dal suffered a precipitous fall: from 8.08 to 3.24 in terms of vote percentage and from 23.47 to 3.14 in terms of seat percentage. Both the Janata Dal and Congress(I) faced a major decline owing to the rebellion of some of their state units which proceeded to form separate state parties, namely, the RJD

TABLE 7.1 Performance of Parties in the 1996 and 1998 Lok Sabha Elections in State/Union Territories and All-India

State	*BJP*				*INC(I)*				*JD*				*CPI(M)*			
	% votes		*No. of seats*		*% votes*		*No. of seats*		*% votes*		*No. of seats*		*% votes*		*No. of seats*	
	1996	*1998*	*1996*	*1998*	*1996*	*1998*	*1996*	*1998*	*1996*	*1998*	*1996*	*1998*	*1996*	*1998*	*1996*	*1998*
Andhra Pradesh	5.65	18.30	0	4	39.66	38.46	22	22	—	0.87	—	1	2.91	2.89	1	0
Arunachal Pradesh	17.41	21.75	0	—	28.83	23.90	0	—	—	1.89	—	0	—	—	—	—
Assam	15.92	24.47	1	1	31.64	38.97	5	10	0.65	0.12	0	0	3.94	3.27	1	0
Bihar	20.54	24.03	18	20	12.99	7.27	2	5	31.88	8.72	22	1	0.84	0.40	0	0
Goa	13.75	30.04	0	—	34.37	31.59	0	2	—	—	—	—	—	—	—	—
Gujarat	48.52	48.28	16	19	38.69	36.49	10	7	0.42	2.94	0	0	0.2	—	0	—
Haryana	19.74	18.89	4	1	22.64	26.02	2	3	1.54	0.38	0	0	—	0.34	—	0
Himachal Pradesh	39.62	51.43	0	3	54.33	41.90	4	1	0.22	0.88	0	0	0.95	—	0	—
Jammu & Kashmir	19.04	28.64	1	2	27.46	19.24	4	1	17.63	0.50	1	0	—	—	—	—
Karnataka	24.85	26.95	6	13	30.29	36.22	5	9	34.91	21.69	16	3	0.38	0.04	0	0
Kerala	5.61	8.02	0	—	38.01	38.67	7	8	4.40	3.90	1	0	21.16	21.00	5	6
Madhya Pradesh	41.32	45.73	27	30	31.02	39.40	8	10	1.05	1.22	0	0	0.05	0.11	0	0
Maharashtra	21.81	42.49	18	4	34.78	43.64	15	33	3.30	1.67	0	0	1.10	0.61	0	0
Manipur	5.25	12.61	0	—	40.17	18.60	2	—	1.76	—	0	0	—	—	—	—
Meghalaya	5.93	9.01	0	—	53.64	47.62	1	2	—	—	—	—	—	—	—	—
Mizoram	—	2.94	—	—	42.50	34.86	1	—	—	—	—	—	—	—	—	—
Nagaland	—	—	—	—	62.31	86.70	1	1	—	—	—	—	—	—	—	—
Orissa	13.42	21.19	0	7	44.90	41.04	16	5	30.05	4.93	4	0	1.69	0.41	0	0
Punjab	6.48	11.67	0	3	35.10	28.85	2	—	2.66	4.18	0	1	2.68	1.06	0	0
Rajasthan	42.36	41.65	12	5	40.51	44.45	12	18	2.63	2.31	0	0	0.44	1.28	0	0
Sikkim	—	—	—	—	—	33.11	—	—	—	—	—	—	—	—	—	—
Tamil Nadu	2.93	6.86	0	3	18.26	4.78	0	—	1.53	—	0	—	1.82	0.63	0	0
Tripura	6.50	8.19	0	—	34.13	42.12	0	—	0.29	—	0	—	52.41	48.80	2	2

(contd.)

TABLE 7.1 (*contd.*)

State	CPI				Samata Party				BSP	
	% votes		*No. of seats*		*% votes*		*No. of seats*		*% votes*	*No. of seats*
	1996	*1998*	*1996*	*1998*	*1996*	*1998*	*1996*	*1998*	*1998*	*1998*
Andhra Pradesh	2.39	2.56	2	2	0.04	0.02	0	0	0.21	0
Arunachal Pradesh	—	—	—	—	—	—	—	—	—	—
Assam	—	0.95	—	0	—	—	—	—	—	—
Bihar	5.08	3.40	3	0	14.45	15.74	6	10	0.53	0
Goa	0.92	—	0	—	—	—	—	—	—	—
Gujarat	0.09	0.09	0	0	0.09	0.07	0	0	—	—
Haryana	0.36	0.15	0	0	19.01	—	0	—	7.68	1
Himachal Pradesh	0.42	0.56	0	0	0.04	—	0	—	1.15	0
Jammu & Kashmir	—	—	—	—	—	—	—	—	4.97	0
Karnataka	0.38	0.06	0	0	—	0.08	—	0	0.56	0
Kerala	8.22	8.32	2	2	0.01	0.00	0	0	0.13	0
Madhya Pradesh	0.73	0.66	0	0	0.06	0.38	0	0	8.70	0
Maharashtra	0.61	0.07	0	0	0.05	—	0	—	0.75	0
Manipur	4.01	20.47	0	1	1.74	0.59	0	0	—	—
Meghalaya	1.41	1.44	0	0	—	—	—	—	—	—
Mizoram	—	—	—	—	—	—	—	—	—	—
Nagaland	—	—	—	—	—	—	—	—	—	—
Orissa	0.34	0.99	0	0	1.55	0.08	1	0	0.32	0
Punjab	1.60	3.40	0	0	—	—	—	—	12.65	0
Rajasthan	0.19	0.62	0	0	0.85	0.06	0	0	2.12	0
Sikkim	—	—	—	—	—	—	—	—	—	—
Tamil Nadu	2.33	2.45	2	1	0.01	0.01	0	0	0.23	0
Tripura	—	—	—	—	—	—	—	—	—	—

(*contd.*)

TABLE 7.1 (*contd.*)

State	*BJP*				*INC(I)*				*JD*				*CPI(M)*			
	% votes		*No. of seats*		*% votes*		*No. of seats*		*% votes*		*No. of seats*		*% votes*		*No. of seats*	
	1996	*1998*	*1996*	*1998*	*1996*	*1998*	*1996*	*1998*	*1996*	*1998*	*1996*	*1998*	*1996*	*1998*	*1996*	*1998*
Uttar Pradesh	33.44	36.49	52	57	8.14	6.02	5	—	4.26	0.47	2	0	0.66	0.23	0	0
West Bengal	6.88	10.20	0	1	40.09	15.20	9	1	0.40	—	0	—	36.70	35.41	23	24
A & N Islands	24.25	35.53	0	—	58.22	35.91	1	1	—	—	—	—	14.32	5.67	0	0
Chandigarh	39.05	42.36	1	1	29.79	38.70	0	—	0.93	—	0	—	2.33	—	0	—
Dadra & Nagar Haveli	42.42	53.73	0	1	55.62	4.13	1	—	—	—	—	—	—	—	—	—
Daman & Diu	40.45	41.96	0	1	50.62	1.98	1	—	—	—	—	—	—	—	—	—
Delhi	49.62	50.73	5	6	37.29	42.64	7	1	4.24	2.46	0	0	0.27	—	0	—
Lakshadweep	—	—	—	—	51.71	51.55	1	1	48.29	48.45	0	0	—	—	—	—
Pondicherry	4.42	—	0	—	39.97	32.12	1	0	—	—	—	—	—	—	—	—
All India	20.29	26.59	161	179	28.80	25.82	140	141	8.80	3.24	46	6	6.12	5.16	32	32
			29.65	33.21			25.80	23.56			23.47	3.14			42.67	45.07

(*contd.*)

TABLE 7.1 (*contd.*)

State	CPI				Samata Party				BSP	
	% votes		No. of seats		% votes		No. of seats		% votes	No. of seats
	1996	1998	1996	1998	1996	1998	1996	1998	1998	1998
Uttar Pradesh	0.38	0.18	0	0	0.93	0.79	1	2	20.90	4
West Bengal	3.81	3.64	3	3	0.01	0.00	0	0	0.24	0
A & Islands	—	—	—	—	—	—	—	—	—	—
Chandigarh	—	—	—	—	17.59	—	0	—	—	—
Dadra & Nagar Haveli	—	—	—	—	—	—	—	—	—	—
Daman & Diu	—	—	—	—	—	—	—	—	—	—
Delhi	0.12	—	0	—	0.12	—	0	—	2.34	0
Lakshadweep	—	—	—	—	—	—	—	—	—	—
Pondicherry	—	—	—	—	—	—	—	—	0.63	—
All India	1.97	1.75	12	9	2.17	1.76	8	12	4.67	5
			27.91	15.92			9.88	21.5		1.99

Notes:

	1996		1998	
	% vote	% seats	% vote	% seats
All National Parties	69.08	22.17	67.98	25.92
All State Parties	21.34	28.16	18.79	21.44
Registered (unrecognised) Parties	3.29	0.38	10.87	5.63
Independents	6.28	0.08	3.37	0.31

Source: Election Commission of India (1996 and 1998), vol. 1 of both.

Note: BSP was recognised as a 'national party' by the Election Commission in summer 1997 on the basis of its performance in the 1996 Lok Sabha election.

and BJD (Janata splinters) and the Trinamool Congress and Tamil Maanila Congress (Congress splinters). A new tendency caused by these elections was the increase in the number and strength of regional parties.

A look at the party scenario as it varies from state to state brings out some interesting characteristics of the configuration of parties (Table 7.1). These two elections revealed that the Congress(I) still continued to be the most widely spread party throughout the country, followed rather closely on its heels by the BJP. The percentage of votes that the former registered was over 30 in as many as 18 of the 25 states in 1996, and in 16 states in 1998. The BJP had a comparable share in the vote percentage in only five states in 1996, which remained the same in 1998, but it is significant that these states were the larger ones. In all-India terms it increased its vote percentage by over six points. All other national parties, including the Janata Dal were by and large more narrowly rooted in the regional context. To come back to the two main national parties, the major gains registered by the BJP between the two elections were in Andhra Pradesh, Arunachal Pradesh, Assam, Bihar, Goa, Himachal Pradesh, Jammu and Kashmir, Kerala, Manipur, Orissa, Tamil Nadu, Uttar Pradesh and West Bengal, mostly breaking new grounds. Notably, its vote percentage did not fall in any significant way anywhere. The main losses suffered by the Congress were in Arunachal Pradesh, Bihar, Goa, Himachal Pradesh, Jammu and Kashmir, Manipur, Meghalaya, Mizoram, Orissa, Punjab, Tamil Nadu and West Bengal. Its principal gains were in Assam, Haryana, Karnataka, Madhya Pradesh, Maharashtra, Nagaland, Rajasthan and Tripura, mostly the states it had lost in recent decades. These were apparently explicable less in terms of all-India factors than various state-specific and local, sociological and political variables.

The Indian electoral history suggests that no single party can hope to gain a majority and form a government of its own unless its vote percentage hovers around 40 and above. Neither of the two main parties in 1996 and 1998 was anywhere close to that point nationally. In the states, the Congress won such 'first-past-

TABLE 7.2
Performance of Major Regional Parties in the 1996 and 1998 Lok Sabha Elections

States and Parties	*1996*		*1998*	
	% votes	*Seats won*	*% votes*	*Seats won*
Andhra Pradesh				
TDP	32.40	16	31.97	12
Assam				
AGP	27.17	5	12.72	10
UMFA	—	—	4.27	1
Bihar				
RJD	—	—	26.58	17
Haryana				
HVP	15.19	3	11.60	1
HLD(R)	—	—	25.90	4
Jammu and Kashmir				
National Conference	—	—	36.35	3
Karnataka				
Lok Shakti	—	—	11.50	3
Maharashtra				
Shiv Sena	16.83	15	19.66	6
RPI	—	—	4.14	4
Mizoram				
MNF	37.63	0	—	—
Orissa				
BJD	—	—	27.50	9
Punjab				
SAD	28.72	8	32.93	8
Tamil Nadu				
AIADMK	7.84	0	25.89	18
DMK	25.63	17	20.08	5
PMK	—	—	6.05	4
MDMK	—	—	6.26	3
TMC	27.00	20	—	—
Uttar Pradesh				
Samajwadi Party	20.72	16	28.70	20
West Bengal				
Trinamool Congress	—	—	24.43	7

(contd.)

Source: Election Commission of India (1996 and 1998).
Note for Table 7.2: In terms of the Election Commission's categories, the AIADMK, DMK, National Conference, HVP, MDMK, MNF, PMK, Shiromani Akali Dal, Shiv Sena, TDP, Samajwadi Party and TMC were listed as 'state parties' in 1996 and UMFA, RPI as registered (unrecognised) parties. MDMK became a registered (unrecognised) party in 1998. HLD(R), West Bengal Trinamool Congress, BJD, Lok Shakti, and RJD are listed as registered (unrecognised) parties in 1998. A state party is defined as one which has been politically active continuously at least for five years, returning at least one member for every 25 members of the Vidhan Sabha/Lok Sabha from the state concerned, and polling no less than four per cent of valid votes there. A national party is one which is recognised as a state party in four or more states/union territories (Election Commission, 1998), vol. 1.

the-post' victory only in Himachal Pradesh, Meghalaya, Nagaland and Rajasthan (both in 1996 and 1998). In Maharashtra it scored a similar success in 1998. It is notable that all the above states, except for Maharashtra and Rajasthan, are relatively smaller states. Such a winning percentage was achieved by the BJP only in Gujarat, Madhya Pradesh and Rajasthan, but they were the relatively bigger states.

A glance at the performance of major regional or state parties in Table 7.2 (in comparison with Table 7.1) brings out some interesting aspects of the politics of regionalism in India. Old regional parties predominate in the states of Jammu and Kashmir, Punjab and Tamil Nadu. The roots of the Dravidian parties go back to 1914, to the non-Brahmin movement in the Tamil-speaking part of the Madras Presidency; those of the Akali Dal to the early 1920s in the Punjab, during the Gurdwara reform movement; and those of the National Conference to the late 1930s in Kashmir, during the land-reform agitations against the princely order. All these states are marked by a stronger sense of regional identities rooted in religion/caste and language, or both. The RPI in Maharashtra is also a party of pre-independence antecedents going back to the Scheduled Castes Federation founded by Dr B.R. Ambedkar. A second category of regional parties comprises the Shiv Sena in Maharashtra and MNF in

Mizoram that surfaced in the 1960s, the former fuelled by Maratha chauvinism in Mumbai and subsequently in the rest of the state, and the latter by tribal insurgency in the north-eastern state which was later contained. The AGP and UMFA are the products of the movements for and against the Assamese linguistic group (mostly Hindus) and Bangladeshi migrant Muslims that peaked in the late 1970s and the first half of the 1980s. Finally, the rest of the new regional parties have mostly been formed in the 1980s and 1990s; they have generally been spurred by regional issues or the fragmentation of national parties such as the Janata Dal, Congress and BJP. Peeved by the supposed cavalier treatment of the Andhra chief ministers by the Congress high command, the Telugu matinee idol, N.T. Rama Rao, plunged into politics and formed the TDP in less than a year before the 1983 elections and led it to power, dislodging the Congress for the first time in the state. The Samajwadi Party in U.P., the VHP and HLD(R) in Haryana, the RJD in Bihar, the BJD in Orissa and the Lok Shakti in Karnataka are all offshoots of the Janata Dal. The Tamil Maanila Congress formed on the eve of the 1996 Lok Sabha elections and Trinamool Congress formed on the eve of the 1998 polls were break-away parties of the Congress(I), in protest against the highhandedness of the Congress high command. The most recent (May 1998) regional split in the Congress(I) for more or less the same reasons as above is the one that produced the Rashtravadi (National) Congress with its centre in Maharashtra. The RJP was born as a result of factionalism in the Gujarat unit of the BJP that was spearheaded by Shankarsinh Vaghela, an OBC leader, in 1994.

The extent of fractionisation of the party system since the 1990s, appeared to bring the effect of proportional representation even under the pluralistic electoral system. This is presumably because of the exacerbation of sharper social cleavages in an already extremely complex, divided and hierarchical society.

The increasing fragmentation of the party system along regional and ethnic lines has given rise to a situation when the performance of even national parties can no longer be explained in terms of factors and forces operating at the all-India level. It is necessary now to take into account state and region-specific causes. For example, the decimation of the Janata Dal must be explained mainly in terms of the decision of the regional lords, such as Mulayam Singh Yadav, Laloo Prasad Yadav and Naveen Patnaik to carve out their own fiefdoms in U.P., Bihar, and Orissa, respectively. The two Yadavs also successfully tried to build up winning caste coalitions of populous Yadavs, Muslims and Dalits, especially the former two. Similarly, the misfortunes of the Congress in Tamil Nadu, Haryana and West Bengal may be mainly attributed to the rebellion of sizeable sections of the Pradesh Congress parties against the national Congress(I) leadership for its patent disregard of the views of the former on local, factional or political issues. This happened in Tamil Nadu on the eve of the 1996 Lok Sabha elections, when P.V. Narasimha Rao decided to have an electoral alliance in the state with Jayalalitha's AIADMK, and overruled the TNCC, the Congress unit in the state. Almost the entire state unit of the party deserted the parent organisation to form a regional outfit, Tamil Maanila Congress. This new regional party aligned itself with the DMK. The Congress(I) in the state failed to win a single seat. The Tamil Maanila Congress performed reasonably well and joined the United Front cabinet at the centre. In 1996, the national Congress(I) leadership under Sitaram Kesari, itself badly divided, failed to manage the Bhajan Lal-Bansi Lal factional feud in Haryana. Bansi Lal formed the Haryana Vikas Party, aligned with the BJP and formed a coalition government in the state after the elections. In West Bengal, on the eve of the 1998 Lok Sabha elections, Kesari failed to evenly balance the factional equations in the West Bengal Pradesh Congress(I). This alienated the firebrand mass leader, Mamata Banerjee, and her cohorts who floated the West Bengal Trinamool Congress which joined the BJP-led alliance. In Maharashtra the Congress(I) continued to be the major opposition after losing to the Shiv Sena-BJP alliance in 1995, but, Sharad Pawar, who maintained an evident mass support in the state, was often treated with suspicion by Sonia Gandhi, the new Congress president. In fact, it would be tautological to explain the Bansi lal and Mamata Banerjee episodes in factional terms alone. The post-economic liberalisation of the Congress(I) had caused a loss of its pro-peasant and pro-poor image, important factors in the political realignments in Haryana and West Bengal, which affected the Congress(I). Bansi Lal was able to combine sizeable sections of the Jat peasant vote plus the migrant Sikh settlers who obviously trimmed their sails to the anti-Congress temper of the Shiromani Akali Dal in the post-Operation Blue Star phase of Punjab politics. (Both the HVP and Akali Dal happened to be allies of the BJP at the time.) Mamata Banerjee was able to bank on the support of the petty bourgeois and urban poor in Kolkata and in the hinterland, on Bengali chauvinism, and the Bengali Muslim vote. Despite her alliance with the BJP, which helped her to rope in the sizeable non-Bengali migrant vote in Kolkata, she has always taken care to assure the support of the Muslim and Bangladeshi migrant sections. The accent on regional identities in recent years and the vested interest in floating regional parties that have come to acquire an influence disproportionate to their size in national-coalition politics are also, here, new factors in the reckoning.

Demographic Correlates

It is a herculean task to unravel the factors that influence Indian elections on account of an extremely complex web of causation operating in a polity of sub-continental diversities and complexities. No wonder, competing subjective interpretations at election time masquerade as valid explanations. In previous chapters we have already offered detailed accounts of political factors such as parties and personalities, issues and campaigns at work and the broad contexts in which the Lok Sabha elections in 1996 and 1998 were held. The discerning reader would be able to get an intuitive grasp of the panoply of political forces that impinged on the overall electoral outcomes. Here, we fall back on some survey data that provide an interesting peep into some demographic and sociological variables that appear to have significantly influenced the party preferences of the voters in 1996 and 1998.

A nationwide exit poll was conducted by the Centre for the Study of Developing Societies, Delhi, on all three days of polling in 1996. It interviewed a national probability sample of voters outside the polling booths after they had cast their votes (in which the senior author was a member of the Advisory Board and the junior author participated as an investigator in the New Delhi Lok Sabha constituency). The poll revealed that the Congress(I) received disproportionately larger votes from the scheduled tribes (47 per cent), scheduled castes (31 per cent) and forward castes (29 per cent). The Congress vote among the OBCs stood at 25 per cent. The BJP vote was relatively higher among the forward castes (33 per cent) and the OBCs (23 per cent) than among STs (17 per cent) and SCs (11 per cent). The National Front-Left Front vote was somewhat more evenly distributed across various ethnic categories: 25 per cent among OBCs, 21 per cent among SCs, 17 per cent among forward castes, and 15 per cent among STs. The BSP was mainly backed by SCs (16 per cent); its vote shares among OBCs, STs and forward castes were rather negligible, ranging between 1–2 per cent. State parties were mainly backed by OBCs and SCs (18 per cent and 14 per cent, respectively); they were backed by only 10 per cent from forward castes and 7 per cent from the STs. The vote shares of other parties among the scheduled tribes stood at 12 per cent, among the forward castes at 10 per cent, and among the OBCs and SCs, 7 per cent each. The Muslim vote predominantly flocked to the National Front-Left Front (48 per cent) and Congress(I) (28 per cent). The modal category of the Christian vote stood by the Congress(I) (46 per cent), the Sikh voters in disproportionately larger numbers supported either the state parties (36 per cent) or the Congress(I) (29 per cent); ten per cent of them voted for the BJP, eight per cent for the BSP, and seven per cent for the National Front-Left Front. In terms of the rural-urban divide, the BJP appeared to be the most visible in the urban areas, and the Congress(I) in the rural areas (32 per cent to each of the parties in their respective areas of prominence). The National Front-Left Front parties were evenly balanced in rural and urban areas with 21 per cent votes in each. More or less similarly balanced in terms of the rural-urban divide were the state parties, with 14 per cent from rural voters and 13 per cent from the urban.[1]

To follow the tack of the 1998 Lok Sabha elections, in a post-poll survey commissioned by *India Today* and conducted by the Centre for the Study of Developing Societies, it was found that the BJP alliance got disproportionately larger shares of votes from both the upper castes (56 per cent) and the OBCs (42 per cent). The mainstay of the Congress support was from the SCs and STs (43 per cent), while the Congress and the United Front were modally backed by the Muslim voters (39 per cent and 30 per cent, respectively). Moreover, upper-caste support for Congress stood at 28 per cent and for the United Front at 11 per cent. The remainder of the OBCs were equally divided among the Congress and the United Front at 21 per cent for each. The Muslim support for the BJP alliance was at a rather low seven per cent. The BJP's predecessor, the BJS, had originated mainly as an urban party, but its successor has now a more or less balanced presence across the urban-rural divide. It received 40 per cent of the votes in urban constituencies and 35 per cent in the rural. The Congress which earlier straddled the rural-urban cleavage like a colossus, received 32 per cent of the rural vote and 29 per cent of the urban. The United Front support was more or less evenly matched with a rural vote of 21 per cent and an urban vote of 20 per cent.[2]

A broad comparison of the demographic profiles of the support enjoyed by various parties between 1996 and 1998 does not suggest any dramatic realignments, except for some notable gains for the BJP among some politically strategic social groups, both at the cost of the Congress and National/United Front, but which were not so substantial as to give it a decisive majority. But for Sonia's belated decision to take the plunge into the electoral vortex, the Congress may have suffered a more ignominous defeat.

Among the 112 seats reserved for the scheduled castes and scheduled tribes, the BJP won 35 and 29 went to the Congress. Regional parties bagged 24 of these seats and 10 were taken by other national parties. Thus, the traditional dominance of the Congress in reserved constituencies during the eras of Nehru and Indira Gandhi, and that somehow continued until the Rajiv Gandhi premiership, has been subject to pluralistic forces in the 1990s. The break up of party performance in terms of SC and ST reserved constituencies is as follows: the BJP and Congress, the two largest single parties, won 24 and 15 SC seats, respectively. Their shares of the ST seats were 11 and 14, respectively. Thus, the BJP had more support among the SCs, while the support for the Congress was greater among the STs. The Left parties won seven SC seats and five ST seats (mainly in West Bengal and Kerala where they are major players). Other national parties (excluding the foregoing) wrested 12 SC seats and six ST seats. The various regional parties together (again major contenders in their respective states) posed a serious challenge to the BJP and Congress, but only in reserved SC constituencies. They had a poor tally of only two seats in the reserved ST constituencies (Table 7.3).

TABLE 7.3
Performance of Parties in Reserved Constituencies, 1998

Parties	*SC seats*	*ST seats*
BJP	24	11
INC	15	14
Left wing	7	5
Other National Parties*	12	6
Regional Parties	22	2
Independents	2	2

*BSP, a party of the SC Reservation Aristocracy, surprisingly won only two SC seats and one ST seat. Interestingly, the bulk of its winning candidates were voted from unreserved constituencies.

Source: Computed from the Election Commission (1998, vol. III), detailed constituency-wise results.

Women candidates contested a total of 539 seats in 1998, but only 43 of the contingent of 271 women were voted to the Lok Sabha. As many as 182 of these candidates forfeited their security deposits.[3] The BJP accounted for 15 women candidates and there were ten from the Congress. The distribution of seats won by women candidates, party-wise, for the remaining seats worked out as follows: three from the CPI(M), three from the Samajwadi Party, two from the RJD, two from the West Bengal Trinamool Congress, one from the CPI, one from the AIADMK, one from the TDP, one from the BSP, one from the HLD(R), and there were two independents.[4]

Inefficacy of Political Engineering?

India's transition from an earlier one-party (Congress) dominant system, with a brief stint towards a two-party system in 1977 and a return of Congress dominance in 1980, to a multi-party system since 1989 is rather intriguing. For, the parameters of the political institutional complex under the 1950 Constitution would appear to be more conducive to the gradual development of a two-party system, at least, at the national level and in most states. The parliamentary system of government at both levels of the polity, albeit in combination with federalism, along with the plurality or first-past-the-post electoral system in single-member constituencies (except for a brief experiment of double-member constituencies to accommodate reserved representation for SCs in 1962), are known to have mostly produced two-party systems in Anglo-American democracies and the older British Commonwealth. This is because the structural logic of the parliamentary system as well as the plurality (not majority) representation generally tend to reward larger parties. Even the American presidential-federal system using the plurality electoral system in single-member constituencies has given rise to a broadly two-party system, though the two American parties are really state-based and decentralised. Contrariwise, parties in parliamentary systems are generally more centralised with the centre of political gravity located in the parliamentary leadership of the party, though the organisational mass membership party leadership is not entirely inconsequential. It is, indeed, this element of party cohesion and discipline that is the principal factor that lends stability to parliamentary governments. On the other hand, parliamentary systems using proportional representation commonly tend to engender multi-party systems as is typical of continental European democracies.

Why have India, and to a lesser extent Canada,[5] been exceptions to the generalisation that plurality-electoral-system-based parliaments are conducive to the growth of two-party systems? One explanation for this, of course, could be that this is due to the confounding effect of the federal component of the Indian —and Canadian—political systems. For, while parliamentarianism is based on the centralisation of powers and government-opposition duality, federalism is founded on decentralisation of powers and the regional multiplier effect on the number of parties, especially regional parties.

Social diversities and complexities of India and Canada are another reason why the growth of two-party systems is hampered in these two countries. In India the caste-class nexus—further complicated by tribal, religious and linguistic pluralities spread across the nation or federality, rooted in territorial configurations in a sub-continental polity—create fertile conditions for a multiplicity of party formations.

The Indian and Canadian experience thus suggest a modification of the hypothesis of the parliamentary systems of the first-past-the-post electoral system which produce two-party systems. Even federalism and presidentialism per se do not as much vitiate the initial formulation as much as the social diversities do. Australia and the USA, despite their vast size and federal constitutions, have evolved into two-party systems. In sum, the original hypothesis that served as our point of departure in this discussion appears to be valid in only relatively homogeneous societies.

The Indian case, in fact, suggests that with the increasing political articulation of social cleavages of the 1990, even a bi-coalitional division of political forces in the parliament has been an elusive goal. Instead, what we find is a tripartite configuration of political parties—the BJP and its allies, Congress and its allies, and the 'third-force' of the Janata Dal, Left parties and some regional parties in-between. The enervation of the Janata Dal and signs of revival of the Congress under Sonia Gandhi have given a fillip to a bi-coalitional pattern, but as shown by the failure of Mrs Gandhi to form an alternate Congress-led coalition government in the wake of the fall of the BJP-led coalition government in mid-April (1999), the tripartite configuration of parties is likely to continue. Indeed, the Rashtriya Congress formed by Sharad Pawar, Poorno Sangama and Tariq Anwar in the wake of the fall of the Vajpayee government and the failure of the Congress(I) to form an alternative administration confirms this trend. These rebel Congressmen from Maharashtra, the Northeast and Bihar, respectively, have announced their intention to keep themselves equidistant from both the Congress(I) and BJP. One must hasten to add, however, that, as yet, this event has failed to trigger a chain response from the disintegrating erstwhile third-force parties. For the moment, neither is Sonia Gandhi willing to countenance a communist-led coalition government headed by Jyoti Basu nor is there any support for a Congress-led dispensation from Mulayam Singh Yadav and the RSP and Forward Bloc. The exits of the AIADMK from the BJP coalition and of the Pawar-Sangama-Anwar group from the Congress(I) are, thus, minor ripples in the party politics of India that would have gone practically unnoticed had not the idealistic images of Vajyapee, Sonia Gandhi and Jayalalitha come under question.

Elections in India must perform their representation and legitimation function by a complex intermediation between ethnicity and class structures, on the one hand, and party and interest-group structures on the other. An important dimension of this intermediation is the territorial factor that varies in size as one moves from a Vidhan Sabha constituency to a Lok Sabha constituency and from the state level to the national level. The larger the unit of analysis, the more complex and varied the social and political formations contained within it. For example, caste-settlement patterns count for much more in the panchayat and Vidhan Sabha constituencies than in the Lok Sabha constituency and state and national aggregation of politics. At higher levels the factors of social dominance are negated by the growing diversities and pluralities that increase the manoeuvrability of political factors. During the period of Congress dominance, the party image and the power and charisma of the prime ministers were fairly effective in churning out a political framework for stable governance. In the more federal phase since 1989, the party organisational factor and the charisma of prime ministers have become variables of diminishing efficacy. Hence, the resultant uncertainties in the outcome of elections. Uncertainty also pervades the increasingly complex tapestry of caste, tribal and religious groupings in shifting patterns and the shaky coalitions of political parties and electoral adjustments which overlie them. These intricate formations are ingeniously crafted by party and community leaders before or after each election that often turn out to have unpredictable consequences. The two policies that require attention with regard to the foregoing are: (1) simultaneous holding of elections to the Lok Sabha and Vidhan Sabha, and (2) legal intervention aimed at the structuring of parties into democratically disciplined instruments of election and governance. These interventions will invest the political factors with greater mileage over the primordial variables and render political parties as institutionalised, legal and democratic instruments linking the civil society and the State. Indian democracy would otherwise fail in its 'tryst with destiny' and get lost in the 'dreary desert sand of dead habits'.

India at the Polls Again

For the fifth time in the short span of a decade India went to the polls again in September 1999. With uncertain mandate and vanished parliamentary majority, the Vajpayee government had to eat humble pie because of the president's order for a new mandate, despite the scramble for power in the existing House among the Congress(I), BJP, communists, Loktantrik Morcha, AIADMK, etc. Neither the dissolution nor the timing of the election was of the prime minister's choice. The BJP's preference for an early/immediate election in June was overruled by the Election Commission on the plea that it needed more time to revise the electoral rolls to ensure free and fair polls. The prime ministers in the UK and prime ministers of India in the past have usually exercised these prerogatives as a matter of right. The enhanced powers of the Election Commission in India are also explained by the federal nature of the Indian Constitution and its growing accent in practical politics.

It proved to be easier for the opposition to pull down the BJP-alliance government than to put together even a ramshackle coalition. President K.R. Narayanan's discretion in obtaining a recommendation for dissolution from the cabinet has at least two merits: it cut short the unseemly horse-trading and it offered the electorate the chance to give itself an alternative dispensation. It is difficult not to feel, however, that the outcome of the bid for a new mandate for a more stable government may not be very different from what we have been witnessing since 1989. This surmise is inescapable in view of the sharpened social divisions and fragmented political culture at the mass as well as elite levels as also the absence of appropriate constitutional, party and electoral reforms.

In addition to the fragmented society and a scam-infested economy, the political processes have become cesspits of the legislative-bureaucratic, criminal-political nexus. Organisations masquerading as political parties do not really offer much of an alternative to the electorate, to say nothing of the areas of 'parallel politics—by other means' in parts of some states where the Naxalites and terrorists call the shots and cause localised breakdown of constitutional order and a crisis of regime on a limited scale. Recent elections have shown the bewildered voters yielding one-party majorities at least in some states but desperately turning away from the incumbent parties in erratic and fickle swings to those in the opposition such that the 'incumbency factor' has come to be dreaded by parties almost as a 'military draft' for mobilisation on a political front, where defeat in the very next election is almost certain. Elections have turned into an expensive ritual—a game of musical chairs without purpose and principles.

Notes

1. *India Today*, 31 May 1996: 47–50.
2. See M.P. Singh and Rekha Saxena, 1998b, *Political Science Annual 1997*.
3. Election Commission, 1998, *Stat. Rep. on Gen. Elections, 1998 the Twelfth Lok Sabha*, vol. I: 96.
4. *Ibid*, figures reported yielded by my computation carried out on detailed constituency-wise results therein.
5. See M.P. Singh and Rekha Saxena, 1998a, *Punjab Journal of Politics*: 499–500.

CHAPTER EIGHT

Mandate 1999: Continuity with Stability?

The drama is make-believe. It does not deal with truth but with effect.

— W. Somerset Maugham

The Backdrop

The 1999 mid-term Lok Sabha elections marked the continuity of federal-coalitional governance within the framework of a multi-party system that had made its first appearance in 1989. It was held in the backdrop of ambiguous tendencies and perceptions in the trail of Pokharan-II, Vajpayee's bus diplomacy to Lahore and India's undeclared limited war with Pakistan in Kargil. All these major events were rather complex and open to divergent interpretations. Depending on the level of voters' awareness and information, or the lack of it, these events could influence the Indian elections differentially. India's second nuclear explosion in Pokharan (the first in 1974) in May 1998, could be interpreted either as a momentous success which ushered it into the exclusive nuclear club or as a dubious achievement that only underlined its status as a nuclear eunuch, inasmuch as nuclearisation of defence seemed to offer no respite from conventional limited war and cross-border terrorism from Pakistan. Pakistan's own nuclear tests followed closely on the heels of India's. Similarly, Vajpayee's diplomatic breakthrough in Lahore in the spring of 1999, could not be taken at face value as the euphoria of the event was marred by the lukewarm attitude of the army in Pakistan to the Lahore peace process. In any case, Lahore was soon followed by the discovery, in early May 1999, of Pakistan's aggression and occupation of Indian Kashmir in the Kargil area across the Line of Control. The conflict remained a local and low-intensity one, thanks to India's universally acclaimed restraint. Yet, Indians had to fight through a bitter summer and pay in blood, tears and sweat to push the intruders back across the Line of Control.

The ambiguous impact of these events appeared, on the balance, to be a sort of boost to Indian nationalism, which the BJP-led coalition government tried its level best to exploit. However, no one, even the BJP, expected the 1999 polls to offer an 'exit' from the contemporary history of coalitional governance of the last two decades of the 20th century in India. For, it contested 43 seats less than in the preceding election—339 as against 384. Instead, it tried to accommodate its regional allies as much as it could to expand its national reach. Priority to consolidate the coalition overrode the BJP's megalomaniac gamble to come to power on its own.

Indeed, the three major pivot parties in coalition politics at the centre since 1989—the Congress under P.V. Narasimha Rao, the Janata Dal under V.P. Singh and the BJP until 1996—had initially all tended to be either reluctant coalition partners or tended to regard each coalition they entered into as the terminal episode from which their parties could emerge as a single majority capable of forming a government on their own. This attitude prevailed at least until the mid-1990s. By this time all the major players had reconciled to the inevitability of coalitional governance. From 1996 onwards, this realistic appraisal seemed to have dawned upon all concerned. Everyone tried to live with the realities of coalition politics and largely avert the necessity of mid-term polls. Yet, they did not overcome the temptation to topple an incumbent government and put in its place an alternative one by 'internal' realignment among parties in the parliament, if it would enhance their manoeuvrability. Strategic miscalculations on the part of political entrepreneurs did, however, occasionally backfire resulting in mid-term polls, as it did in 1998 and then again in 1999. The former was caused by miscalculations of the Congress president, Sitaram Kesari, who miserably failed for lack of allies in his game plan of engineering a Congress-led coalition government to replace the United Front. The latter was destabilised by the AIADMK supremo, J. Jayalalitha.

When Jayalalitha dramatically withdrew her party's support from the BJP-led coalition government on 17 April 1999, after months of her lobbying for the reinstatement of Admiral Vishnu Bhagwat—earlier sacked by the government for allegedly showing signs of defying the principle of cabinet control of the armed forces—she possibly relied on an internal realignment of political parties in the twelfth Lok Sabha. This was also the game plan of her abettors in the Congress, the CPI(M) and the Rashtriya Loktantrik Morcha of Mulayam Singh Yadav and Laloo Yadav. All of them worked on the logistics of their pulling down the Vajpayee government and putting in place an alternative dispensation. Mulayam Singh Yadav of the Samajwadi Party said the successor to Vajpayee will be found 'within hours' of his deposition. But that was not to be. For, the opposition was more agreed on the removal of the incumbent than supporting a successor. The CPI(M) wanted the Congress to lead the coalition supported by itself and others such as the AIADMK from outside, without joining the cabinet. The Loktantrik Morcha was divided; Mulayam Singh Yadav of the Samajwadi Party opposed the idea of the Congress's heading the coalition, while Laloo Prasad Yadav of the Rashtriya Janata Dal was inclined towards the Congress. Mulayam would not support a government led either by the Congress or BJP, but would instead support a 'third-force' candidate as the prime minister who should be acceptable to the Congress as well. However, the Congress, RJD and the left wing were not inclined to explore the possibility of the third force forming the government, presumably because of the extreme fragmentation and decimation of the Janata Dal and the loss of the Telugu Desam Party to the BJP-led alliance. Within the Left Front, the CPI(M) sought to build bridges with the Congress, but the RSP and Forward Bloc preferred to maintain an equal distance from both the Congress and BJP. Jayalalitha, then out of power in Tamil Nadu, apparently wished to return to the seat of power, but the DMK, Tamil Maanila Congress as well as smaller parties from the left wing would have nothing to do with an arrangement that included the AIADMK, whose primary objective was to bail out Jayalalitha who was accused in a number of corruption-related cases.[1] Laloo Prasad Yadav, too, was embroiled in cases of a similar nature. But neither the Congress nor the Left Front appeared to have any reservations about associating with his Rashtriya Janata Dal. In 1996, Laloo, the then national Janata Dal president and the Bihar chief minister, had campaigned in his state, presenting himself as the prospective prime minister. But he was thwarted by the corruption cases against him which cost him the office of chief minister, though he managed to put his wife in his place as a puppet chief minister. In 1997, he had parted company with the Janata Dal, forming his own regional outfit in Bihar, the Rashtriya Janata Dal, which despite its prefix 'Rashtriya' was a party confined to the state of Bihar.

Intense political activities in the two major camps culminated on 21 April with Sonia Gandhi and L.K. Advani separately meeting President K.R. Narayanan to present unverified lists of the MPs who they claimed were supporting them—Sonia Gandhi claimed she had the support of 272 MPs and L.K. Advani said he had the support of 270 MPs. Two days later Sonia's list came down to 233 and she asked for and was given more time to fabricate a majority. The CPI(M) general secretary, Harkishan Singh Surjeet continued to lobby for a Congress-led government, and even the enigmatic Jayalalitha obliged with a letter supporting the Congress. At a meeting of non-Congress, non-BJP parties hosted by the RLM on 21 April, to which the former prime minister, Chandrashekhar, was a special invitee,

Mulayam Singh Yadav ruled out 'blind support' to the Congress. He instead proposed the name of Jyoti Basu, the CPI(M) chief minister of West Bengal, as the prime minister. The CPI(M) did not take the bait for the same reason that it did not do so in 1996. It was not prepared to join a coalition government in which it did not have a position of dominance, a decision that was reiterated at the CPI(M)'s Kolkata Congress in 1998.[2] In 1996, the UF had offered to make Jyoti Basu the prime minister, but his party did not accept the offer. Basu had later lamented his party's decision as being a 'historic blunder', but his party remained unmoved.

Faced with the continuing deadlock, the president dissolved the twelfth Lok Sabha on 26 April and ordered fresh polls.[3] Ten days earlier, the BJP-led coalition government had already lost the confidence of the Lok Sabha by a single vote cast by Giridhar Gamang, a Congress MP who had in the meantime shifted to Orissa as the chief minister but whose membership of the House was still technically valid. In a wrangle between the government and the opposition over the propriety of his presence, the speaker, G.M.C. Balayogi (Telugu Desam Party), allowed him to vote on his own 'conscience'.[4] In the confidence vote on 17 April the parliamentary division since 1996 was largely maintained, except for the major shifts in the inter-party alliances in Tamil Nadu and their impact on the coalition government at the centre. The smaller allies of the AIADMK gradually deserted it and stayed in the BJP-led coalition at the centre even though Jayalalitha drifted to the opposition. The ruling DMK, which was earlier with the opposition in New Delhi, finally joined the federal coalition at the centre. There was a last-minute surprise in the confidence vote in the Lok Sabha when the BSP voted against the Vajpayee government, reversing its stand of abstaining which it had announced a day earlier during the debate (Table 8.1).

The Vajpayee government wanted an immediate election (in June–July) presumably to reap the electoral harvest of nationalistic fervour in the wake of the Kargil conflict. However, the Election Commission, after consultations with all political

TABLE 8.1
Division in the Confidence Vote in the Lok Sabha Lost by the Vajpayee Government on 17 April 1999

Against		*For*	
Congress	139	BJP	182
CPI(M)	32	Samata Party	12
Samajwadi Party	20	Telugu Desam	11
AIADMK	17	BJD	9
RDJ	16	Akali Dal	8
CPI	8	Trinamool Congress	7
Janata Dal	6	DMK	6
RSP	5	Shiva Sena	6
BSP	5	PMK	4
RPI	4	INLD	4
TMC	3	MDMK	3
Forward Bloc	2	Lok Shakti	3
IUML	2	National Conference	2
Janata Party	1	TRC	1
Majlis (Owaisi)	1	RJP (Anand)	1
ASDC	1	Arunachal Congress	1
Arunachal Congress(M)	1	HVP	1
AILC (Ola)	1	SDF	1
SJP	1	MCCP	1
NC (Soz)	1	Maneka Gandhi	1
Kerala Congress	1	Independents (Satnam Singh, Lallungmauna, S. Biswamuthiary)	3
UMF	1		
PWP	1		
Buta Singh	1	Nominated	2
Total	270	Total	268

Source: *Indian Recorder*, 14–20 May 1999, p. 4466.
Note: Total seats 545, including the speaker. Vacancies 2. An AIADMK member did not vote. A CPI and an RJD member were absent.

parties in the system, decided to conduct the polls from September–October. Thus, the monsoon could be avoided and would also allow the completion of the revision of the electoral rolls. An immediate poll was also considered inadvisable by the union home secretary, B.P. Singh, in view of the difficulties involved in rapidly deploying the central paramilitary forces on election duty from one state to another within the short period before the onset of rains.[5] The home secretary was promptly replaced. But the Election Commission stuck to its poll schedule which was to be completed in five phases between 4 September to 1 October 1999.

The electorate was called upon to vote on the government's performance during its short span of nearly nineteen months, of which five months was in the capacity of a caretaker government on the request of the president until it came back to power after the elections. The government was constantly dogged by bickerings in the coalition and criticism of its policies on the way the Kargil war was conducted (which was unavoidable) but also on economic matters, issues on which a caretaker government does not normally suffer.[6] Our surmise, however, is that the Indian voters' resistance to misgovernment and corruption has become rather weak. It may be recalled that stronger electoral reaction against authoritarianism was seen in 1977 and against corruption in public life in 1989. This state of affairs may presumably be attributed to the growing cynicism, though perhaps not apathy, of the voters, with the amoral profession of politics that has been flourishing in the country over the years.

The Contestants

The mid-term polls enlarged the arena as well as the number of effective contenders for power owing to the realignment of political forces after the fall of the Vajpayee government. The continuing fragmentation and regrouping of political parties provided a wider opening and space for smaller political formations as well as primary groups and identities such as castes and communities as determinants of coalition politics. Like other elections since 1989, this was also an election in which national-level factors and issues probably played as much of a role as the regional and local ones. It was, thus, unlike the plebiscitary elections of the era of Congress predominance or the first post-Emergency Janata poll of 1977 when uniformity of electoral responses in the north favoured one party across the board over large parts of the country.

National Democratic Alliance

The political scene in 1999, appeared to be as chequered as that in the recent elections in the 1990s. The 14-party BJP-led alliance remained reasonably cohesive despite the fall of its government. One ally, the AIADMK, deserted it, but the AIADMK's main rival in Tamil Nadu, the DMK, made good the loss by joining the BJP alliance. Throughout the tenure of the Vajpayee government, the AIADMK had clamoured for the dismissal of the DMK government in Tamil Nadu. This was resisted by the centre in the name of federalism. The smaller erstwhile allies of the AIADMK—the PMK, MDMK and TRC—stayed in the BJP-led coalition and later, in a shift of loyalties, allied with the DMK. However, the DMK's erstwhile ally in Tamil Nadu, the TMC, snapped its ties with the DMK after the DMK general council formally resolved to join the NDA, led by the 'gentleman politician' (A.B. Vajpayee) who was 'committed to federalism'. Karunanidhi later explained that his party's joining the NDA did not mean its endorsement of the 'Hindutva' concept; 'we will continue to be committed to the minority community'.[7] The DMK would thus strengthen the 'secular bloc' in the NDA, which consisted of, informally, the Samata Party, TDP, National Conference, BJD, etc. Besides the BJP-DMK and Congress-AIADMK alliances in Tamil Nadu, the TMC leader, G.K. Moopanar, and Puthiya Thamilagam leader, K. Krishnasamy, formed a third front in the state, the Progressive People's Front including also the JD (Secular), RPI and Dalit Panthers. The main plank of the front was its campaign against religious fundamentalism and corruption.

The BJP-led federal alliance included three regional parties in the north-west: the National Conference, Akali Dal (Badal), and Indian National Lok Dal led by Omprakash Chautala. The Akali Dal and National Conference stood firmly by the BJP-led coalition government. The presence of these two parties both ruling at the time in Punjab (in coalition with the BJP) and Jammu and Kashmir, lent to the BJP-coalition government in New Delhi greater representativeness and legitimacy among Sikhs and Muslims. In July 1999, the HVP government in Haryana led by Bansi Lal suddenly fell because of the withdrawal of Congress support from the floor of the assembly as well as because of a split in the HVP. That offered an opening to Chautala to form an alternative government as the joint candidate of INLD, BJP and HVP rebels. But relations between INLD and BJP were not without problems. Chautala was inclined to vote against the Vajpayee government on the crucial confidence motion, ostensibly on the issue of the withdrawal of subsidies to farmers, but, he was finally won over at the eleventh hour. He contested the mid-term polls as an ally of the NDA.

The BJP-led allies met on 15 May 1999 and gave their alliance a formal collective name, the National Democratic Alliance. The constituents retained their separate identities but decided to contest the forthcoming election using a common manifesto under the leadership of BJP's Atal Behari Vajpayee. The Telugu Desam, Trinamool Congress and Jammu and Kashmir National Conference, who were apparently worried about the impact of their aligning with the Hindu-right BJP on their sizeable or dominant Muslim electorate in their respective states, were not represented in this meeting,[8] but, they eventually stuck to the alliance.

Besides the DMK, another major group to join the NDA in July 1999, was a major faction of the Janata Dal. The JD chief minister of Karnataka, J.H. Patel, unilaterally decided to join the NDA. The move was opposed by the majority in the national Political Affairs Committee of the party, but the Sharad Yadav faction in the committee rebelled and joined forces with the majority faction in the Karnataka Janata Dal in their move to build bridges with the NDA. Indeed, the NDA allies, the Samata Party and Lok Shakti also merged with the rebel Janata Dal and formed a new party, Janata Dal (United). The main Janata Dal under H.D. Deve Gowda now became the Janata Dal (Secular). It stayed out of the NDA.

The NDA still remained a confederal inter-party formation. There was no move to form a federal party like the Janata Party in 1977 (which later became the Janata Dal in 1988). The constituent parties in the Janata Party had at least *formally* merged into one. But then, the composition of the NDA is much more diverse in regional and cultural terms than the Janata Party and which was essentially a north-Indian phenomenon. The NDA has become an all-India affair.

The Congress-Led Front

The six-party, Congress-led alliance included, among others, two major regional parties, the AIADMK and RJD. In the period, which extended to a year, preceding the mid-term polls, the Indian National Congress went through the motions of reorganising itself according to an amended party constitution accepted at the All India Congress Committee on 18 December 1998. These amendments increased the membership of the top executive committees of the party (the members in the Congress Working Committee was increased from 21 to 25 and the Congress Parliamentary Board from seven to nine), created bodies for conducting regular organisational elections in the AICC and Pradesh Election Committees and reserved 33 per cent of all seats for women and 20 per cent for SCs/STs/OBCs in all party committees at all levels.[9] Moreover, in the run-up to the 1999 Lok Sabha elections, the Congress party unit in Gujarat was reinforced by the merger with the Rashtriya Janata Party on 1 July 1999 led by Shankarsinh Vaghela, the ex-chief minister of the earlier Congress-backed RJP government in the state. He had led a faction out of the BJP in the early 1990s. However, the verve and vibrancy that was evident in the party when Sonia Gandhi became the party president and during her campaign in the 1998 Lok Sabha election was missing from the party in the 1999 polls.

On 15 May 1999, the Congress headed for a split. Three senior CWC members—Sharad Pawar, P.A. Sangama and Tariq Anwar—suggested to Sonia Gandhi in a letter handed to her at the meeting of the party's national executive committee that the party should consider including in its election manifesto a promise to propose an amendment to the Indian Constitution to ensure that only a 'natural-born' Indian citizen was eligible to hold the offices of president, vice-president or prime minister of the Republic. The letter added that leading India was 'probably the single most difficult job in the world today' and that a person 'taking the reins of this country' needed a large measure of 'experience and understanding of public life'.[10] The letter could be interpreted as a move to take the wind out of the sails of the BJP's attack on Sonia's foreign origin and political inexperience. But it could be equally construed to be anti-Congress as well as anti-Sonia. Its real motive was, in all probability, to enhance the career prospects of Pawar and Sangama and whom the Congress establishment had been trying to sideline. Sonia promptly resigned in anguish as the party president and the Congress Working Committee and PCC presidents summarily expelled the three rebels from the party. Then, there followed a melodrama in which all the Congress Working Committee members and the four chief ministers of the party in Madhya Pradesh, Rajasthan, Orissa and Delhi offered to resign, saying: 'We do not think that the Congress will have any future without your [Sonia's] leadership'. Sonia was thus finally prevailed upon to resume the presidency of the party.

The rebels proceeded to form a new party, the Nationalist Congress Party, with evident prospective support from the capitalist sugar farmers in Pawar's home turf in western Maharashtra and a sizeable Christian vote from Sangama's home state, Meghalaya. Anwar could probably bring some Muslim votes in Bihar and the neighbouring states. The split resulting in the formation of the NCP considerably weakened the Congress; the followers of Pawar in Maharashtra took away the majority of the Congress legislators in both the Houses of the Maharashtra legislature. The NCP adopted a constitution which broadly replicated the organisational structure of the Indian National Congress. Later, it issued an election manifesto which was the most comprehensive and detailed election-related party document of 1999 (NCP, 1999).

The Congress and CPI joined in a poll pact nationally that cleared the way for state-level alliances 'which can pave the way for emergence of a third force at the national level'. In addition, the Congress and AIADMK forged an electoral arrangement that included the CPI(M), CPI and Indian National League in Tamil Nadu and Pondicherry. The front's seat-sharing formula resolved that out of the 40 Lok Sabha seats from Tamil Nadu and Pondicherry together, the AIADMK would contest 23, Congress 12 (reduced from 27 seats in 1996, then also in alliance with the AIADMK), CPI(M) and CPI two each and Indian National League, one. In addition to Tamil Nadu, the CPI(M) and CPI would also align with the Congress in Bihar and lend 'tacit' support to the Congress in Uttar Pradesh, Maharashtra, Punjab, Haryana and Madhya Pradesh. Besides, the Congress also entered into poll alliances with the RPI in Maharashtra and the MGP in Goa.[11] It is notable that the two major Congress allies—the AIADMK and RJD—were regional parties badly embroiled in corruption cases.

A Muslim convention called by Jamaat-e-Ulema-i-Hind and addressed by the Congress president, Sonia Gandhi, decried the disunity among secular parties and dismissed the talk about the secular third force as wishful thinking and urged the Muslim voters to vote for Congress and avoid division of their vote.[12]

The Disunited Front

The parties remaining outside the major two blocs described above were often lumped in a residual category the 'third force'. The so-called third force in 1999 was a misnomer inasmuch as it was a divided lot. The National Front, Federal Front, RLM, had all by now disintegrated and were history. The only surviving front was the Left Front consisting of five parties and led by the CPI(M). The National/United Front that ruled in New Delhi in the first half of the 1990s was particularly unhinged by the fissioning of the Janata Dal, which, despite the formation of the Janata Dal (United) in 1999, remained hopelessly fragmented into its regionally personalised splinters such as the RJD of Laloo Yadav, BJD of Naveen Patnaik, Janata Dal (Secular) of H.D. Deve Gowda, Samajwadi Party of Mulayam Singh Yadav, and Samajwadi Janata Party of Chandrashekhar. Other major regional constituents of the United Front such as the DMK and Telugu Desam had, meanwhile, shifted to the National Democratic Alliance as had the JD (United). The remaining ones such as the AGP and Samajwadi Party did not have any alliances in 1999, as did the BSP that decided to contest alone in U.P., M.P. and Bihar in the Lok Sabha election but settle for seat adjustments with regional parties in Punjab and Haryana.

A belated attempt to unite the third force was made by the NCP and Samajwadi party in mid-June 1999. These two parties entered into a poll pact to work together in the forthcoming election. Sharad Pawar and Mulayam Singh Yadav, besides bringing their parties closer, also tried to form a common front with some other like-minded parties including the Left and RJD. However, this effort to revive a third front with non-BJP and non-Congress parties did not fructify. The CPI(M) was not convinced of the strategy of their keeping an equal distance from *both* the BJP and Congress. Both the CPI(M) and RJD were anti-BJP in the interest of secularism but were inclined towards the Congress. The two smaller Left parties—Forward Bloc and RSP—and Janata Dal (Secular) were the only ones to respond positively to the call to join the front floated by the NCP and Samajwadi Party.[13]

Another attempt to underline the need for unity among what it called 'secular parties' was made by five leading Muslim organisations—Jamaat-e-Ulema-i-Hind, Jamaat-i-Islami-Hind, All India Milli Council, All India Muslim Personal Law Board and All India Majlis-e-Mushawarat. Former union minister Saifuddin Soz and former Janata Dal MP, Sayed Sahabuddin released the common document urging secular parties to consider the inclusion of considerations for the welfare of Muslims in their manifestos. Sahabuddin urged the secular parties to 'close their ranks through alliances, adjustments or understanding to give a one-to-one fight to the communal forces'. Soz identified the secular parties as the Left parties, Congress, RJD, Samajwadi Party and Bahujan Samaj Party.[14]

However, in 1999, prospects of a left-of-centre alliance such as the National/United Front or of non-BJP 'secular' parties coming to power in New Delhi appeared very bleak.

Inter-Party Alliances

It is evident from the foregoing that the broadly threefold clustering of parties in the preceding years came in for realignment in 1999. This was clear from the attempt of parties to form an alternative coalition in the wake of the fall of the Vajpayee government as well as from the inter-party alignments while they contested the mid-term polls that followed. Instead of the earlier pattern of two major polar parties, i.e. the BJP and Congress, with the third-force parties in alliance with either the National Front or United Front, there was a more chequered field outside the major bloc represented by the NDA. Besides the NDA, there were at least four party fronts, some of which were partly overlapping and one, the Tamil Nadu PPF, limited to one state only. The CPI(M) and CPI were present in the Congress-led front as well as in the Left Front, while the smaller Left parties such as the Forward Bloc and RSP belonged to three fronts simultaneously (Table 8.2). The single most important political factor responsible for the unhinging of the earlier National Front and United Front was the decimation and fragmentation of the Janata Dal. The major Left parties tried in vain to substitute the Janata Dal with the Congress as the axis of the non-BJP front. But their strategy came to naught by the lukewarm response of the Congress to their overtures and the anti-Sonia posture of the Samajwadi Party and NCP.

TABLE 8.2
Inter-Party Alliances in the 1999 Lok Sabha Elections

NDA	*Congress*	*Left*	*NCP-SP*	*Tamil Nadu Progressive People's Front*
BJP	INC	CPI(M)**	NCP	TMC
Shiv Sena	AIADMK	CPI**	Samajwadi Party	Puthiya Thamilagam
JD(U)	RJD	Forward Bloc***	RSP***	RPI
BJD	CPI**	RSP***		Dalit Panthers
Trinamool Congress	CPI(M)**			
Akali Dal	Forward Bloc***			
National Conference	RSP***			
TDP				
INLD				
DMK				
PMK				
MDMK				
TRC				

Notes: No(s) of asterisks marked against a party indicate the presence of that party in that many alliances.
BSP decided to contest on its own in the 1999 polls except for seat adjustments with some regional parties in Punjab and Haryana.

Candidate Selection

An analysis of an aspect of candidate selection by major parties in 1999, revealed certain interesting patterns (Table 8.3). The

TABLE 8.3
Candidate Selection by National and Major Regional Parties in the 1999 Lok Sabha Elections

Parties	*Renominated*	*New*	*Fielding a candidate in 1999 where the party did not contest in 1998*
BJP	214 (61.7%)	112 (32.3%)	21 (6.0%)
INC	165 (36.5%)	267 (59.1%)	20 (4.4%)
CPI(M)	38 (53.5%)	15 (21.1%)	18 (25.3%)
CPI	19 (46.3%)	10 (24.4%)	12 (29.3%)
BSP	41 (18.7%)	131 (59.8%)	47 (21.5%)
JD(U)	—	—	53
JD(S)	—	—	82
Other major state/UT parties	194 (23.1%)	273 (32.5%)	373 (44.4%)

Sources: Compiled from comparisons carried out between the data reported in *Statistical Report on General Elections, 1998 to the Twelfth Lok Sabha*, vol. 3 Detailed Results (New Delhi: Election Commission of India, 1998) and *Statistical Report on General Elections, 1999 to the Thirteenth Lok Sabha*, vol. 3, Parts I and II (New Delhi: Election Commission of India, 1999).

Note: JD(U) and JD(S), being election-eve splinters of JD in 1999, did not exist in 1998. Hence, there are no entries in the relevant cells of the Table pertaining to 1998 elections. Since both these parties were formed in 1999, all their candidates are here reported as fielded in 1999, even though some of these candidates had contested in the previous elections under different party labels.

two largest parties—the BJP and Congress—did the opposite of each other while nominating their candidates: the former renominated nearly 62 per cent of the sitting MPs in the dissolved Lok Sabha, and 59 per cent of the Congress candidates were new. The CPI(M) renominated 53.5 per cent of its candidates and the CPI, 46.3 per cent. Nearly 60 per cent of the BSP candidates were new. When it came to contesting new seats, which were earlier left uncontested, over 44 per cent of the new constituencies were contested by the regional parties, which in 1998, were conspicuous by their absence. Other such expanding parties were the CPI (over 29 per cent) and the CPI(M) (over 25 per cent). Notably, neither the BJP nor Congress displayed any marked interest to cover the entire nation. Despite the 'pop patriotism' showcased by news-bytes during the Kargil war, the largest two all-India parties were not exactly upbeat in 1999.

An organisation called the Lok Satta Election Watch in Andhra Pradesh headed by A. Lakshman Rao, former chief justice of the Allahabad High Court, announced that 46 of the candidates contesting the simultaneous Lok Sabha and Vidhan Sabha polls in the state in 1999, had a 'criminal background'. The list was compiled from 1,538 letters from the public and scrutinised by a committee of 15 eminent persons.[15] Similar civic action from other states would be most welcome.

Issues and Campaign

An Indian election is a huge affair, the outcome of which depends on a large number of complex and indeterminate issues which include economic, cultural, administrative and civic matters. Since 1991, when the Rao Congress government accelerated the process of liberalisation of the economy, there has been a growing convergence of ideological perspectives at least, among the larger parties and alliances. Thus, both the NDA and Congress and its allies were broadly in favour of neo-classical, pro-market economic reforms, without fully writing off the role of the State in the economy and dispensing with protectionist policies for domestic industries. The common manifesto of the NDA, which was largely recycled from the *National Agenda for Governance* (1998), but, issued before the polls this time, observed:

> The old leftist approach sought complete state control of industry while the rightist approach wanted to leave it to the market. We reject both. Government and industry must work together to achieve key objectives aimed at enhancing the

> dynamism of the market with effective and efficient regulatory mechanisms. In fact the issue is not about capitalism or socialism, nor is it about more of market or less of state. It is about better society, about improving the way citizens can demand and obtain all sorts of public goods. It is about dignity for all (NDA, 1999: 4).

A similar neo-liberal economic posturing, albeit with a certain degree of Keynesian welfarism born of a string of electoral reverses since 1991, was to be found in the Congress manifesto for 1999:

> The Congress reiterates its firm commitment to faster economic reforms with a human face. Higher growth is possible only if we invest more productively in physical and social infrastructure and only if the pattern of public expenditures at all levels reflects pressing socio-economic priorities and needs of the poor, the unemployed, the deprived, the malnourished and the disadvantaged of India (INC, 1999: 14).

In contrast to these right-of-centre views—discounting the rhetorics of course—the left-of-centre perspective on economic issues was espoused by the Left parties, which, in 1999, did not issue a joint manifesto in addition to their separate one, as they did in 1998. The CPI(M) manifesto called the BJP and its allies 'the swadeshi agents of MNCs thanks to whose policies MNCs are taking over Indian companies and buying up the Indian partners' share in joint ventures'. The Marxists also criticised the indiscriminate privatisation of the public sector. And, they promised a better deal to the workers, unemployed, Dalits and Adivasis, women, youth and children. They urged and promised land reforms. They also advised a 'critical review' of the agreements made in the Uruguay Round during the reappraisal of the WTO regime in 1999 [CPI(M), 1999: 3–18]. With a similar litany of criticisms on the 'neo-liberal economic policies' introduced by the Congress and 'aggressively pursued' by the BJP-led governments 'under the diktat of the IMF, World Bank and international capital', the CPI offered similar solutions (CPI, 1999: 8–13). For the Left, neither the BJP nor Congress offered a meaningful alternative, but the former was definitely a greater evil. In the given situation, they appealed to the electorate to vote for 'the Left, Democratic and Secular forces'.

The Samajwadi Party and RJD echoed sentiments on economic and cultural issues that were reminiscent of the Left. Both were highly critical of the religious communalism practised by the BJP. Their relations with the Congress diverged in 1999: the SP was hostile to it but the RJD aligned itself with it (Samajwadi Party, 1999).[16]

Thus, the differences among parties on economic and cultural/ identity issues broadly coincided. The divide among parties on economic issues expressed itself between neo-liberal market reforms and economic nationalism/public welfarism. The cultural cleavage was between Hindu nationalism and Indian secularism. However, the ruling NDA coalition effectively put a moratorium on the secular-communal conflict by dropping the contentious issues of the Ram temple, Common Civil Code for all Indians and Article 370 of the Constitution in relation to Jammu and Kashmir from the common manifesto of the NDA parties, even though the BJP manifestos of the pre-1999 elections had included them and the RSS/VHP leaders and some members of the BJP still harped on them even during the 1999 campaign. (The BJP did not issue a separate manifesto in 1999.) Yet, the parties which were not in the NDA, and therefore in opposition, continued to accuse the BJP, in no uncertain terms, of professing and practising Hindu communalism to the disadvantage of the minorities.

A puzzling aspect of the election manifestos of the major political parties in 1999, was the issue of ecological and environmental concerns that had begun to be included in these documents in the mid-1990s, but, were again on their way out. These issues were conspicuous by their absence in the Congress, CPI(M) and CPI manifestos. The NDA did, however, promise to 'establish an appropriate legal framework for the protection of the environment and unveil a National Environment Policy to balance development and ecology' (NDA, 1999: 8).

On India's foreign policy the national consensus on non-alignment and nuclearisation for peaceful purposes (without closing the option for weaponisation) that was evident in the past, tended to break down in the post-Cold War and post-Pokharan-II periods. Neither the NDA nor the Congress manifesto mentioned non-alignment in the recent elections. The NDA manifesto did, however, obliquely add: 'We are committed to making the voice of India as the voice of the developing world' (NDA, 1999: 8). There was also no attempt to develop India's nuclear doctrine in popular discourse in the changed context of both India and Pakistan going nuclear. Not even in the Congress manifesto which in 1999, underlined the need for the foreign policy to be 'supported by the vast majority of the people'. 'Foreign policy must have strong domestic roots and must reflect domestic priorities and concerns' (INC, 1999: 75). The Congress and BJP seem to display a syndrome of being nationalists when in opposition and globalists when in government. They have, of course, come to power in the 1990s only in a minority or coalitional dispensation. Hence, the compulsion to act on a multi-party consensus or create one when required.

The Left parties still continue to abide by a foreign policy of non-alignment and 'anti-imperialism'. The CPI(M) manifesto was critical of the BJP-led government's having 'reversed the course of India's foreign policy whose foundations were based on non-alignment and independence in decision making' [CPI(M), 1999: 4–5]. The CPI manifesto warned: 'When NATO is mounting its offensive worldwide, India has to pursue a consistent anti-imperialist foreign policy. The BJP-led government has been softening up to the USA. India has to be [on] guard against any move for its mediation on bilateral issues' (CPI, 1999: 15).

Recent electoral trends have shown that the 'incumbency factor' has emerged as a good predictor of elections in the sense that a party in power is rarely returned to office in the following election. This is arguably construed as the emergence of the mature voter's evaluating the performance of governments in office. The 1999 mid-term polls were held in an unusual atmosphere. Although the previous election had been under normal circumstances and the inflation rate had been below 2 per cent for some years, the Kargil war was thrust upon the nation unexpectedly between the fall of one government and the holding of the resultant polls. This was both a bane as well as a boon for the government. For, there was unprecedented publicity and assessment of its actions or inactions in the media and the larger matrix of political institutions at the crucial time when elections were imminent. Elections even in normal circumstances are a comprehensive focal event when the political community, in a manner of speaking, is exposed to observation and scrutiny. To make things more complicated, the 1999 polls were held under the shadow of a low-intensity war.

However, Kargil also whipped up nationalist fervour in the face of blatant aggression. Almost all parts of the country mourned deaths of officers and *jawans* on the front. Fortunately for India, there was unprecedented diplomatic support from the international community, including, for a change, the USA. Finally, India succeeded in its limited military objective of repelling the intruders from the Line of Control. The nationalist upsurge engendered by these events came to the rescue of the beleaguered Vajpayee government. The BJP tried to harness this patriotic windfall to its advantage.

Yet, the caretaker government was also constantly dogged by controversies on all sorts of issues ranging from inexcusable intelligence and security lapses to the impropriety of taking policy decisions in various areas, e.g., allowing private operators to migrate from license-fee in the telecom sector, privatised in 1994, to a profit-sharing arrangement under pressure from the business lobby. The government evaded the request from the president and pressure from the opposition to convene a session of the Rajya Sabha (which being a permanent chamber is never dissolved) to discuss the situation arising in the wake of Kargil. Instead, it called a meeting of the chief ministers, but, at this forum too, the government had to face scathing criticisms from the Congress chief ministers for the lapse in allowing the circumstances leading to the war. The president kept a vigilant eye on the caretaker government, having written to the prime minister as many as seventeen times to give advice or seek explanations.[17] Not all of these were heeded by the Vajpayee government.

Despite the long shadow cast by Kargil on the mandate of 1999, political parties stepped up a vigorous campaign spread over almost two months owing to the five-phase polling in different parts of the country. Indeed, it was a swift shift of the scene from the war front to the hustings. Electioneering moved in three different beats conducted largely by different sets of personnel: national, regional and local. The national circuit this time was almost entirely monopolised by the BJP's Atal Behari Vajpayee and from the Congress, Sonia Gandhi's son Rahul, daughter Priyanka, and son-in-law Robert Vadhera. There were high-powered airdashes and motorcades to major rallies. Wherever expectant crowds had gathered, they were addressed by the representatives of the parties. They made it a point to cover at least the major regions of the country. The hordes of media persons accompanying the prime ministers in government planes were missing this time, thanks to the Election Commission's instruction that it would amount to a misuse of government machinery and be an unfair advantage over the opposition constrained to move in hired, smaller aircraft.

The regional campaign circuit was dominated in different states by Farooq Abdullah, Prakash Singh Badal, Omprakash Chautala, Mulayam Singh Yadav, Laloo Prasad Yadav, Naveen Patnaik, Jyoti Basu, Mamata Banerjee, Prafulla Kumar Mahanta, Poorno Agitok Sangama, Sharad Pawar, Bal Thackray, Chandrababu Naidu, S.M. Krishna, M. Karunanidhi, J. Jayalalitha, etc. Without pretentions of any claim to their being national leaders, the regional satraps travelling by air or by road fought hard on their home turfs. Many of them, especially the larger regional players, were contesting in alliance with one or the other major national parties, but these alliances were mostly loaded in favour of the regional partners, especially when it came to the division and sharing of Vidhan Sabha and Lok Sabha seats. Even so, going by press reports, Jayalalitha's keeping Sonia Gandhi waiting during the campaign for nearly an hour at a joint Congress-AIADMK rally in Tamil Nadu before finally regretting her absence was atypical of the relationship between national and regional parties aligned for the 1999 polls.

The focus was on the locality—clusters of village settlements and urban *mohallas*. This network spread out over a larger area, e.g., several constituencies in Rajasthan where Jats traditionally supported the Congress, rose in ire against the party because it prevented, in their perception, the granting of OBC status to them and the resultant loss of reservation in government jobs. As an observer reported: 'The Jat Mahasabha, which was still recently a social organisation dealing with matrimonial and such other matters, has issued an edict that the Congress should be defeated in the Lok Sabha polls.'[18] Or to sample a vignette from Tamil Nadu: 'While [P.] Chidambaram [TMC, Sivaganga] is touring villages, [H.] Raja [BJP, backed by DMK, MDMK, PMK, and TRC] is concentrating in towns such as Karaikudi, Tirupattur and Sivaganga. ... The DMK has plunged headlong into the battle, and wants to put up a stiff fight against Chidambaram who has won consecutively for the last five times from the constituency.'[19]

As in the recent previous elections, the Election Commission of India played an eminently salutary role in ensuring a free and fair poll. It again worked out a schedule of campaign broadcasts and telecasts on the government-managed electronic media by the recognised political parties, free of cost. However, it proscribed paid advertisements by parties on private TV channels to reduce the influence of money power during elections and ensure a level-playing field for all parties. The commission kept a vigilant eye on the enforcement of the model code of conduct and did not hesitate to cross swords with the high and mighty in the land, e.g., with the Government of India on the policy change from fixed licence-fee-based private telecom operations to revenue-sharing operations, which was allowed sensitively close to the elections. Also, the presence of the three chiefs of the armed forces at a meeting addressed by the prime minister in Haryana was a blatant exploitation of the Kargil war for electoral gains.[20]

The commission also attempted to stop the dissemination of 'exit-poll' results conducted during the early phases of the polls until after the completion of the last phase of voting so that early voting trends do not influence the voting behaviour of the latter voters. However, the commission's order to this effect was challenged in the Supreme Court and invalidated which betrayed the institutional rivalry of the judges against the commissioners. Moreover, the third phase of polling was marred by excessive violence, with over 45 persons being killed in Bihar and the Kashmir valley.[21]

The Question of Political Financing

Party funding and electoral expenses are a grey area in Indian democracy. It is an aspect of fundamental significance to both democratic and developmental performance of the Indian political system. Yet, it continues to be largely neglected owing to deep-seated vested interests in the polity and economy. In terms of comparative political experience in this matter, there are, broadly speaking, three patterns of party and electoral financing in the world. The first is the maximalist pattern of state funding of parties as well as elections that is prevalent in continental Europe (Scandinavia, Germany, Austria, the Netherlands, Italy). The second is the minimalist pattern of subsidising only elections (not parties) by way of specific grants or state-provided services with the obligation on the recipients to render accounts to public authorities. This practice is typical of the UK, Ireland, Australia and New Zealand. Limits on campaign expenditure are fairly common in these countries. The United States of America and Japan have, also, a variant of this pattern as they limit contributions to parties and candidates with an intent to broad base fund-raising instead of their depending on a few large donors. The USA, in particular proscribes direct corporate or trade union contributions to parties. The third is the mixed pattern, where public and private political financing, in more or less equal measure, is allowed, with an obligation to be publicly accountable. Even in the preceding models that mainly rely on public or state funding, private contributions are also allowed (Sridharan, 1998: 62 and 1999: 231–32).

Political financing in India does not fall into any of the above three categories. The pattern is one of largely private donations on a quid pro quo basis, mostly on a clandestine basis with no accountability. The two sets of relevant legal provisions relate to corporate donations under the Companies Act (1956, amended severally) and Limits on Election Expenses under the Representation of the People Act, 1951. Both these sets of provisions are completely ineffective and unrealistic. Even after repeated amendments, the impractical low expenditure limits bear no relationship to actual electoral expenses that have increased enormously over the recent decades. Company donations to parties are legally allowed, but, the legal channel is largely ignored by companies for fear of objections by shareholders and political victimisation by the party that was refused donations if it was to come to power.

The legal provision relating to company donations to parties in India, has seen several changes. In 1969, after the major split in the Congress party, Indira Gandhi banned company donations with the intent to stop the flow of funds to the opposition parties. This was reversed in 1985 by Rajiv Gandhi, with the professed objective of 'permitting the corporate sector to play a legitimate role within the defined norms in the functioning of our democracy'. Yet, for reasons mentioned above, companies have been generally reluctant to opt for the transparency of political contributions under the law. In the era of permit-quota-license-raj, the big businesses were obliged to make political funds available to the ruling parties: With the growing liberalisation of the economy since 1991, the big business houses are no longer constrained to donate money to politicians and parties as in the past. Paradoxically, despite the quick turnover of governments, there has been a remarkable continuity of economic policies. The general direction of economic reforms has been in the reduction and simplification of taxation, removal of controls and the opening of the economy to international finance and technology. It is in this changed context that some companies like the Tatas and the Aditya Birla group have set up trusts for channelising political donations to parties on some objective criteria. The Tata Trust is open to any company, though the Birla Trust consists of the companies of its own group. However, these commendable experiments are still very limited. None of the major chambers of commerce and industries has succeeded in persuading all its members to set up a common organisation to manage political donations according to some set criteria. It is, perhaps, for this reason that companies still want to buy certain political favours, both in the interest of their business and politics.[22]

In the most recent phase, the major recipients of company donations have been the BJP and the Congress. The national bourgeoisie has mainly preferred to back these two parties and is often baffled at the inability of these two parties to move ahead to form a coalition government.[23] Going by political arithmetics in the Lok Sabha, such a government would certainly be politically more stable but this viewpoint is oblivious of the political and cultural issues that divide these two single largest parties in the system. The regional bourgeoisie likewise backs the major state parties several of whom have been ruling in a number of states.

The prevailing condition pertaining to political financing is not a very happy one. This is mainly for two reasons. One, growing, clandestine black money is coming to rule the roost gradually. This does not imply that the political class is covered in glory. Yet, a more balanced relationship between a reformed political class and a reformed business elite is in order in the interest of democratic politics and civic virtues. Two, a package with regard to the state funding of elections as suggested by an All Party Parliamentary Committee,[26] headed by Indrajit Gupta, ought to be legislated to promote a healthy politics-business relationship that is premised on the principle of autonomy of the democratic state.

Interpreting and Explaining the Outcome

Overview

The electoral outcome in 1999, marked a continuity as well as a departure from the political patterns established in 1998. The continuity lay in the coming to power again of a right-centrist coalition led by the BJP. The departure was that for the first time in the decade, a coalition government was voted to power that was no longer dependent on support from 'outside'. All the coalition partners joined the cabinet, excepting the TDP whose representative, G.M.G. Balayogi, became the speaker of the Lok Sabha. This was, thus, not a minority government dependent on parliamentary support of parties that were half inside and half outside the coalition. This was, indeed, the factor that had brought down all the previous coalition governments in the decade. With this crucial destabilising factor out of the way, the NDA government could look to the future with a greater degree of confidence. Yet, for the leading party in the coalition there was not much to rejoice about. For, even though the BJP towered over other allies, its parliamentary seats did not register an increase (182 as against 182 in the previous Lok Sabha). Its vote share percentage declined from 25.47 to 23.75. However, its main adversary, the Congress, suffered a precipitous decrease in its number of seats from 141 to 114, even though its vote stood at 28.30, that is, 4.55 per cent higher than that of the BJP. The Congress also increased its vote percentage from 25.88 to 28.30 (see Table 8.4).

If we compare the electoral performance of the two largest single parties leading the two major coalitional blocs, we find that the Congress secured over 30 per cent votes in 16 states and six union territories. In terms of its parliamentary seat share, it was on or above the 40 per cent mark in seven states and four union territories. Evaluated on the same criteria as applied to the Congress above, the BJP crossed the 30 per cent mark in terms of vote share in six states and four union territories. In terms of seat share, it won over 40 per cent in eight states and two union

TABLE 8.4
Lok Sabha Elections 1999: Performance of Parties in States, Union Territories and All-India

Parties	*% votes*	*No. of seats*	*% of seats*
	Andhra Pradesh		
BJP	9.90	7	16.7
INC	42.79	5	11.9
CPI(M)	1.40	0	0.0
CPI	1.33	0	0.0
JD(S)	0.05	0	0.0
TDP	39.85	29	69.0
	Arunachal Pradesh		
BJP	16.30	0	0.0
INC	56.92	2	100.0
	Assam		
BJP	29.84	2	14.28
INC	38.42	10	71.4
CPI(M)	1.77	0	0.0
CPI	0.58	0	0.0
AGP	11.92	0	0.0
	Bihar		
BJP	23.01	23	42.5
INC	8.81	4	7.40
CPI(M)	0.98	1	1.85
CPI	2.69	0	0.0
BSP	0.95	0	0.0
JD(U)	20.77	18	33.3
JD(S)	0.14	0	0.0
RJD	28.29	7	12.96
	Goa		
BJP	51.49	2	100.0
INC	39.01	0	0.0
CPI	2.93	0	0.0
	Gujarat		
BJP	52.48	20	76.92

(*contd.*)

Parties	*% votes*	*No. of seats*	*% of seats*
INC	45.44	6	23.07
CPI	0.04	0	0.0
JD(U)	0.40	0	0.0
JD(S)	0.06	0	0.0
Haryana			
BJP	29.21	5	50.0
INC	34.93	0	0.0
CPI(M)	0.15	0	0.0
BSP	1.96	0	0.0
JD(S)	0.02	0	0.0
HVP	2.71	0	0.0
INLD	28.72	5	50.0
Himachal Pradesh			
BJP	46.27	3	75.0
INC	39.52	0	0.0
CPI	0.46	0	0.0
BSP	0.31	0	0.0
JD(S)	0.19	0	0.0
HVC	12.30	1	25.0
Jammu and Kashmir			
BJP	31.56	2	33.3
INC	17.83	0	0.0
CPI(M)	1.00	0	0.0
BSP	4.84	0	0.0
JD(U)	0.14	0	0.0
JD(S)	0.92	0	0.0
JKNC	28.94	4	66.66
Karnataka			
BJP	27.19	7	25.0
INC	45.41	18	64.2
CPI(M)	0.08	0	0.0
BSP	0.65	0	0.0
JD(U)	13.28	3	10.7
JD(S)	10.85	0	0.0

(contd.)

Parties	*% votes*	*No. of seats*	*% of seats*
	Kerala		
BJP	6.56	0	0.0
INC	39.35	8	40.0
CPI(M)	27.90	8	40.0
CPI	7.57	0	0.0
BSP	0.09	0	0.0
JD(U)	1.35	0	0.0
JD(S)	2.17	0	0.0
KC	2.38	1	5.0
KC(M)	2.32	1	5.0
MUL	5.27	2	10.0
	Madhya Pradesh		
BJP	46.58	29	72.5
INC	43.91	11	27.5
CPI(M)	0.05	0	0.0
CPI	0.23	0	0.0
BSP	5.23	0	0.0
JD(U)	0.02	0	0.0
JD(S)	0.07	0	0.0
	Maharashtra		
BJP	21.18	13	27.1
INC	29.71	10	20.8
CPI(M)	0.52	0	0.0
CPI	0.06	0	0.0
BSP	0.32	0	0.0
JD(S)	0.91	1	2.1
NCP	21.58	6	12.5
SHS	16.90	15	31.2
BBM	2.10	1	0.0
PWPI	0.90	1	0.9
	Manipur		
BJP	1.02	0	0.0
INC	25.29	0	0.0
CPI	3.95	0	0.0
JD(U)	3.19	0	0.0

(*contd.*)

Parties	*% votes*	*No. of seats*	*% of seats*
MPP	16.25	0	0.0
MSCP	24.90	1	50.0
NCP	13.50	1	50.0
	Meghalaya		
BJP	9.45	0	0.0
INC	32.75	1	50.0
CPI	0.68	0	0.0
NCP	27.90	1	50.0
	Mizoram		
One seat won by independent			
	Nagaland		
BJP	5.12	0	0.0
INC	71.18	1	100.0
	Orissa		
BJP	24.63	9	42.8
INC	36.94	2	9.5
CPI(M)	0.20	0	0.0
CPI	1.18	0	0.0
BSP	0.33	0	0.0
JD(U)	0.03	0	0.0
BJD	33.00	10	47.6
	Punjab		
BJP	9.16	1	9.6
INC	38.44	8	61.5
CPI(M)	2.18	0	0.0
CPI	3.74	1	7.6
BSP	3.84	0	0.0
JD(U)	0.10	0	0.0
JD(S)	0.03	0	0.0
SAD	28.59	2	15.3
SAD(M)	3.4	1	7.6
	Rajasthan		
BJP	47.23	16	64.0
INC	45.12	9	36.0

(*contd.*)

Parties	*% votes*	*No. of seats*	*% of seats*
CPI(M)	0.49	0	0.0
CPI	0.42	0	0.0
BSP	2.76	0	0.0
JD(U)	1.60	0	0.0
JD(S)	0.06	0	0.0
	Sikkim		
SDF	52.56	1	100.0
	Tamil Nadu		
BJP	7.14	4	10.2
INC	11.10	2	10.2
CPI(M)	2.35	1	2.5
CPI	2.56	0	0.0
JD(S)	0.15	0	0.0
AIADMK	25.68	10	25.6
DMK	23.13	12	30.8
PMK	8.21	5	12.8
MDMK	5.95	4	10.2
MADMK	1.46	1	2.5
	Tripura		
BJP	12.82	0	0.0
INC	13.88	0	0.0
CPI(M)	56.24	2	100.0
	Uttar Pradesh		
BJP	27.64	29	34.1
INC	14.72	10	11.8
CPI(M)	0.03	0	0.0
CPI	0.28	0	0.0
BSP	22.08	14	16.4
JD(U)	0.59	0	0.0
JD(S)	0.09	0	0.0
SP	24.06	26	30.5
SJP(R)	0.50	1	1.1
ABLTC	1.51	2	2.3
RLD	2.49	2	2.3
Inds.	3.60	1	1.1

(contd.)

Parties	*% votes*	*No. of seats*	*% of seats*
	West Bengal		
BJP	11.13	2	4.8
INC	13.29	3	7.1
CPI(M)	35.57	21	50.0
CPI	3.47	3	7.1
BSP	0.24	0	0.0
JD(S)	0.02	0	0.0
AITC	26.04	8	19.0
RSP	4.25	3	7.1
FB	3.45	2	4.8
	Andaman & Nicobar		
BJP	52.74	1	100.0
INC	43.17	0	0.0
	Chandigarh		
BJP	45.07	0	0.0
INC	47.00	1	100.0
BSP	2.75	0	0.0
	Dadra and Nagar Haveli		
BJP	20.83	0	0.0
INC	14.74	0	0.0
Ind.	44.90	1	100.0
	Daman and Diu		
BJP	43.13	0	0.0
INC	49.48	1	100.0
	National Capital Territory of Delhi		
BJP	51.75	7	100.0
INC	41.96	0	0.0
BSP	2.24	0	0.0
JD(S)	1.39	0	0.0
	Lakshadweep		
INC	53.96	1	100.0
JD(U)	43.28	0	0.0
JD(S)	1.82	0	0.0

(*contd.*)

Parties	*% votes*	*No. of seats*	*% of seats*
	Pondicherry		
INC	37.17	1	100.0
	All India		
BJP	23.75	182	33.5
INC	28.30	114	21.0
CPI(M)	5.40	33	6.1
CPI	1.48	4	0.1
BSP	4.16	14	2.6
JD(U)	3.10	21	3.9
JD(S)	0.91	1	0.2

Source: *India, Republic. Statistical Report on General Elections, 1999, to the 13th Lok Sabha*, vol. I, National and State Abstracts and Detailed Results (New Delhi: Election Commission of India, 2000).

Note: National Parties taken together polled 67.11 per cent votes, winning 369 seats. The corresponding figures for the state parties in aggregate are 26.93 per cent of votes and 158 seats. The registered unrecognised parties polled 3.22 per cent of votes and bagged 10 seats, independent candidates registered 2.74 per cent of votes and 16 seats.

territories. None of the other national parties secured even six per cent of the national vote or seven per cent of the parliamentary seats. The best performance among these minor national parties was that of the CPI(M) with 5.4 per cent of votes and 6.1 per cent of seats nationally.

Among the major regional parties, counting the largest ones in their respective states, we get nine state parties with their seat shares in their respective states ranging between 69 per cent (TDP in Andhra Pradesh) and 13 per cent (RJD in Bihar). Their respective vote shares in the limited arenas of their states ranged between 39.9 per cent (TDP) and 16.9 per cent (Shiv Sena in Maharashtra).

Electoral Pacts

It would be interesting to compare the impact of some inter-party alliances in some states on the electoral outcome. To begin with, in Tamil Nadu the DMK replaced the AIADMK in the

BJP-led alliance in 1999. The largest two parties in the alliance in the state in 1998 had registered 32.7 per cent votes and 21 seats. The altered combination of the largest two parties together secured 30.3 per cent of votes and 16 seats. Whereas the BJP's performance in both these elections remained more or less constant in terms of votes, its seats increased from 3 to 4 in 1999. It meant that the replacement of the AIADMK by DMK more or less compensated for the alliance.

In Andhra Pradesh, the BJP and TDP were not aligned in 1998, whereas they joined hands in 1999. Here again, the combined performance of the two parties remained more or less constant. However, the alliance did make some internal difference between the relative position of the two parties such that the BJP vote share declined from 18.3 per cent to 9.9 per cent. The corresponding vote shares of the TDP in the two elections were 32 per cent and 39.8 per cent, respectively. In terms of seats, BJP's share increased from 4 to 7, while that of TDP from 12 to 29. Thus, the alliance primarily worked to the advantage of the regional partner.

The merger of a faction of the JD, Samata Party and Lok Shakti and the resultant split in the JD produced notable realignment of political forces in Karnataka and Bihar on the eve of elections in 1999. Even though the BJP national leadership was somewhat skeptical of aligning with the JD, then ruling in Karnataka and hence susceptible to the adverse operation of the incumbency factor, it finally acquiesced in the coalition. In Karnataka, the hesitation of the BJP leadership was justified as far as voting percentage was concerned. In 1998, the combined votes of these parties, had the JD been in alliance, would have been 60.2 per cent. But, their combined vote in 1999 declined to 51.3 per cent. In fact, their seat share also went down from nineteen to ten. BJP's own vote percentage remained largely constant (26.9: 27.2). However, its number of seats went down from thirteen to seven. Thus, the alliance in Karnataka worked neither in favour of the national party nor the regional one. Confirming the worst fears of the BJP, the Congress was voted to power in the state in the simultaneous elections to the Vidhan Sabha. Even in the parliamentary contingent from the state, the Congress secured 18 seats as against seven for the BJP-JD(U) alliance. The BJP-JD(U) alliance was, however, more fruitful in Bihar where it improved upon the performance of the BJP-Samata alliance in 1998, both in terms of votes and seats. Their vote percentage of 39.6 in 1998 jumped to 43.8 in 1999. Similarly, their seat share of 29 went up to 41.

The BJP-BJD alliance in Orissa worked better in 1999 than in the previous election. Its vote percentage increased from 48.7 per cent to 57 per cent and seats from 16 to 19. Both the parties benefitted from the alliance. The BJP's vote increased from 21.2 to 24.6 and seat share improved from seven to nine. Similarly, the BJD's vote share increased from 27.5 to 33 per cent and seats from 9 to 10. Yet, the regional partner was relatively much better off than the national one. The fact that the Congress happened to be the ruling party in the state at the time of the election augured well for the BJP-BJD alliance. For, the incumbency factor negatively worked against the Congress.

The National Conference in Jammu and Kashmir and Shiromani Akali Dal in the Punjab also contested the 1999 Lok Sabha elections in alliance with the NDA. Compared to 1998, when the BJP and National Conference were not electoral partners, the two parties together increased their vote from 59.2 to 60 per cent and seats from three to six. The individual gain of the BJP was more marked, especially in terms of votes: from 23.3 to 31.6 per cent; its seats went up from one to two. The National Conference found its vote declining from 35.9 to 28.9, though its seats did improve from two to four.

The BJP and Akali Dal in Punjab were allies both in 1998 and 1999. Both the partners found their fortunes diminished in terms of votes as well as seats in the subsequent polls: the BJP's decline was from 11.7(3) to 9.2(1) and Akali Dal's from 32.9(8) to 28.6(2). (The figures in parentheses stand for seats).

In Maharashtra, the BJP-Shiv Sena alliance suffered a decline in terms of votes (from 42.1 to 38.0 per cent), yet they improved their seats share (from 10 to 28). In terms of individual party gains and losses, the BJP's vote share went down from 22.5 per cent to 21.2 per cent though its seats went up from four to thirteen. The comparable figures for Shiv Sena were 19.7: 16.9 per cent in terms of vote and 6:15 in terms of seats for the two successive elections. This finding was consistent with the negative operation of the incumbency factor in some other alliances reported here where the regional partner happened to be in power in the state concerned, e.g., Karnataka, Orissa, Punjab. The two exceptions to this rule were Jammu and Kashmir and Tamil Nadu, where the BJP's alliance with the National Conference and DMK did not suffer from the fact that the state parties in the combination were ruling parties in the respective states.

The Congress-RJD alliance in Bihar was operative in both 1998 and 1999. The pact worked to the advantage of both the partners individually as well as collectively, though there was growing pressure from the BJP-led alliance in both the elections. The NDA improved its vote/seat share from 33.7 (22) to 37.1(11) the figures within the parentheses being seats. The Congress shares in the booty were 7.4 (5) and 8.8 (4) and those of the RJD 26.3 (17) and 28.3 (7) in 1998 and 1999, respectively.

The electoral impact of the Nationalist Congress Party's split from the Congress in Maharashtra on the parent party was disastrous: its vote went down from 43.6 to 29.7 per cent and seats from 33 to 10. There was some consolation for it in its electoral performance vis-a-vis its rebellious splinter. The Congress registered 29.7 per cent of the votes compared to 21.6 per cent for the NCP. And, the former won ten seats as against six won by the NCP. In Meghalaya, the one other state where the split had considerable impact, the Congress vote share went down from 47.6 to 32.7 per cent and its seats from two to one. In 1999, the Congress polled 32.7 per cent of votes as against NCP's 27.9. Both parties captured one seat each.

Simultaneous Polls

It has often been argued that elections to the assembly and local bodies arouse greater political involvement in the voter than the parliamentary polls. This may be because of the immediacy of the issues and the institutions to the constituents. National and state elections were held simultaneously until before the 1971 snap Lok Sabha polls when Mrs Indira Gandhi first delinked the two sets of elections arguably to carve out a national arena of political mobilisation less constrained by local and regional issues. The strategy apparently brought rich electoral windfalls to Mrs Gandhi which enabled the Congress party to reverse the trend of its decline by an emotive pro-poor, left-of-the-centre ideological campaign. The assumption that simultaneous assembly and parliamentary polls generate a greater political activity is borne out by Table 8.5, as far as the electoral turnout figures are concerned. In all the six states that simultaneously went to the polls to elect their MLAs and MPs the turnout percentages were consistently higher than the comparable statistics for all India. However, the hypothetical localising or nationalising effect of simultaneous elections on the campaign is difficult to determine precisely and conclusively. In Andhra Pradesh, the combined vote percentages for national parties (52.69) was higher than that for the dominant regional party, the TDP, that won the assembly polls. The BJP and TDP who fought the election in alliance with each other together polled 49.75 per cent votes. The Congress vote in the state (42.79 per cent) was higher than the votes won singly by either the BJP, which was ruling in New Delhi at the head of a coalition, or the TDP in Hyderabad. But for the BJP-TDP alliance, the anti-incumbency factor would have probably helped the Congress to regain power in the state after a lapse of several terms. The situation was similarly complicated in other states. In Arunachal Pradesh, the Congress in alliance with a regional outfit, then in opposition, carried the day and unseated the dominant regional party, the Arunachal Congress. In Haryana, the major regional party, Indian National Lok Dal, in alliance with the BJP-led National Democratic Alliance was voted to power. In Karnataka, despite the BJP-JD(U) alliance formed just before the election, the incumbent Janata Dal government in the state was checkmated by the Congress that swept the polls. The

Congress vote in the state for the Lok Sabha polls too was very impressive (45.41) and way ahead of both the JD(U) (13.28 per cent) and BJP (27.19). In Maharashtra, despite an alliance between the Shiv Sena and BJP ruling both in Mumbai and New Delhi, the Indian National Congress outpaced both the ruling parties with a 29.71 poll percentage and captured power in the state in a post-election alliance with its own rebellious splinter, the Nationalist Congress Party, that had parted company with the parent party on the eve of elections. In Sikkim the regional party, Sikkim Democratic Front, had a field day, winning 52.56 per cent votes for the Lok Sabha.

TABLE 8.5

Aspects of Electoral Behaviour at the All-India Level and in States where Simultaneous Lok Sabha and Vidhan Sabha Elections were Held in 1999

Area/Unit	*% turnout*	*% BJP vote*	*% Congress vote*	*% vote major regional party or 3rd party*
All India	59.99	23.75	28.30	26.93 All state parties
Andhra Pradesh	69.14	09.90	42.79	39.85 TDP
Arunachal Pradesh	72.16	16.30	56.92	16.62 AC
Haryana	63.68	29.21	34.93	28.72 INLD
Karnataka	67.58	27.19	45.41	13.28 JD(U)
Maharashtra	60.94	21.18	29.71	16.86 SS
Sikkim	81.71	00.00	04.76	52.56 SDF

Source: Compiled from *Election Commission of India* (1999), vol. 1.

Demographics

Some rare data from the National Election Study 1999, based on a cross-country probability sample survey conducted soon after the polls by the Centre for the Study of Developing Societies, Delhi, enables us to probe into some demographic factors affecting party votes in 1999. Table 8.6 shows that the upper castes (UCs) were more likely to vote for the BJP-led NDA (50.5 per cent) than any other party front or party; the remainder of their vote is plurally divided with 21.7 per cent for Congress and allies, and 5.9 per cent for the Left Front. The other backward castes (OBCs) vote was divided between the BJP and its allies, on the one hand, the Congress and its allies, on the other, to the ratio of 30.9 to 38.5 per cent, respectively. Thus, with the largest party-divided blocs of UCs and OBCs supporting the NDA, there may be some temptation to interpret the 1999 mandate in terms of Hindu-right consolidation. But it is important to remember that the NDA included ten parties that profess the secular values of the Constitution. Only the BJP and Shiv Sena in the lot sweared by Hindu nationalism. In the total tally of 300 NDA seats, the BJP and its Maharashtra ally together accounted for 197 seats. As Ashutosh Varshney (2000: 4) reminds us: 'While Hindu nationalists have indeed, come to power in Delhi, Hindu nationalism as an ideology has not.'

TABLE 8.6
Caste and Community by Party Vote in the 1999 Lok Sabha Elections, Row Percentages (Ns)

Caste/ Community	*Congress and allies*	*BJP and allies*	*Left Front*	*BSP*	*Others*	*D.K./ N.A.*
Upper Caste	21.7	50.5	5.9	0.5	11.0	10.3
	(498)	(1,158)	(135)	(12)	(253)	(235)
OBCs	30.9	38.5	4.7	1.3	13.2	11.4
	(987)	(1231)	(151)	(43)	(421)	(365)
SCs	37.0	20.6	9.7	11.0	11.6	10.2
	(615)	(342)	(161)	(183)	(192)	(169)
STs	41.7	29.3	6.0	0.1	10.3	12.5
	(300)	(211)	(43)	(1)	(74)	(90)
Muslims	52.9	11.2	9.7	1.6	15.3	9.4
	(475)	(101)	(87)	(14)	(137)	(84)
Others	32.7	32.4	11.4	0.6	11.7.	11.4
	(112)	(111)	(39)	(2)	(40)	(39)

Note: Congress and allies include the RJD, Muslim League, Kerala Congress, AIADMK, RPI (Prakash). BJP and allies in the NDA alliance include Shiv Sena, JD(U), Akali Dal, HVP, BJD, HVC, TDP (Naidu), DMK, PMK, TRC, MDMK, MGP, Trinamool Congress. Left Front includes CPI(M), CPI, Forward Bloc, RSP.

Just as the UCs and OBCs modally tended to support the BJP and is allies, scheduled castes and scheduled tribes modally voted for the Congress and its allies: 37.0 per cent and 41.7 per cent, respectively. The rest of the SCs voted as follows: 20.6 for the BJP and its allies, 9.7 per cent for the Left Front and 11.0 per cent for the BSP. The rest of the STs' vote was likewise divided as follows: 29.3 per cent for the BJP and its allies, 6.0 per cent for the Left Front, and 0.1 per cent for the BSP.

The Muslims predominantly voted for the Congress alliance in 1999—52.9 per cent. The BJP and its allies got only 11.2 per cent votes from the Muslims and the Left Front, 9.7 per cent. An indicator of 'tactical' voting by Muslims in a large number of constituencies was perhaps, reflected by the fact that as many as 16.3 per cent of the Muslims voted for nondescript parties desultorily put in the residual category 'Other (Parties)'. Tactical voting is defined as the voters' calculated exercise of their franchise for *any* party that seems poised to defeat a hated party even though such a vote may not lead to the success of the party they identify with. The press reported that the Muslim voters negatively targetted the BJP's defeat in many constituencies across the country in 1999.

The relationship between the rural/urban location and party vote is presented in Table 8.7. While the Congress and its allies received more or less comparable levels of support from rural and urban voters—32.8 and 32.9 per cent, respectively, the BJP and its allies were more popular in urban areas (38.0 per cent) than in the rural (33.7 per cent). The Left Front's share in the party-divided vote was 8.0 per cent rural and 2.4 per cent urban. The comparable figures for the BSP were 3.2 per cent rural and 1.3 per cent urban.

Table 8.8 displays the relationship between age and party vote. There does not seem to be a marked differential impact of age on party choice. The only clear pattern that emerges from the table is that in all age groups the bulk of the sample voted for either the Congress alliance or the BJP alliance.

TABLE 8.7
Rural/Urban Locality by Party Vote in the 1999 Lok Sabha Elections, Row Percentages (Ns)

Locality	*Congress and allies*	*BJP and allies*	*Left Front*	*BSP*	*Others*
Rural	32.8	33.7	8.0	3.2	12.4
	(2,322)	(2,385)	(568)	(228)	(877)
Urban	32.9	38.0	2.4	1.3	11.9
	(665)	(769)	(48)	(27)	(240)

Note: The category 'D.K./N.A.' with figures 10.0 (707) Rural and 13.6 (275) Urban is dropped from above. Percentages and numbers (Ns) are both given.

TABLE 8.8
Age by Party Vote in the 1999 Lok Sabha Elections, Row Percentages (Ns)

Age	*Congress and allies*	*BJP and allies*	*Left Front*	*BSP*	*Others*	*D.K./ N.A.*
Up to 25 years	31.7	35.6	5.7	3.0	11.7	12.2
	(505)	(567)	(90)	(48)	(187)	(195)
26 to 35 years	32.5	34.8	7.1	3.2	12.6	9.9
	(864)	(925)	(188)	(86)	(334)	(263)
36 to 45 years	31.4	34.4	7.7	2.6	13.4	10.5
	(622)	(680)	(153)	(51)	(265)	(208)
46 to 55 years	36.8	33.9	6.7	2.1	11.2	9.3
	(494)	(455)	(90)	(28)	(150)	(125)
Above 55 years	32.6	34.3	6.2	2.7	11.8	12.4
	(502)	(527)	(95)	(42)	(181)	(191)

Table 8.9 suggests that there was some tendency for the male voters to prefer the BJP alliance (37.4 per cent) and the female voters to vote for the Congress alliance (34.1 per cent). But this probability is not very strong. For other parties there was no marked relationship between gender and party vote.

Table 8.10 shows that education and party vote were correlated. However, whereas this correlation was negative in the Congress alliance, it was positive in the BJP alliance. In other words, the higher the educational standard of the voters, the lower the probability of their voting for the Congress bloc. On the other hand, this relationship was reversed for the BJP bloc such that with rising levels of education the voters were more likely to vote for the NDA. In the case of the Left Front the relation between education and party vote was shown to be curvilinear. That is, at both lower and higher levels of education the voters were less likely to vote Left Front than were the voters at middle levels of education. In the case of the BJP there was no clear association between education and party vote.

TABLE 8.9
Gender by Party Vote in the 1999 Lok Sabha Elections, Row Percentages (Ns)

Gender	*Congress and allies*	*BJP and allies*	*Left Front*	*BSP*	*Others*	*D.K./ N.A.*
Male	31.5	37.4	6.6	3.4	13.0	8.2
	(1,457)	(1,726)	(304)	(157)	(599)	(377)
Female years	34.1	31.8	6.9	2.2	11.5	13.5
	(1,530)	(1,428)	(312)	(98)	(518)	(605)

TABLE 8.10
Education and Party Vote in the 1999 Lok Sabha Elections, Row Percentages (Ns)

Education	*Congress and allies*	*BJP and allies*	*Left Front*	*BSP*	*Others*
Non-literate	36.6	29.6	5.1	3.8	13.0
	(1,365)	(1,105)	(190)	(140)	(486)
Up to primary	33.8	33.4	9.4	2.0	12.0
	(743)	(735)	(207)	(43)	(263)
Up to matriculation	29.4	39.4	7.5	2.6	11.6
	(585)	(785)	(149)	(52)	(230)
Up to college	24.9	44.8	5.3	1.8	11.5
and above	(282)	(508)	(60)	(20)	(130)
Missing information	21.1	36.8	17.5	—	14.0
	(12)	(21)	(10)	—	(8)

Note: The category 'D.K./N.A.' (don't know/not applicable) was dropped from the above. The relevant row percentages and numbers (Ns) for the corresponding Education/Party cells were as follows: 11.9 (445), 9.5 (209), 9.5 (189), 11.7 (133), and 10.5 (6).

Table 8.11 demonstrates the relation between voters' occupation and party vote. Although the construction of finer categories on the occupation side has proliferated cells some of which are left with too few cases to allow generalisation, certain patterns of relationship between voters' occupation and party vote are in fact faintly evident from the table. For example, comparing the row percentages we find that higher and lower professionals, big and medium and other businessmen, owner cultivators of all sizes of landholdings, tenants, and non-workers were more likely to vote for the NDA. The service class and non-cultivators were more inclined to vote for the Congress and its allies. The Left Front had the vote of the tenants, non-cultivators, and 'non-workers'. The row percentages do not reveal a relation between occupation and party vote. Yet, the column percentages reveal that the BSP voters were more likely to be in service or were agricultural workers, tenants of 0–5 acres, and owner cultivators with 0–5 acres.

TABLE 8.11
Occupation by Party Vote in the 1999 Lok Sabha Elections, Ns, Row and Column Percentages

Occupation	*Party*					
	Congress and allies	*BJP and allies*	*Left Front*	*BSP*	*Others*	*D.K./ N.A.*
Higher professional	22	43	3	—	8	21
	22.7	44.3	3.1	—	8.2	21.6
	0.7	1.4	0.5	—	0.7	2.1
Lower professional	323	416	74	11.0	104	159
	29.7	38.3	6.8	1.0	9.6	14.6
	10.8	13.2	12.0	4.3	9.3	16.2
Big and medium business	51	87	7	—	21	18
	27.7	47.3	3.8	—	11.4	9.8
	1.7	2.8	1.1	—	1.9	1.8
Small business	277	341	66	21.0	99	86
	31.1	38.3	7.4	2.4	11.1	9.7
	9.3	10.8	10.7	8.2	8.9	8.8
Service	699	504	147	75.0	257	181
	37.5	27.1	7.9	4.0	13.8	9.7
	23.4	16.0	23.9	29.4	23.0	18.4

(contd.)

Occupation	*Party*					
	Congress and allies	*BJP and allies*	*Left Front*	*BSP*	*Others*	*D.K./ N.A.*
Owner cultivator 20+ acres	56 32.7 1.9	85 49.7 2.7	1 0.6 0.2	— — —	20 11.7 1.8	9 5.3 0.9
Owner cultivator 10–12 acres	68 29.8 2.3	106 46.5 3.4	5 2.2 0.8	1.0 0.4 0.4	25 11.0 2.2	23 10.1 2.3
Owner cultivator 5–10 acres	173 35.2 5.8	190 38.7 6.0	4 0.8 0.6	4 0.8 1.6	64 13.0 5.7	56 11.4 5.7
Owner cultivator 0–5 acres	557 33.6 18.6	617 37.2 19.6	53 3.2 8.6	54 3.3 21.2	200 12.0 17.9	179 10.8 18.2
Tenant 0–5 acres	35 15.5 1.2	81 35.8 2.6	25 11.1 4.0	14 6.2 5.5	49 21.7 4.4	22 9.7 2.2
Other agricultural work	644 33.9 21.6	591 31.2 18.7	188 9.9 30.5	64 3.4 25.1	236 12.4 21.1	174 9.2 17.7
Non-cultivators	34 29.1 1.1	26 22.2 0.8	17 14.5 2.8	4 3.4 1.6	17 14.5 1.5	19 16.2 1.9
Non-workers	48 24.0 1.6	67 33.5 2.1	26 13.0 4.2	7 3.5 2.7	17 8.5 1.5	35 17.5 3.6

Note: The residual category 'Non-worker' is vague and therefore not very illuminating.

Governmental Performance

The National Election Study's post-poll survey (1999) also enables us to explore the voters' perception and evaluation of some recent governments in New Delhi and their actions and inactions. Question 8 of their schedule asked the respondents to specifically indicate which of the three recent governments of India—the Rao Congress, BJP and its allies and United Front —they liked the best. The responses are cross-tabulated with the party vote in Table 8.12. Although the 'can't say/D.K. (don't know)' responses are rather high, yet party vote and the evaluation of 'best of three governments', or rather the vice versa, were strongly correlated. Those voting for the Congress alliance were likely, with a probability of 71 per cent, to evaluate the Rao Congress government as the best. Those voting for the BJP alliance rated the Vajpayee government as the best to the tune of 66.5 per cent. The Left Front voters thought, with a probability of 40.3 per cent, that the UF governments headed by H.D. Deve Gowda and I.K. Gujral were the best of the lot. The largest proportion of voters perceiving no difference among these governments were the Congress voters (31.5 per cent). The Congress voters also outnumbered others in the 'can't say/D.K. (don't know)' response.

TABLE 8.12

Government Performance by Party Vote in the 1999 Lok Sabha Elections, Ns and Row and Column Percentages

	Party Vote					
Best performing government	*Congress and allies*	*BJP and allies*	*Left Front*	*BSP*	*Others*	*D.K./ N.A.*
Congress	1,410	139	56	30	176	175
	71.0	7.0	2.8	1.5	8.9	8.8
	47.2	4.4	9.1	11.8	15.8	17.8
BJP and allies	336	2,094	69	34	317	301
	10.7	66.5	2.2	1.1	10.1	9.6
	11.2	66.4	11.2	13.3	28.4	30.7
United Front	180	84	286	13	84	62
	25.4	11.8	40.3	1.8	11.8	8.7
	6.0	2.7	46.4	5.1	7.5	6.3
No difference	357	252	73	79	233	141
	31.5	22.2	6.4	7.0	20.5	12.4
	12.2	8.0	11.9	31.0	20.9	14.4
Can't Say/D.K.	704	585	132	99	307	303
	33.1	27.5	6.2	4.6	14.4	14.2
	26.6	18.5	21.4	38.8	27.5	30.9

Pokharan-II and Kargil

Another set of questions sought to measure the impact on the elections of Pokharan-II and the Kargil conflict. The responses to the questions about these two events in relation to the party vote are presented in Table 8.13 and 8.14. Table 8.13 shows that the Pokharan nuclear explosion was approved by those voting for the BJP alliance by a majority (51.2 per cent). The approval tapered off with the electorate voting for other combinations of parties: the Congress alliance (22.9 per cent), the Left Front (4.1 per cent), others (11.2 per cent), and the BSP (1.8 per cent). It is notable that the category 'Inapplicable' that includes those who have not heard about Pokharan is rather large, as much as 60.1 per cent among Congress-alliance voters and 69.0 per cent among BSP voters. The proportion of such ill-informed voters is relatively lower yet as high as 45.2 per cent among the BJP-alliance voters and 39.8 per cent among the Left Front voters.

TABLE 8.13
Pokharan-II by Party Vote in the 1999 Lok Sabha Elections, Ns and Row and Column Percentages

	Party Vote					
Voters' perception of Pokharan	*Congress and allies*	*BJP and allies*	*Left Front*	*BSP*	*Others*	*D.K./N.A.*
Disapprove	362	158	200	9	93	77
	40.3	17.6	22.2	1.0	10.3	8.6
	12.1	5.0	32.5	3.5	8.3	7.8
Approve	615	1,372	110	47	300	236
	22.9	51.2	4.1	1.8	11.2	8.8
	20.6	43.5	17.9	18.4	26.9	24.0
No opinion	215	197	61	23	116	51
	32.4	29.7	9.2	3.5	17.5	7.7
	7.2	6.2	9.9	9.0	10.0	5.2
Inapplicable	1,795	1,427	245	176	608	618
	36.9	29.3	39.8	3.6	12.5	12.7
	60.1	45.2	100.0	69.0	54.4	62.9

Table 8.14 shows that satisfaction with the government's handling of the Kargil was the highest, though still short of the

majority mark, in those voting for the BJP and allies (49.5 per cent). Those voting for the Congress alliance were dissatisfied with Kargil in more or less similar proportion—48.3 per cent.

TABLE 8.14
Kargil by Party Vote in the 1999 Lok Sabha Elections, Ns and Row and Column Percentages

	Party Vote					
Evaluation of government's handling of Kargil	*Congress and allies*	*BJP and allies*	*Left Front*	*BSP*	*Others*	*D.K./ N.A.*
Not satisfied	551 48.3 18.4	135 11.8 4.3	206 18.1 33.4	26 2.3 10.2	111 9.7 9.9	111 9.7 11.3
Satisified	887 23.5 29.7	1,871 49.5 59.3	149 3.9 24.2	70 1.9 27.5	450 11.9 40.3	355 9.4 36.2
Can't say/D.K.	357 34.7 12.0	264 25.7 8.4	91 8.8 14.8	43 4.2 16.9	159 15.5 14.2	115 11.2 11.7
Inapplicable	1,192 37.7 29.9	884 28.0 28.0	170 5.4 27.6	116 3.7 45.5	397 12.6 35.5	401 12.7 40.8

The Left Front voter was less satisfied with the government's handling of the Kargil conflict (3.9 per cent). The satisfaction level went down to a mere 1.9 per cent among those voting for the BSP. It was a bit higher, 11.9 per cent, among those voting for the residual party category 'Others'. Notably, the proportion of the sample that had not heard about Kargil was somewhat large, especially among the Congress-alliance and BJP-alliance voters—37.7 and 28 per cent, respectively. These respondents are included in the category 'Inapplicable' in the table.

Leadership Image

It is common knowledge that the prime minister's image is larger than the party's image among the Indian electorate. To measure the impact of this variable in the 1999 election, the respondents were asked who their choice was for the next prime minister of the country. The responses are reported in Table 8.15. Over 37 per cent of respondents preferred Vajpayee as against nearly 27 per cent for Sonia Gandhi. Jyoti Basu was the choice of 4.05 per cent of the respondents. Predictably, each of these prime ministerial choices were predominantly favoured by their own alliance-party voters; Vajpayce was the choice of 71 per cent of the BJP-alliance voters; Sonia Gandhi of 76.5 per cent of the Congress-alliance voters, whereas Jyoti Basu was the top choice of the 89 per cent of the Left Front voters.

TABLE 8.15

Choice of Prime Minister by Party Vote in the 1999 Lok Sabha Elections, Ns and Row Percentages

	Parties					
Leader(s)	*BJP and allies*	*Congress and allies*	*Left Front*	*BSP*	*Others*	*D.K./ N.A.*
Sonia Gandhi	107	1,941	80	20	168	222
	4.2	76.5	3.2	0.8	6.6	8.7
A.B. Vajpayee	2,482	279	67	23	326	320
	71.0	8.0	1.9	0.7	9.3	9.2
Jyoti Basu	2	16	339	—	3	21
	0.5	4.2	89.0	—	0.8	5.3

Note: The question 'Who in your opinion should be the next PM?' included other leaders as well: George Fernandes, Kanshi Ram, Mayawati, Manmohan Singh, Digvijay Singh, Mamata Banerjee, Sharad Pawar, Moopanar, Bal Thackray, L.K. Advani, Kalyan Singh, Mulayam Singh Yadav, Naveen Patnaik, Laloo Prasad Yadav, Chandrashekhar, Devi Lal, P.S. Badal, P.K. Mahanta, Karunanidhi, Jayalalitha, R.K. Hegde and N. Chandrababu Naidu. But outside the regions from where these leaders held sway the voters' choice of them as PMs was negligible. Since these figures are omitted from the table, percentages do not add up to 100.

The 1999 mid-term polls were particularly marked by a hot controversy regarding Sonia Gandhi as a prime ministerial candidate, both within her own party, that split on this issue, and outside. To as many as 63.72 per cent of voters interviewed, this was a non-issue. As Table 8.16 shows that among those who considered her unsuitable for the job, did so mainly for two reasons, in that order: foreign origin (15.2 per cent) and inexperience (10.3 per cent). In terms of major party divisions, 57 per cent of the BJP alliance voters disqualified her for her inexperience whereas only 13.3 per cent of Left Front voters and 9.4 per cent of Congress-alliance voters did so. Poor leadership skill was cited by 57.3 per cent of the BJP-alliance voters against 17.8 per cent and 7.1 per cent of the Left Front and Congress-alliance voters, respectively. The factor of foreign origin weighed most heavily with the BJP-alliance voters: 61.2 per cent in contrast to only 5.3 per cent of Left Front voters and 6.4 per cent of the Congress-alliance voters. Her being a woman mattered most in this context to the BJP-alliance voters: 52.3 per cent; the comparable percentages relating to the Left Front voters and Congress-alliance voters were 15.6 and 7, respectively.

TABLE 8.16
Sonia Gandhi's Suitability or Otherwise for Prime Ministership by Party Vote in the 1999 Lok Sabha Elections, Ns and Row Percentages

	Parties					
Suitable/If not why?	*BJP and allies*	*Congress and allies*	*Left Front*	*BSP*	*Others*	*D.K./ N.A.*
Suitable	2,799	1295	337	170	699	701
	46.6	21.6	5.6	2.8	11.6	11.7
Inexperience	91	55	129	10	93	95
	9.4	57.0	13.3	1.0	9.6	9.8
Poor leadership	16	129	40	3	27	10
	7.1	57.3	17.8	1.3	12.0	4.4
Foreign origin	92	879	76	36	224	129
	6.4	61.2	5.3	2.5	15.6	9.0
Poor	23	121	10	2	14	15
communication	12.4	65.4	5.4	1.1	7.6	8.1
Female	9	67	20	—	26	9
	7.0	52.3	15.6	—	20.3	4.7
Any other	13	73	20	9	23	15
	8.5	47.7	13.1	5.9	15.0	9.8
Can't say/D.K.	27	153	28	25	45	39
	8.5	48.3	8.8	7.9	14.2	12.3

Conclusion

The 1999 Lok Sabha elections will go down in history as a definite mandate for the NDA in a decade of uncertain verdicts. But it is a mandate for a disparate set of parties led by the Hindu-right BJP, but, subscribing to many other tendencies of the centre-left as well as of the regional bent. In order to make this unlikely combination possible, the BJP had to put its own radical Hindu nationalist agenda in cold storage and rub shoulders with parties who were more liberal on secular-pluralist issues or frankly more regional and even casteist. BJP's pragmatism engendered by its promising electoral successes in the 1990s plus Vajpayee's liberal, national image prepared the BJP for this historic role. Federal-coalitional power is perhaps the most important cementing bond that aids and abets this combination. Another important negative factor is the disinclination of these parties to align with either the Congress or communists. The political untouchability of the BJP—demonstrably present in the party system as recently as in 1996, when the Hindu-right forces failed to make good the presidential invitation to form a coalition government—had become a thing of the past. This was mainly because of the decimation of the Janata Dal and the disintegration of the third front (National and United Fronts). There are still third-force parties but hardly a third front.

Besides the NDA, the BJP has on the other flank its own 'Sangh Parivar' to keep in line in order to be able to govern, its 'cultural' allies (as distinct from the political)—the RSS, VHP Bajrang Dal, Swadeshi Jagaran Manch, and the like. This flank is more steeped in Hindu nationalism and even more conservative than the BJP's political allies. To a certain extent, they set a limit to the political compromises the BJP can make in pursuit of federal-coalitional power. However, the cultural allies also know the limits of their pressure on and persuasion of the parliamentary leadership of the BJP. And, going by the experience so far, the internal relations in the Sangh Parivar, while not entirely free from tensions, have not been overly conflictual. The RSS experienced the change of guard—

Sarsanghachalak—from Rajendra Singh to K.C. Sudarshan early in 2000 in a smooth way. And, the BJP itself had geared itself to elect a new president on the completion of Kushabhau Thakare's term, apparently without any impending turmoil between the organisational and parliamentary wings of the party.

In addition to a fairly stable set of economic policies over the 1990s despite governmental turnovers, the electoral victory of the NDA in 1999 may perhaps be able to offer India a certain degree of governmental stability as well. Signs of a government more firmly in command in relation to the allies in the coalition in comparison to the period between the 1998 Lok Sabha election and the mid-term polls of 1999 are already evident. Harish Khare observes in this change, Prime Minister Vajpayee's bringing back the authority of his office in the wake of a new set of equations in the political system. He goes on to cautiously elaborate:

> Mercifully, Mr Vajpayee has only the bare minimum control over institutional authority vested in his office. He has not become an insufferable overlord who can ignore the constitutional parameters of his authority, he is not even in a position to roll back the encroachments the judiciary and Rashtrapati Bhawan have made on prime ministerial authority. But he has his acceptability to retrieve just about enough power to lend credibility and efficacy to the governing arrangement at the Centre.[25]

This illustrates the style of prime ministerial leadership, elsewhere conceptualised by the senior author [M.P. Singh (1994: 203)] as being 'federal' and different from 'parliamentary' and 'neo-patrimonial'.

Thus, the parliamentary elections in the federal phase have radically altered the parameters of politics prevailing before 1989. This new federal tempe1 is manifest in the whole institutional matrix ranging from the parliament, president and governors, prime ministers and chief ministers, the judiciary, Election Commission and the inter-governmental agencies.

Without any major, formal constitutional amendments, India today is functionally far more federal than ever before. The general direction of change has resulted in greater autonomy for state governments and constitutional offices of the president and governors; a greater opening for regional forces in the central government and inter-governmental agencies; and activism on the part of the judiciary, Election Commission of India, Central Vigilance Commission, Central Bureau of Investigation and the like, often under judicial diktat. This radical transformation in the political scenario is mainly attributable to the new patterns of elections and reconfiguration of political parties in the system in the 1990s and beyond, in response to the changes in social and psychological bases of politics in India (M.P. Singh, 2000).

The party system in India today is obviously a multi-partisan one. It tends towards a bicoalitional configuration of parties, with a declining 'third' force between a BJP-led NDA and a Congress-led bloc. In terms of Giovanni Sartori's sevenfold typology of party systems (1976: 125, Chaps. 5–7), the contemporary Indian variant is a borderline case overlapping a multi-party system of (1) limited or 'moderate pluralism' and (2) that of extreme or 'polarised pluralism'. Indeed, the presence of nearly two dozen parties in the ruling NDA additionally lends the flavour of a third category which Sartori called 'atomised pluralism'. The tendencies of polarisation and moderation and atomisation are all simultaneously present in the system in a dialectical idiom. The core of the party system is constituted by two larger all-India parties—the Congress and BJP—the latter a far Hindu-right nationalist party is ambivalent about some basic constitutional values such as secularism and minority rights. Yet, it has put some of its extremist Hindu nationalist agenda in cold storage in order to forge a ruling coalition with parties with secular tendencies and a socialist past. The second girdle of parties in the system are the smaller, national, regional and ethnic parties, some of which are ruling parties at the state level, either singly or in coalitions. These are the parties that have offered support to the two major (and one minor) coalitional blocs at the centre. There is, indeed, a third girdle of political forces in the system comprising anti-systemic and extremist organisations such as the People's War Group and other Naxalite formations some of whom double as political parties, e.g., People's Front, CPI(M-L), etc. Also falling in this category are some separatist political forces in the north-west and north-east areas which usually go through phases of negotiated legality and underground illegality. The latest instances in this context are the JKLF and the Hurriyat Conference in Jammu and Kashmir.

Notes

1. *Economic Times*, 1, 3, 5, 6 April 1999; *The Hindu*, 1, 3, 4, 5 April 1999; *The Pioneer*, 3, 4, 5 April 1999.
2. *Ibid*, 22–27 April 1999.
3. *The Hindu*, 27 April 1999.
4. *The Hindustan Times*, 18 April 1999.
5. Election Commission of India, Press Note, No. MCS/PN/12/99, New Delhi, 11 July 1999, signed by Subas Pani, deputy election commissioner. Also, the national newspapers around 11 July 1999 cited above.
6. M.P. Singh, 'The Status of a Caretaker Government', *The Hindu*, 24 July 1999: 10.
7. *Indian Recorder*, 2–8 July 1999: 4587.
8. *The Hindu*, 16 May 1999.
9. *Indian Recorder*, 8–14 January 1999: 4188.
10. *Ibid*, 18–24 June 1999: 4554–4555.
11. *Ibid*, 13–19 August 1999: 4685.
12. *Ibid*, 27 August–2 September 1999: 4714.
13. *Ibid*, 16–22 July 1999: 4615.
14. *Ibid*, 6–12 August 1999: 4668.
15. *Ibid*, 1–7 October 1999: 4791.
16. *Ibid*.
17. *Ibid*, 3–9 September 1999: 4729.
18. *Frontline*, 10 September 1999: 116.
19. *Ibid*: 121.
20. Press releases from the Election Commission of India during the pendency of the poll and the *Indian Recorder*, 1999.
21. *Indian Recorder*, 1999.

22. 'Cover Story: Big Business and Elections', *Frontline*, 31 July–13 August 1999.
23. See Lyla Bhavadam's interview with Rahul Bajaj, president of the Confederation of Indian Industry (CII), *Ibid*: 8–9.
24. *IIPA Newsletter*, vol. XLIII, No. 9, September 1999: 5.
25. Harish Khare, 'Vajpayee Brings Back the PM', *The Hindu*, 31 May 2000: 10.

CHAPTER NINE

Party System and Electoral Reforms

By any minimal definition of democracy in relation to both elections and governance, India stands out as a relative democratic success story. Yet, the fact remains that elections as well as governance in India leave much to be desired. It is axiomatic that as the most vital link between the civil society and the State, a representative and internally democratic set of political parties is a *sine qua non* of both orderly elections and stable governance. Parties are additionally required to be disciplined in a parliamentary form of government. Political reformers and founding fathers of republics have, however, generally been prone to express anti-party sentiments. For parties tend to divide the organic unity of the nation and subserve special and corrupting interests and influences.[1] Early modern royalists were also inclined to trust a socially responsible prince who symbolised the nation's unity much more than a party.[2] Yet, in comparative political theory and practice, parties are an essential mechanism of representative governance. It is difficult to imagine a contemporary developed or developing political system that can do without its institutionalising parties and elections effectively rooted in social cleavages and voter alignments (Lipset, 2000). Democratic elections and parties are the patent ways of reconciliation of conflicts in governance. Political parties are amphibious creatures equally at home in electoral and governmental arenas.

There are three, major theoretical perspectives on political parties: (1) society-centred, (2) state-centred, and (3) party-centric. The first approach may be called communitarian; the second statist; and the third, organisational. These are, of course, ideal types relating to party formation, and the parties in the real world may often present mixed cases with conceptual overlaps. Roughly, these three ideal types may also appear to represent various phases of evolution of political parties in various parts of the world. Modern political parties first arose in America and Western Europe. The earliest European political parties typically had their birth in elitist parliaments elected on limited franchise and dominated by the monarchy and aristocracy. The classical conservative and liberal parties first emerged in this context as representing the political tendencies favouring status quo or moderate reforms. These parties typically operated with parliamentary notables who gradually struck up and extended grass-roots constituency support as franchise was extended to a larger electorate. Since these parties arose in societies with a feudal history, the approach of the party elites to the issue of political mobilisation was at worst one of resistance to change, and at best one of restrained receptivity to reforms.

Political parties in America developed in a society with greater equality and without a feudal past. Hence, the American parties have generally displayed a greater propensity towards populism. American parties, to be sure, had been greatly vulnerable to bossism called 'machine politics', but the American political system has always been more inclined to embrace anti-bossism reforms than those in any other parts of the world. The so-called progressive movements in American states and the introduction of 'primary' elections to select party candidates by all registered voters belonging to a particular party are illustrations of this trend in American parties.

We may call the West European and American approach to parties society-centred, because parties in this liberal tradition subscribe to a theory of representation that envisages the role of a party legislator either as a trustee or a delegate.[3]

The state-centred approach to parties is reflected in the Marxist theory. Lenin regarded the communist party as the sole representative and the vanguard of the proletariat. The Leninist idea of party organisation and ideology is premised on militant ideological mobilisation by professional revolutionaries and a rigid principle of 'democratic centralism'. This means absolute subordination of lower party organs to higher ones once a party line is laid down, supposedly, on the basis of debate and deliberations in all party organs.[4] Louis Althusser conceptualises parties as parts of what he calls the 'ideological state apparatus', as distinguished from the 'coercive state apparatus'.[5] There is, of course, some difference between the Leninist and the Althusserian concept of parties. To Marx and Lenin, not only parties but even the entire state apparatus were superstructural entities rooted in the more fundamental structures of the mode of production or economy, consisting of the class relations and forces of production of technology. Whereas, neo-Marxists like Althusser are prepared to concede that at certain historical junctures, state structures and ideologies could assume structural importance, which may be as determinative as the mode of production itself, even though in the long run the economic structures turn out to be the ultimate determinants of the superstructural entities. There are other revisionist streams in Marxism such as social democracy dating back to the last quarter of the 19th century and Euro-communism of a more recent post-war vintage. These revisionist schools have abandoned the classical Marxist revolutionary strategy in favour of a parliamentary road to socialism. Euro-communism has gone so far as to eschew the dictatorship of the proletariat, not only as a matter of tactics but also as an article of democratic faith.

The third approach to parties is the one that regards them neither as a part of the state apparatus nor of the social structure. Instead, parties are conceptualised as vital links between the State and the civil society. The accent is on their autonomy as organisational entities which articulates the demands of the society to the political authorities and serves as autonomous agencies of governance. This approach to parties thus puts a premium on their resistance to populist pressures and their refusal to be used as subservient agents of state power such as the bureaucracy, police and the army.[6]

The Functional Context of Party Growth in India

Political parties, as Lapalambara and Weiner (1966: 3) aptly observe, are a feature of 'modern and modernising societies.' In modernising societies, party formation is often delayed or distorted. For, many of the objective conditions associated with vigorous party growth and functioning may be lacking or slow in appearing. For example, absence of a large number of secondary associations or voluntary organisations in neo-traditional or developing countries may result in primordial groups gatecrashing into the political arena and masquerading as parties. However, wherever political development leads to the introduction of institutions of representative democracy, either in a colonial or post-colonial context, political parties inevitably emerge as instruments of articulation and aggregation of demands into political platforms and policy outputs as governing or oppositional forces.

Political parties in India first emerged in the context of local, self-governing institutions such as district boards and municipal councils in the last quarter of the 19th century. A political anthropologist has called such early parties (e.g., 'kayastha party', 'Khatri party', etc.) as 'micro-parties' (Harold Gould, 1994). The term is not very apt, because these parties included elements other than the castes after which they were named and were very different from the traditional caste categories. They were still a far cry from the model of modern political parties. They are better called pre-party factions or cliques. In that sense such organisations existed even in pre-British times, e.g., liberal and orthodox factions in the Maurya and the Mughal courts.[7] In any case, as the British Raj introduced partly elected councils and assemblies, such pre-party formations tended to acquire more and more the characteristics that we usually associate with political parties.

Another and more important context which facilitated the emergence of parties in India was the nationalist movement. Various political organisations which first emerged in British Indian provinces and princely states as pressure groups, with both secular and communal overtones, clamoured for representation in administration. Subsequently, they turned into mass movements agitating for independence. In the most comprehensive of the nationalist movements in India led by the Indian National Congress, the dominant tendency was to give primacy to agitational politics, though the Congress also occasionally joined the limited assemblies as a secondary strategy of constitutional politics. The centre of political gravity, of course, remained the mass movement rather than the legislative parties. It was only after independence that the parliamentary and assembly wings of the movement started in right earnest the transformation of the movement into a party. Similar tendencies with some variations may be observed in the left wing and in religion-based parties on the Right as well as in regional parties.[8]

The third and the most important context of emergence and growth of political parties in India was the universal-adult-franchise-based parliamentary and assembly elections in the country since 1952. Since then thirteen Lok Sabha general elections and numerous rounds of assembly general elections have regularly been held, to say nothing of thousands of by-elections at both the levels. This has been the most fecund arena and phase of party growth, indeed their mushrooming. In a perceptive study of competitive elections in India, Myron Weiner (1987: 54–57) addressed the problem of delineating the social bases of voter alignments as follows. In addition to non-ethnic-based parties such as the Congress, Janata, socialists and communists, he proposed a classification of 'ethnic-based' parties in the following terms: (1) Hindu nationalist BJS/BJP; (2) parties of 'cultural regionalism', e.g., the Dravida parties; (and we may add the AGP in Assam; the National Conference in Jammu and Kashmir; and the TDP in Andhra); (3) parties of 'religious regionalism', e.g., the Akali Dal; (4) parties of 'middle peasant-caste politics', e.g., the Lok Dal (and we may add, JD, Samajwadi Party, and RJD in Bihar); (5) nativistic parties, e.g., the Shiv Sena; and (6) tribal parties, e.g., Jharkhand parties (and we may add some such parties from the Northeast). Reflecting on the tangled web of ethnic versus class politics, Weiner (1987: 68) makes the following apt comparative observation:

> The Indian experience suggests an important variant [to the trend of reduction in class cleavages giving rise to new political ethnic pluralism in Belgium, Canada, France and Spain]: The decline of one ethnic cleavage may give rise to another ethnic cleavage rather than to a class cleavage. Caste politics may be subsumed under linguistic politics and not be replaced by class conflicts. Tribes may band together to make regional claims. Several castes may come together, redefining themselves as a new multicaste collectivity (backward castes, scheduled castes). In a society of such multiple and overlapping group affiliations, politics plays a critical role in defining group identities.

Phases of Party-System Evolution in India

In his comparative study of political parties, Maurice Duverger (1963), proposed the hypothesis that the plurality electoral system in single-member constituencies (also called first-past-the post-system) generally leads to two-party systems, while proportional representation tends to engender multi-party systems. This probablistic generalisation is statistically defensible, but it conceals some important deviant cases that do not exactly conform to Duverger's generalisation. Such deviant cases are both from the economically developed as well as developing countries and at different stages of political development. For example, Canada since 1867 and India since 1950 have given rise to party systems very different from England, the USA and Australia. In contrast to these other countries which have more or less settled with a party configuration that can be broadly characterised as two-party systems, both Canada and India have experienced varying patterns of party systems at various points of their histories. Canada's aggregate party system—taking into account parties both at the national and provincial levels—can only be described as a multi-party system. Even at the national level alone, Canada has had either a one-party dominant system or a two-party system with a minor 'third' party in the parliament that has never alternated in power. Canadian political scientists have popularly called it a 'two-party plus' system. Besides, the Liberals, Conservatives and New Democrats at the federal level, there have always been in Canada a number of provincial parties, some of them including the New Democrats, holding the reins of power in some provinces. Examples of these provincial parties were/are the Social Credit Party in Alberta and Saskatchewan, Union Nationale and Party Quebecoi in Quebec, etc. Moreover, the 1993 House of Commons elections witnessed the sudden emergence of two new parties—one professedly national but de facto regional and the other, a province-based party but seeking elections to the national parliament. These are the Reform Party led by Preston Manning, the son of a former Social Credit premier of Alberta, and the Bloc Quebecoi led by a separatist Quebec leader.

In India, too, the configuration of parties since independence cannot be categorised under any single label. We can delineate at least six different phases of party-system evolution: (1) one-party dominance model (until 1969); (2) coalition model at the state level (1967–71); (3) second one-party dominance model at the centre (1971–77); (4) coalition model at the centre (1978–79); (5) third one-party dominance model (1980–89); and (6) multi-party coalitional or minority governments model (1989 onwards to-date). (Rekha Saxena, 1998).[9]

The major tendencies in the above and other periodisations are basically two: (1) the pull towards one-party dominance, and (2) the pull towards multi-party coalitions. Of course, this classification is complicated by the lead or lag in the emergence of these tendencies at the centre or in the states. In other words, the tendencies of dominance or coalitions do not appear simultaneously at both the levels of the political system. For example, when the coalitional tendency first appeared at the state level in 1967, the Congress rule continued at the national level with reduced dominance. Similarly, when the Congress lost power at the centre for the first time in 1977, it continued to be a dominant force in such major south-Indian states as Andhra Pradesh and Karnataka. Likewise, when the Congress was restored under Indira Gandhi and further registered a landslide victory in 1984 under Rajiv Gandhi in New Delhi, it suffered a series of electoral defeats in the 1980s, and lost power in states such as Andhra Pradesh, Karnataka, Punjab, Assam, Sikkim and Haryana. Moreover, the Congress dominance under Nehru, on the one hand, and Indira Gandhi and Rajiv Gandhi, on the other, were very different despite the fact that all these periods are referred to as a period of dominance by that party. The Congress party led by Nehru was a much more institutionalised party organisation characterised by more or less regular organisational elections and a federally segmented framework of power in the sense that the Congress chief ministers of that period enjoyed greater regional or federal autonomy. The Indira Gandhi and Rajiv Congress dispensed with internal organisational elections and turned the party into a pack of personal followers and dynastic loyalists. Besides, state party organisations as well as state governments under Indira Gandhi and to a lesser extent under Rajiv Gandhi were turned into neo-patrimonial entities, with even chief ministers being nominated from the top rather than being a representation of the structure of interests and opinions in the state legislatures.

The decline of Congress dominance did not result in the emergence of dominance by an alternative party. Instead, a heterogeneous set of parties replaced the Congress. Broadly speaking, three or four types of parties have filled the spaces vacated by the Congress. First, alongside the previously left-of-the centre Congress (but now somewhat right-of-the centre), another centrist party leaning to the left emerged by way of the Janata Party in 1977, which came to be the Janata Dal in 1988, but in the 1990s it suffered hopeless fragmentation. The Janata Party was formed during the Emergency in the trail of the Navanirman movement in Gujarat and the JP movement against corruption among the powerful, and the authoritarianism of the Congress. Originally it amalgamated the Bhartiya Jan Sangh, Bhartiya Lok Dal, Congress(O), Socialists and the Congress for Democracy. Subsequently, some of its constituents deserted it to form new parties, but in 1988, the Jan Morcha, founded by V.P. Singh and his cohorts who left the Congress, merged with it. Since then it has been called the Janata Dal. It headed the National/ United Front governments in New Delhi between 1989 and 1998, except during the interlude of the Congress minority government from 1991–96.

The second category of parties to occupy the space vacated by the Congress was the major party of the right wing, namely, the Bhartiya Janata Party. The merger of the Bhartiya Jan Sangh with the Janata Party and the subsequent splitting of the BJP from it, marks some important landmarks of political realignment in the country. The BJP in its present form represents the 'cultural' (real Hindu) nationalism of the 1980s and 1990s. It has won and lost power in several states in this period and headed the coalition governments at the centre formed in the wake of the 1998 and 1999 Lok Sabha elections.

A third category of non-Congress parties is the left wing consisting of a number of parties and headed by the CPI(M) and CPI, in that order. The Left Front has ruled in West Bengal, Kerala and Tripura and was a partner in the United Front governments headed by H.D. Deve Gowda and I.K. Gujral. The United Front was led by the Janata Dal and comprised the Left Front and some major regional parties, including such Janata parivar parties as the Samajwadi party led by Mulayam Singh Yadav in Uttar Pradesh, the Rashtriya Janata Dal led by Laloo Prasad Yadav in Bihar, and the Biju Janata Dal led by Naveen Patnaik in Orissa. The convenor of the United Front was the TDP chief minister, Chandrababu Naidu of Andhra Pradesh, who is now in the NDA boat led by the BJP.

The last category of non-Congress parties is that of regional or state parties whose ranks have of late multiplied to an unprecedented extent. These parties can be sub-divided into two major classes, mainly, old regional parties and the new ones. The examples of the former are the DMK, AIADMK, Akali Dal, National Conference, Jharkhand Mukti Morcha, etc. The direct or indirect roots of these parties go back to the nationalist movements during the British Raj. The new regional parties like Telugu Desam, Asom Gana Parishad, Tamil Maanila Congress, and parties of the Northeast have all emerged in the post-independence period, especially after the decline of the Congress.

As is evident from the brief narrative above, the party system of India consists of very different parties at varying levels of organisational and ideological development. Only the communist parties and the BJP appear not only to be structured around stable interests and classes but also based on periodically organised internal party organisations and conferences. The rest of the parties do articulate some vaguely recognisable interests and classes either at the national or the regional level, but they are erratic in terms of organisational elections and conferences. They appear to be more in the nature of personalised, ethnic or regional following of some prominent national and regional leaders. They are notoriously negligent of their own constitutions, to the chagrin of the Election Commission.

Degeneration of Political Parties in India

Political parties in any democratic polity are supposed to be vital links between the State and the civil society. Parties in India have failed to perform the basic functions of government and opposition on account of a number of reasons. As already pointed out above, very few parties take their own constitutions seriously. For this reason they have come under personalised and dynastic dominations.

Another aspect of the degeneration of the party political processes in the country is what has commonly come to be known as criminalisation of politics. There is probably no political party today that does not harbour a number of criminals who hold party and even legislative/ministerial posts, the figure, in some parties, running into double digits as revealed by press reports. In the 1990s, economic scams and political scandals reached huge proportions. The octopus-like hold on politics and the economy by the business-politics-administration-crime nexus has reached a stage where even JPC investigations have proved to be an utterly ineffective, fruitless and farcical exercise. In July 1993, the Government of India established a committee at the administrative level, headed by the then home secretary, N.N. Vohra 'to take stock of all available information about the activities of crime-syndicate/mafia organisations which had developed links with and were being protected by government functionaries and political personalities' (Vohra Committee Report, 1993: 1). The report submitted in October 1993, made the following sinister submission among others: 'CBI has reported that all over India crime syndicates have become a law unto themselves ... the nexus between the criminal gangs, police, bureaucracy and politicians has come out clearly in various parts of the country. The existing criminal justice system which was essentially designed to deal with the individual offences/crimes, is unable to deal in the activities of the Mafia...' There is evidently little follow-up action on the report notwithstanding a Supreme Court directive to the Government of India in 1997 to report what steps had been taken to implement its recommendations. The Court's directive was made in the course of the Jain hawala case when it was examining the question of granting autonomy to investigating agencies (*The Indian Express*, New Delhi, 22 August 1997).

Another dimension of political corruption is the so-called politics of defection, which since 1967, has turned the legislatures and ministries into licensed casinos for political opportunists and defectors. The Anti-Defection Act, 1985, has been largely unsuccessful in stemming the tide. The fear of individual disqualification under the Act has turned defection into a 'one-third' group behaviour. For, if a one-third or more of members of a party in a legislature desert it, the law treats it as a split rather than defection and exempts it from penal disqualification of membership of the House. The speakers, too, have exercised their power under the Act in a partisan manner often resulting in litigation. Huge sums of money change hands and to stem defections plane-loads of legislators are flown to five-star tourist facilities to insulate them from temptations offered by other parties. Formerly known to have taken place only in state capitals, a similar vice for the first time surfaced at the national level in the notorious JMM bribery case adjudicated by the Supreme Court in 1998. The Supreme Court ruling in this case was: (1) An MP is a public servant under the provisions of the Prevention of Corruption Act 1988; since there is no competent authority under the provisions of the Act to remove an MP from his office, the court can take cognisance of his offence without seeking sanction from any other authority. (2) However, the prosecuting agencies need to seek sanctions from the speaker of the Lok Sabha or the chairman of the Rajya Sabha before proceeding to frame charges. (3) MPs charged with taking bribes to vote against a no-confidence motion enjoy immunity from the courts under Article 105 of the Constitution relating to the parliamentary privileges. (4) Bribe-givers enjoy no such immunity. (5) It is for the competent parliamentary authority to take proper action against offending MPs (Supreme Court, 1998).

It may bear pointing out that the speaker's ruling in the matter is subject to judicial review. Also a public interest litigation may arise if competent parliamentary authorities fail to take proper action in the matter.

Ergo

A notable development of the 1990s, is the emergence of the Election Commission of India as an activist, federal agency. The commission under T.N. Seshan and his successors appear to have brought about a sea change as far as the conducting of elections was concerned. In the elections of the 1990s, there was visible impact of the commission in their curbing electoral abuses by the ruling and opposition parties, e.g., compelling the parties to adhere to a code of conduct formulated by the commission, which was in the past followed more in the breach than in the observance, reduction of election expenses by a more rigorous rendering of accounts, control over noisy, communal and polluting campaigns, filing of affidavits regarding non-involvement in criminal convictions and activities and so on. The commission has also considerably checked mass transfer of government officers for electoral purposes, misuse of government machinery by the party in power, announcement and inauguration of schemes for particular sections of the population just before the electoral schedule to influence voting and so on. Moreover, the commission has also been presenting a variety of proposals for electoral and party reforms to the government.

The recent proposals of the Election Commission to the government broadly cover a wide range of issues concerning delimitation of constituencies, conduct and administration of elections and political parties and candidates. In view of the fact that the degeneration of parties and criminalisation of politics have assumed alarming proportions in more recent times, we review here mainly proposals relating to these problems. To begin with regarding the registration of political parties with the commission, the commission recommends measures to discourage frivolous party formations and deregistration of non-serious and defunct parties. At present, parties are registered with the commission under the provisions of Section 29A of the Representation of the People Act, 1951. A total of 650 parties are so registered, of which around 150 contested in the 1998 Lok Sabha elections and 169 in the 1999 mid-term polls. The commission has categorised these parties into a threefold classification: (1) national parties, i.e. a recognised political party in four or more states; (2) state parties, i.e. recognised in less than four states; and (3) registered unrecognised parties, which is a residual category. According to the latest notification of the commission, a recognised political party must have been active continuously for five years and won at least four per cent of the seats in the last Lok Sabha elections or 3.33 per cent of the seats in the assembly elections from the state. Else, it should have polled at least six per cent of the total valid votes in the last Lok Sabha or assembly elections in the state. Or else, such a party's total votes (excluding votes secured by the party candidates in constituencies where it bagged less than 1/12th of valid votes) must be at least four per cent of the total valid votes (Internet, *Discover India, Twelfth Lok Sabha Elections*, 1998). These criteria remained unchanged in 1999 (Subhash Pani, deputy election commissioner, May 2000). Even with these formulations, the Election Commission's criteria for recognition of political parties appear to be minimalist and fairly easy. But under the plurality or first-past-the-post system of representation, these criteria should not perhaps be made more restrictive. At present, there is no specific provision for deregistration of parties. So, parties once registered stay unscrutinised on the records. The commission has recommended to the government that a provision in the RPA for deregistration of parties should be made.

The commission ought to devise more stringent requirements relating to the parties' organisational structure. Indeed, the commission requires parties to submit copies of their constitutions and election manifestos to it. Until T.N. Seshan's incumbency as the CEC, this was a fairly ritualistic affair. Moreover, the commission has since then started to insist on the adherence of parties to their own constitutions when they constitute party organs and hold regular organisational elections. The commission should also find ways and means to register manifestos and electoral promises by parties and coalitions. Enforcement of these rules and regulations will force parties to structure themselves democratically, develop grass-roots and constituency organisations, and define themselves more sharply in ideological terms.

On the important issue of donations by companies to political parties, the commission is inclined to go along with the current law whereby a company in existence for more than three years may contribute an amount to party funds not exceeding five per cent of its average net profit. The commission is against a total ban on company donations on the ground that political parties do need funds coming through certain channels for legitimate political activities. Besides, as trade unions and other organisations are allowed under the law of the land to contribute funds to parties, a ban on company donations would appear to be unjustified in the commission's view. All that the commission requires is that 'such contributions should be limited to a reasonable level and all transactions in this regard must be made in a completely transparent manner' (Election Commission, 1998: 7). Moreover, it also commends to the government that parties must be required to maintain their accounts and get them audited by agencies specified by it. But, it covers a rather small fraction of the expenses involved.

Further, the commission also recommends that it should be empowered to fix a ceiling on election expenses before every general election and that the expenditure incurred by a political party and other organisations should be included in the election expenses of a candidate for purposes of ceiling on election expenses. Besides, it is also in favour of some sort of state funding of elections to a certain extent. The commission has, indeed, already worked out and implemented a scheme of allocation of free time to parties on an equitable basis on the state-owned electronic mass-media.

One other serious problem which the Election Commission has recently been seized with is the difficulty to define a criminal and to prevent his/her entry in politics:

> The commission is conscious of the fact in the eye of law a person is presumed to be innocent unless proved guilty… In the commission's considered opinion, a person who is facing trial in a serious offence, if kept out of the electoral fray till he is exonerated of the charge, should not have a legitimate grievance, as such restriction on his right to contest election would be a reasonable restriction in the greater public interest and for bringing sanctity to the august Houses which are the supreme law-making bodies of the country (Election Commission, 1998: 24–25).

Pending government action on this proposal, the commission has already initiated some steps in this direction. In August 1997, it invoked Article 324 of the Constitution to oblige all candidates then contesting to file affidavits along with their nomination about their convictions in cases covered by Section 8 of the Representation of the People Act, 1951, which disqualifies persons convicted of those specified offences. In view of the judgments of several high courts the commission has come to the opinion that a person remains disqualified even during pendency of appeal or release on bail.

Two Parliamentary Committees

Two all-party parliamentary committees on electoral reforms have deliberated on the problems of electoral and party reforms in the last decade. These were chaired by Dinesh Goswami and Indrajit Gupta, respectively. The former reported in May 1990 and the latter in 1998. The important recommendations of the Goswami committee included the following: a three-member Election Commission and the appointment of the chief election commissioner in consultation with the chief justice of India and the leader of the opposition, and the appointment of election commissioners in consultation with the CEC; issuing of multi-purpose photo-identity cards to voters; disallowance of contesting of candidates from more than two constituencies, the raising of security deposits of independent candidates and forfeiture of security of all candidates securing less than 1/4th of the votes polled; a statutory status to the model code of conduct formulated by the Election Commission in consultation with political parties; better administration in conducting elections aided by suitable legislative measures; fresh delimitation of constituencies on the basis of the 1981 census to be frozen for three decades and rotation of seats reserved for SCs/STs; taking cognisance of party whips by the speaker only in cases of confidence votes, money bills and motion of thanks to the president for his opening address to parliament for determination of defection by a legislator; limited state funding in kind to recognised political parties; a review of the electoral system by a standing committee of the parliament and an expert committee; and deletion of Section 29(A) of the Representation of the People Act, 1951, concerning the registration of political parties and delegation of this power to the Election Commission under the Election Symbols (Reservation and Allotment Order, 1968).[10]

The Indrajit Gupta committee on electoral reforms unanimously recommended state funding of electoral expenses of recognised national and state parties and their candidates—in kind, not cash—by creating an election fund with an annual matching contribution of Rs 600 crores each, from the centre and state governments. Contributions upwards of Rs 10,000 must be accepted by cheque. There must be an obligatory transparency of sources of funds and submission of annual audited accounts to income-tax authorities. Parties must also render complete accounts of each election to the Election Commission. Moreover, the existing ban on donations to parties by government corporations/companies should continue.[11]

The Law Commission

The Law Commission, in a comprehensive review of election-related laws, recommended in 1999, a 25 per cent increase in Lok Sabha and Vidhan Sabha seats, with the new Lok Sabha seats (138 in number) to be filled through the list system on the panels of prospective legislators furnished to the Election Commission by political parties. In apportioning these seats, parties with less than five per cent votes should be eliminated. Old territorial constituencies should also continue, but their number should stand frozen at 550 until the year 2025. If thus reconstituted, the Lok Sabha would have a total of 688 seats. This reform, in the view of the Law Commission, is necessary to rectify the anomaly arising out of the freezing of Lok Sabha seats since the 1981 census. Moreover, the Law Commission also recommended that political parties be brought within the purview of the law by amending the Representation of the People Act, 1951, which requires parties to constitute executive committees every three years, with specific powers to local party units in decision making and elections by secret ballot within the party, and regular maintenance of accounts.[12]

Big Business and Political Financing

The historical coincidence of capitalism and democracy has given rise to a paradox where, 'if parties want to gain or retain the power of office, they have to secure the trust of private investors and of the masses simultaneously' (Habermas, 1987: 346). This paradox is further compounded by the fact that 'the polity and economy operate in India in a manner diametrically different from the formally stipulated model[s]' (K.N. Kabra, 1998: 43). The essential democracy, premised on voters' sovereignty and operated by competitive political parties, and formal captalism predicated on consumers' sovereignty catered to by competitive corporations, are both distorted and flawed in practice.

Corporate funding to political parties in India is legally regulated by the Companies Act, 1956 (with subsequent amendments); Foreign Contribution (Regulation) Act, 1976; and the Income Tax Act, 1961. Under Section 293A of the Companies Act, corporate contributions to political parties are legally permissible with proper accounting up to five per cent of the average net profit of the company for the three preceding financial years. Banned in 1969 by Prime Minister Indira Gandhi, this provision was restored by Prime Minister Rajiv Gandhi in 1985, with the stated objective in Section 4 of 'permitting the corporate sector to play a legitimate role within the defined norms in the functioning of our democracy'. Section 4(1) of the Foreign Contribution (Regulation) Act debars political parties from accepting any foreign contribution, though an 'organisation of a political nature (not being a political party)' can accept such contribution 'with the prior permission of the central government' under Section 5(1). Under the Income Tax Act, 1961, political parties are required to maintain an audited account of their income from various sources, including voluntary contributions exceeding Rs 10,000, with the identification of the donor. Every political party is obliged to file every year a return of total income in terms of sub-section 4(B) of the Taxation Laws (Amendment) Act, 1978.

The framework of law notwithstanding, party financing has been a murky aspect of party politics in India. Membership dues and cess on legislative income of members form only a small fraction of party funds, except perhaps for the left wing. With electioneering costs rising astronomically after the 1957 general elections, the ruling and upcoming opposition parties came to increasingly count on corporate funding. The licence-quota-permit raj set up by the Congress enabled it to grab the lion's share of such funds. In the 1960s, the business groups also made some corporate funds available to the emergent parties, mainly from the right wing, the Bharatiya Jan Sangh and Swatantra Party. The Tatas and Birlas together offered 34 per cent of total company donations between 1962 and 1968.[13] That nearly two-thirds of the contribution came from other big and smaller business houses augured well for competitive politics in the country. From the late 1960s to the late 1970s, the Congress, under threat from the emergent opposition parties, tried hard to reverse the trend by an aggressive populist mass mobilisation as well as by legally seeking to dry the flow of corporate funds to non-Congress parties. Indira Gandhi's Emergency regime (1975–1977) was particularly 'distinguished by massive extortion of corporate donations by the ruling party'.[14] Taking cues from its electoral defeat in 1977, the Congress after coming to power in the 1980s tended to rely less on domestic, business contributions and more on 'huge kickbacks from foreign firms while striking significant deals in the defence and infrastructure sectors'.[15] One such defence deal relating to the purchase of Howitzer guns from the Swedish company, Bofors, and its subsequent exposure turned out to be Rajiv Gandhi's Waterloo.

In the changed context of the failure of the licence-quota-permit raj and the neo-liberal economic reforms, especially since July 1991, the corporate sector is no longer under the same compulsion to make political donations at the beck and call of the political establishment. There has been, additionally, a remarkable continuity of economic policies of the Government of India despite the change of party or coalitions in power over the 1990s—Congress, United Front and NDA. Yet, even in reduced circumstances, government patronage does matter for the business. In the new atmosphere of the political economy, two patterns of business contributions to politics are noticeable. While some big business houses have taken the lead in establishing trusts for channelising funds to political parties on certain objective criteria, others prefer to make individual donations on a quid pro quo basis mostly through underhand deals bypassing the laws. The chambers of commerce and industries generally collectively try to influence the inclusion of certain issues affecting the overall business climate, but they do not proceed to orchestrate political donations from their members through transparent, legal channels. The Tata Electoral Trust, open also to companies outside the Tata Group, have funded political parties since 1998 in proportion to their strength in the outgoing and newly elected parliament. The General Electoral Trust founded in 1998 by the Aditya Birla Group receives money from its own companies and disburses funds to political parties on the basis of suggestions from its Advisory Board in terms of business interests of the contributing companies in each state. The Indrajit Gupta Committee on Electoral Reforms recommended the continuance of the five per cent profit limit for company donations, but added that the decision should be made with the approval of the Annual General Meeting instead of the Board of Directors only, as required by the law at present. 'Approval at the Annual General Meeting', in the opinion of the Gupta committee, 'will ensure a decisive say of the general members of the company in any contributions made by it for political purposes'.[16]

In the recent past, the big business houses have generally backed the BJP or Congress, plus dominant regional parties in the states. They perceive that a coalition of these two major national parties would be desirable for governmental stability at the centre. However, fundamental differences among the two over cultural and ideological issues have precluded such a coalition.[17] Perceptions in politics and business do not always overlap. Regional business groups, especially in economically buoyant states, have become great sources of political funds to the major state parties.[18] In economically stagnant states like Bihar, the political class has easily yielded to the temptation of defrauding the state treasury and extorting contributions from the urban and rural middle classes.

Political parties have yet to do a lot to set their houses in order. This is evident from the writ petition No. 24 of 1995 to the Supreme Court of India by the Common Cause, a registered Society headed by H.D. Shourie. The public-interest case arose out of the alleged violation of the provisions of Section 13-A of the Income Tax Act and Section 293-A of Companies Act, by political parties with regard to their income and expenditure. The Common Cause (1995: 12) argued that these laws 'clearly indicate the legislative scheme, the object of which is to ensure that there should be transparency in the matter of sources of funds of the political parties and of the manner in which the funds are spent'. The laws put 'all political parties … under mandatory obligation to maintain accounts, issue receipts for voluntary contributions … above the prescribed limit and of getting their accounts annually audited' (Common Cause, 1995: 13). Of the major 15 parties approached for confirmation none could claim that the legal requirements were complied with —barring the Janata Party, a rump of its namesake from before and a pocket organisation of Subramaniam Swamy. The response from the concerned Department of Revenue, Ministry of Finance, Government of India confirmed the above fact (Common Cause, 1995: 13). In 1974, the Indira Gandhi government had contrived to exceed the election expense limit in the Representation of the People Act by an amendment to the Act (Section 77) by excluding the amounts spent by a candidate's political party and friends on his account. The Supreme Court in the Common Cause case (1996) did not strike down this new explanation added to Section 77 of the Act but ruled that the limit could be exceeded provided the party reported the additional expenditure in its own account.

An Example India may Emulate

The Election Commission of India as well as many prominent citizens and jurists like Jayaprakash Narayan and Justice (Rtd.) V.R. Krishna Iyer, respectively have been advocating electoral and party reforms over the years (M.P. Singh, 1996 and 1998). In view of the seriousness of the malady, it appears imperative now to entrust the task of considering comprehensive electoral and party reforms to a full-scale constitutional commission like the Sarkaria Panel on centre-state relations. It may be interesting to draw attention here to the valuable work done in this respect by the Royal Commission on Electoral Reform and Party Financing appointed by the Government of Canada in November 1989. This commission sponsored a score of academic studies on the problem as well as held hearings itself and submitted its recommendations in four volumes in 1993.[19]

Some of the recommendations of this commission as well as some Canadian practices in this regard, in vogue since the early years of this century may also be considered for adoption in India. Volume 3 of the report which is presented in the form of a model legislation has some interesting ideas about political parties, constituency associations and party foundations. The proposed legislation lays down detailed legal requirements for registration of parties, their constituency associations and party foundations under this parliamentary law. Each of these organisations is supposed to be registered under Section 24 of the model Act on the condition that they must have a constitution that shall:

(a) Promote democratic values and practices in a manner consistent with the spirit and intent of the Canadian Charter of Rights and Freedoms; (b) Provide clear and consistent rules

> on the selection of candidates, leaders, delegates, if any, and officers; (c) Provide that members of the party who select the party's candidates, select delegates to a leadership convention or select a party leader must be voters....[20]

The proposed legislation goes on to provide other legal requirements to facilitate smooth functioning of these organisations and procedures for settlement of disputes, which need not necessarily detain us here.

A party foundation may be registered under this Act by a recognised party as 'a distinct and permanent institution':

1. to develop and promote public policy options;
2. educate party members on matters of public policy; and
3. provide the party with research and advise on policy.

These party foundations are to be incorporated under the Canada Corporation's Act.[21]

The Canadian Royal Commission believes in full disclosure of the size and source of contributions to parties and candidates to forestall any undue influence on elected officials by contributors of large amounts. It recommends the submission of interim unaudited reports of all contributions by registered parties and their ancillary organisations for the first six months of the year and a 'full audited return on their financial activities for the entire year'.

The Canada Elections Act neither bans nor limits the fund a person, corporation, or trade union can donate to a federal party or candidate. However, all donations over $100 must be disclosed and 75 per cent tax benefit to the donor can be claimed on only the first $100. Moreover, in June 1999, the federal government forbade federal Crown corporations from making contributions to political parties. Bill C-2 proposed most comprehensive amendments to the Canada Election Act since 1974, with a view to rectify 'some of the well-known problems with the regulation of party and candidate financing', though 'some of the most important were ignored' (W.T. Stanbury, 2000).

The combination of parliamentary and federal systems of government in Canada has forced the Canadians to depart from the practice of their electing party leaders by the parliamentary organisations (elected MPs). The Canadian parties early in the 20th century gave up the practice of electing party leaders by the parliamentary caucuses in favour of a national leadership convention composed by provincial party delegates voting as individuals rather than as state delegations en bloc as in the American national party conventions organised every four years for nominating presidential candidates. This device of electing the party leader introduces an overarching national element over the state/province-based national parties in the USA and Canada. The adoption of the party-convention system in Canada was done to make the leadership-selection process more representative and federal. In view of the increasing fragmentation of the Indian party system, the adoption of the Canadian system of party leadership convention here would introduce an element of federal aggregation of political forces in the country. This reform is particularly necessary now that the growing regionalisation of parties in India has rendered the process of formation and maintenance of stable parliamentary government at the centre a highly problematic proposition.

Notes

1. George Washington, the first American president, twice unanimously elected, was among the earliest critics of modern party politics that were still in a nascent state of development in the USA in the garb of the Federalists and Republicians. In his farewell address (1796) he mused on the 'baneful effects of the spirit of party' in a rather ambivalent mood. He earnestly urged the country to preserve 'the unity of government which constitutes you one people'. Richard Hofstadter, William Miller and Daniel Aaron, 1959, *The American Republic vol. 1: To 1865*: 280.

   In India, a day before his martyrdom, Gandhi wrote in a note posthumously published on 15 February 1948 under the title 'His Last Will and Testament' that the Indian National Congress having attained India's freedom ought to be dissolved. This was necessary for keeping out 'unhealthy competition with political parties and communal bodies'. He, instead, proposed the formation of a Lok Sevak Sangh as India had 'still to attain social, moral and economic independence in terms of its seven hundred thousand villages as distinguished from its cities and towns'. Gandhi (1970: 290). After Gandhi, two other Indian political thinkers and activists—Jayaprakash Narayan and M.N. Roy—advocated a partyless democracy. Narayan was a former Marxist-turned Gandhian and Roy a former Marxist revolutionary-turned radical humanist. See M.P. Singh and Himanshu Roy (eds.) 2000, *Indian Political Thought*: chaps. 9 and 10.

2. In the United Kingdom, Henry St. John, later Viscount Bolingbroke, who wrote his *Dissertation Upon Parties* in the backdrop of the uneasy truce negotiated in the Glorious Revolution of 1688 by the Whigs and Tories that soon began to fracture into party strife, attempted to revive a neo-stoic conception of patriotism by his vision of a non-partisan executive in *The Idea of Patriot King*. See Bolingbroke edited by David Armitage, 1997, *Political Writings*.
3. Gandhi and Edmund Burke subscribe to a view of representation that emphasises the larger conscience of the representative as much as his obligation to mirror the narrow interests and views of the constituents or electors. Vulgar and populist views of representation underline only the latter, which is actually a distortion of democratic theory. For sampling a good, sociological approach to political parties, see S.M. Lipset and Stein Rokkan, eds., 1967, *Party Systems and Voter Alignments: Cross-National Perspectives*. See also Samuel J. Elderveld 1971, *Political Parties: A Behavioural Analysis* and Myron Weiner, 1967, *Party-Building in a New Nation: Indian National Congress*.
4. For a good discussion of concepts of the party in Marx, Lenin, Rosa Luxemburg, Trotsky and Gramsci, see John Molyneux, 1986, *Marxism and the Party*.
5. Louis Althusser, 1984, *Essays on Ideology*.
6. Organisational approaches to political parties are best reflected in the works of M. Ostrogorki, 1902, *Democracy and the Organisation of Political Parties*, Robert Michels, 1962, *Political Parties*, Maurice Duverger, 1963, *Political Parties*, Samuel J. Eldersveld, 1971, *Political Parties: A Behavioural Analysis* and Angelo Panebianco, 1988, *Political Parties: Organisation and Power*. There appears to be

a palpable Euro-American schism in theorising about the dominant organisational tendencies in political parties. Michels, Duverger, and Panebianco tend to inconclusively lean towards varying degrees of an 'iron law of oligarchy' which, however, is not entirely rust-proof, given their ambivalence in conceding the possibility of democratic challenges to the party oligarchy. These democratic challenges not only open up avenues for career mobility of competing factions, both young and old, but also help to adapt the party to the society, which, in turn, is also a dynamic structure.

Eldersveld, on the other hand, finds that a party is 'an open, clientele-oriented structure, permeable at its bases as well as its apex' and it is also 'a "stratarchical" control structure, rather than an elitist command structure'. He goes on to say: 'Power is devolved and proliferated to echelon commands, decision-making is autonomised at the lower reaches of the structure, and deference is not exclusively upward, but reciprocal' (pp. 526–27). Parties in the real world seem to alternate between relatively oligarchical and relatively democratic phases.

In the Indian context the above tendencies are roughly indicated in the study of Congress factionalism and the split in 1969 by M.P. Singh, 1981, *Split in a Predominant Party: The Indian National Congress in 1969*. For the preceding phase of Congress politics from this angle, see Stanley Kochanek, 1968, *The Congress Party of India*. For an organisational and sociological study of the BJP, the single, largest party in Indian politics today, see Yogendra Malik and V.B. Singh, 1994, *Hindu Nationalists in India: The Rise of the Bharitya Janata Party*, and Christophe Jaffrelot, 1996, *The Hindu Nationalist Movement in India*. For a similar study of the communist parties in India, see Ross Mallick, 1994, *Indian Communism: Opposition, Collaboration and institutionalization*.

7. See Romila Thapar, 1997, *Ashoka and the Decline of the Mauyras*, I.H. Qureshi (n.d.), *The Administration of the Mughal Empire*, Satish Chandra, 1979, *Parties and Politics at the Mughal Court*.
8. Lipset and Rokkan, 1967, *Party Systems and Voter Alignments*: postulate that in the evolution of European party systems four major lines of social cleavages—centre-periphery, state-church, land-industry, and owner-worker—broadly influenced the formation of parties and their clustering into party systems. The first two of these cleavages were the products of the National Revolution in the 16th to 18th centuries that engendered the European nation-states in the

wake of Reformation and Counter-Reformation in Christianity and related to religion and language. The latter two cleavages were the effects of the Industrial Revolution and the Russian Revolution in the 19th and 20th centuries that gave rise to conflicts between agricultural and industrial interests and bourgeoisie and workers as the main classes of the industrial societies.

Applied to the Indian context, we can build up the argument that the emergence of the Indian National Congress and the Muslim League relates to the freedom struggle and the imperial partition of India; the parties such as the Hindu Mahasabha-BJS-BJP and Akali Dal relate to the role of religion in politics; regional parties such as the AIADMK, DMK, MDMK, TDP, AGP, National Conference, etc, veer around the issues of language and regions; communist parties highlight the issues of class and regions; JD, RJD, RJP, SP, BSP, BJD exacerbate the caste-class religious-minority region nexus; most tribal parties in the country are based on tribal and local identities. Economic liberalisation since 1991 has produced another major political issue which finds the Congress mostly inclined to favour it, the communists most vocally opposed it, while the BJP, Janata Dal, and regional parties somewhere in-between. Thus, the Indian party scene does not neatly conform to the Lipset-Rokkan model. As Weiner, 1987, in *Competitive Elections* in *Developing Countries*: 55, observes: 'The religious, regional, ethnic and class conflicts that in other countries are often sequential are in India all present simultaneously.'

9. For a more nuanced periodisation of the evolution of the party system in India, see M.P. Singh, 1994, *The Indian Journal of Social Science*. The post-independence Indian-party system at the centre is here periodised as follows: (1) 1952–1969 predominant party system; (2) 1969–1971 multi-party system; (3) 1971–1977 predominant party system; (4) 1977–1984 two-party system; (5) 1984–1989 [still-born] predominant party system; and (6) 1989 to date multi-party system.
10. Lok Sabha Secretariat, *Information Bulletin, Electoral Reforms in India*, June 1994.
11. *The Economic Times*, New Delhi, 15 January 1999: 2.
12. *IIPA Newsletter*, Indian Institute of Public Administration, New Delhi, vol. XLIII, no. 9, September 1999: 5.
13. V. Venkatesan, 'Cover Story: Big Business and Elections', *Frontline*, Chennai, vol. 16, no. 16, 31 July–13 August, 1999: 10.

14. *Ibid*: 11.
15. *Ibid*.
16. *Ibid*: 12–13.
17. Rahul Bajaj, president of the Confederation of Indian Industry (CII) said in an interview in answer to the question of what business houses were looking for in the outcome of the mid-term polls in 1999: 'Stability... This means either a BJP or a Congress government or at least a BJP-Congress coalition'. *Frontline*, 31 July–13 August, 1999: 8. This possible coalition has so far been highly improbable in real terms owing to ideological differences between the two largest, single parties. Such a coalition will require a 'historic compromise' like the one between Communists and Christian Democrats in Italy.
18. Sanjay Baru, 1997, *Democracy and Social Transformation: India Fifty Years After Independence*.
19. Government of Canada, 1991–93, *Royal Commission on Electoral Reform and Party Financing Report*.
20. Government of Canada, 1991, *Royal Commission on Electoral Reform and Party Financing Report*.
21. *Ibid*.

Bibliography

Public Documents

Butler, David, Ashok Lahiri and Prannoy Roy, 1995. *India Decides: Elections 1952–1995* (New Delhi: Books and Things, 3rd ed.).

Datta, P.S. (Compiler), 1995. *Ethnic Peace Accords in India* (New Delhi: Vikas Publishing House).

Government of India, 1988. *Commission on Centre-State Relations, Report*, Part I (Nasik: Government of India Press). Part II containing memoranda and submissions to the commission was published in 1987.

Government of Canada, Royal Commission on Electoral Reform and Party Financing, 1991. *Reforming Electoral Democracy, Proposed Legislation* (Ottawa: Minister of Supply and Services Canada).

Government of Canada, 1991–93. *Royal Commission on Electoral Reform and Party Financing, Report*, 4 vols. (Ottawa: Minister of Supply and Services). Chair Pierre Lotie.

Government of India, 1987–88. *Commission on Centre-State Relations, Report*, Parts I and II (Naisik: Government of India Press).

Government of India, May 1990. *Report of the Committee on Electoral Reforms* (New Delhi: Ministry of Law and Justice, Legislative Department). Chair Dinesh Goswami.

Government of India, 1993. *Vohra Committee Report* (New Delhi: Ministry of Home Affairs). Chair N.N. Vohra, Home Secretary.

Election Commission of India, 1991. *Report on the Tenth General Elections to the House of the People in India, 1991* (Statistical) (New Delhi: ECI, Nirvachan Sadan).

Election Commission of India, 1996. *Statistical Report on General Elections, 1996, The Eleventh Lok Sabha*, vol. 1, (National and State Abstracts) (New Delhi: ECI, Nirvachan Sadan)

Election Commission of India, 1998. *Statistical Report on General Elections, 1998, The Twelfth Lok Sabha*, vol. 1 (National and State Abstracts) (New Delhi: ECI, Nirvachan Sadan).

Election Commission of India, 1991. *Model Code of Conduct for the Guidance of Political Parties and Candidates* (New Delhi: ECI, Nirvachan Sadan).

Election Commission of India, 12 April 1997. *Agenda and Notes: Meeting with Recognized National and State Parties* (New Delhi: ECI, Nirvachan Sadan).

Election Commission of India, 1998. *Statistical Report on General Elections, 1998 to the Twelfth Lok Sabha*, vol. I (National and State Abstracts) (New Delhi: Election Commission of India).

Election Commission of India, n.d. but apparently 1998. *Electoral Reforms: Views and Proposals* (New Delhi: ECI, Nirvachan Sadan).

Election Commission of India, 2000. *Statistical Report on General Elections, 1999 to the 13th Lok Sabha*, vol. 1, National and State Abstracts and Detailed Results (New Delhi: Election Commission of India, Nirvachan Sadan).

Parliament of India, June 1994. *Information Bulletin* (On Electoral Reforms) (New Delhi: Lok Sabha Secretariat).

Internet. *General Elections in India: An Overview*, Lttp.WWW indiagov org elec 98 art 6 ltm.

Internet. *Discover India, 13th Lok Sabha Elections, 1998*, ECI Website.

News Services Division, All India Radio, 1991. *Lok Sabha Poll: An AIR Analysis* (Party Position in Lok Sabha Before and After Election 1991) (New Delhi: Government of India).

Sadachar Bharati, 1995. *Report of Justice H.R. Khanna Committee on Code of Conduct for Ministers and People's Representatives* (Bombay: Bharatiya Vidya Bhawan).

Party Documents

All India Congress Committee (I), 1990. *Constitution of the Indian National Congress* (As amended at the Delhi AICC on 22 July 1990) (New Delhi: 24, Akbar Road, 1994, Reprint).

AIADMK, 1996. *Election Manifesto: Parliamentary/State Assembly General Elections 1996* (Madras: AIADMK).

BJP, 1996. *Election Manifesto 1996* (New Delhi: BJP Central Office, 11 Ashoka Road).

BJP and Alliance Partners, n.d. but obviously 1998. *National Agenda for Governance* (New Delhi).

BJP, 1998. *Election Manifesto 1998* (New Delhi: Bharatiya Janata Party, 11 Ashoka Road).

BSP, n.d. *Uttar Pradesh Vidhan Sabha Elections* (New Delhi: BSP Kendriya Karyalaya, 12 Gurudwara Rakabganj Road).

CPI, 1996. *Election Manifesto 1996*, (New Delhi: New Age Printing).

CPI, 1998. *Election Manifesto 1998*, (New Delhi: New Age Printing).

CPI, 1999. *Election Manifesto, 13th Lok Sabha 1999* (New Delhi: CPI).

CPI(M), 1996. *Manifesto: Eleventh Lok Sabha Elections* (New Delhi: A.K.G. Bhawan, 27–28, Bhai Vir Singh Marg).

CPI(M)-CPI-RSP-AIFB, 1998. *Manifesto of the Left Parties for Lok Sabha Elections 1998* (New Delhi: Left Front).

CPI(M), 1999. *Election Manifesto, 13th Lok Sabha 1999* (New Delhi: CPI(M), A.K.G. Bhawan, 27–28 Bhai Vir Singh Marg).

INC, 1996. *Election Manifesto, General Election 1996* (New Delhi: AICC, 24 Akbar Road).

INC, 1998. *Election Manifesto, General Election, Lok Sabha 1998* (New Delhi: AICC, 24 Akbar Road).

INC, 1999. *Manifesto, Lok Sabha Election 1999* (New Delhi: AICC, 24 Akbar Road).

INC, 1999. *Election Manifesto General Elections 1999* (New Delhi: NCP, 10 Dr B.D. Marg).

JD-SP-CPI(M)-CPI-RSP-FB, 21–27 April 1996. 'Platform for Secular Democratic Alternative', *New Age Weekly* (New Delhi): 6.

JD, 1996. *Janata Dal Election Manifesto 1996* (New Delhi: 7 Jantar Mantar Road).

JD, 1998. *Power to Grassroots for Change with Stability: Janata Dal Manifesto, Lok Sabha Elections 1998* (New Delhi: 7, Jantar Mantar Road).

NDA, 1999. *For a Proud, Prosperous India: An Agenda* (New Delhi: NDA, 11 Ashoka Road).

RJD, 1998. *Election Manifesto 1998: RJD's Vision of India in the 21st Century* (New Delhi: Rashtriya Janata Dal, 2 Motilal Nehru Place, Akbar Road).

Samajwadi Party, 1998. *Lok Sabha Nirvachan 1998: Chunav Ghoshanapatra* (New Delhi: Samajwadi Party).

Samajwadi Party, 1999. *Lok Sabha Samanya Nirvachan 1999, Chunav Ghoshanapatra* (New Delhi: Samajwadi Party, 18 Copernicus Lane).

Samata Party, 1996, 1998. *Manifesto 1998* (New Delhi: Samata Party, 220, V.P. House, Rafi Marg).

Telugu Desam Party, n.d. but obviously 1996. *Manifesto of Telugu Desam Party 1996* (Hyderabad).

Note: Manifestos of Asom Gana Parishad, Jammu and Kashmir National Conference, and Shiromani Akali Dal were published in Assamese, Urdu and Punjabi, respectively.

Political Tracts/Personal Papers

Gandhi, M.K. 'His [Gandhi's] Last Will and Testament', written on 29 January 1948, a day before his martyrdom and published posthumously on 15 February 1948, this document is reprinted in V.V. Ramana Murti (ed.), 1970. *Gandhi: Essential Writings* (New Delhi: Gandhi Peace Foundation).

Narayan, Jayaprakash. *Swaraj for the People* (Varanasi: Akhil Bharat Sarva Seva Sangh, n.d. but Preface date 1961). Reprinted by Oxford University Press, Delhi, in volumes on JP edited by Bimal Prasad.

Roy, M.N., 1981. *Politics, Power and Parties* (Delhi: Ajanta Publications; first published 1960).

Case Laws

(Relevant *All India Reporter* Annual Vols., Supreme Court Section).

Common Cause. *In the Supreme Court of India, Civil Extra-Ordinary Jurisdiction, Writ Petition No. 24 of 1995.* H.D. Shourie, Director, Common Cause.

Supreme Court of India, 1977. *Rajasthan vs. Union of India.*

Supreme Court of India, 1978. *Mohinder Singh Gill vs. Chief Election Commissioner and Others.*

Supreme Court of India, 1991. *S.S. Dhanoa vs. Union of India.*

Supreme Court of India, 1994. *S.R. Bommai and Others vs. Union of India and Others.*

Supreme Court of India, 1996. *T.N. Seshan vs. Union of India.*

Supreme Court of India, 1996. *Common Cause* (A registered society) *vs. Union of India and Others.*

Supreme Court of India, 1998. *P.V. Narasimha Rao vs. The State* (CBI/SPE), (JMM Bribery Case).

Papers in Research Journals or Presented in Seminars

Baru, Sanjaya, 16–19 November 1997. 'Economic Policy and the Development of Capitalism in India: The Emerging Role of Regional Capitalists and Regional Political Parties', *Democracy and Social Transformation: India Fifty Years After Independence*, Centre for the Advanced Study of India, University of Pennsylvania, (India International Centre, New Delhi), Seminar Papers.

Blair, Harry W., 12 January 1980. 'Rising Kulaks and Backward Classes in Bihar: Social Change in the Late 1970s', *Economic and Political Weekly.*

Canovan, Margaret, March 1999. 'Trust the People! Populism and the Two Faces of Democracy', *Political Studies*, vol. 7, no. 1.

Centre for the Advanced Study of India, University of Pennsylvania, 11 March 1996. *Emergence of State-Based Parties: Implications for India's Federalism: Workshop Proceedings* (New Delhi: India International Centre).

Duncan, Ian, 1997. 'New Political Equations in North India: Mayawati, Mulayam, and Government Instability in Uttar Pradesh', *Asian Survey.*

Economic and Political Weekly, 21–27/28 August– 3 September 1999. Special Number on 'Electoral Politics in India, 1989–99', vol. XXXIV, nos. 34 and 35.

Habermas, Jurgen. 'New Social Movements', *Telos*, vol. XLX.

Kabra, K.N., March–April 1998. 'Degradation of Democracy and Development: Dangerous Growth of Dirty Economy', *Denouement*, vol. 8.

Kitschelt, Herbert, July 1993. 'Social Movements, Political Parties, and Democratic Theory', The Annals of the American Academy of Political and Social Sciences, 528.

Lijphart, Arend, June 1996. 'The Puzzle of Indian Democracy: Consociational Interpretation', *American Political Science Review.*

Lipset, S.M., January 2000. 'The Indispensability of Political Parties', *Journal of Democracy*, vol. 11, no. 1.

Pai, Sudha, 1998. 'The Indian Party System Under Transition: Lok Sabha Elections 1998', *Asian Survey.*

Saxena, Rekha, June 1998. 'Party System Transition and Electoral Turning Points in India', *Trends in Social Science Research* (Delhi), vol. 5, no. 1.

Saxena, Rekha, 1 April 1998a. 'Viable Coalitions', *The Pioneer.*

Saxena, Rekha, 26 February 1998. 'Political Regionalization', *The Pioneer.*

Saxena, Rekha, 25 April 1998b. 'Coalition Experiment: Problems and Prospects', *Mainstream.*

Saxena, Rekha, January–February 1999. 'Constitutional Reforms Yes, But No Restructuring', *Denouement*, vol. 9.

Singh, M.P., August 1990. 'The Crisis of the Indian State: From Quiet Developmentalism to Noisy Democracy', *Asian Survey*, vol. XXX, no. 8.

Singh, M.P., 1991. 'Ideological Spectrum of Indian Party System: A Middling Pattern with Persisting Multi-Polarity', *The Indian Journal of Social Science* (New Delhi: ICSSR-Sage), vol. 4, no. 3.

Singh, M.P., April 1992. 'The Dilemma of the New Indian Party System: To Govern or Not to Govern?', *Asian Survey*, vol. XXXII, no. 4.

Singh, M.P., 1992. 'From Hegemony to Multi-Level Federalism? India's Parliamentary Federal System', *The Indian Journal of Social Science*, vol. 5, no. 3.

Singh, M.P., 1994. 'Political Parties and Political Economy of Federalism: A Paradigm Shift in Indian Politics', *The Indian Journal of Social Science*, vol. 7, no. 2.

Singh, M.P., December 1996. 'Electoral Politics and Phases of Politicization in India', *Trends in Social Science Research*, vol. 3, no. 2. Forthcoming in a revised version as a monograph from the Indian Council of Social Science Research, New Delhi.

Singh, M.P., December 1996. 'Electoral Politics and Phases of Politicization in India', *Trends in Social Science Research*, vol. 3, no. 2.

Singh, M.P. and Rekha Saxena, 1998a. 'Paradigm Shifts in Canadian and Indian Party Ssytems', *Punjab Journal of Politics* (Amritsar), vol. XXII, nos. 1 and 2.

Singh, M.P., 11 March 1996a. One of the two Keynote Observations in the University of Pennsylvania, Institute of Advanced Study of India, *The Emergence of State-Based Political Parties: Implications for Indian Federalism* (Workshop Proceedings), India International Centre, New Delhi.

Singh, M.P., April 1998. 'The Party Factor in "Dirty" Economy',

Denouement, Special No. on Democracy, Development and 'Dirty' Economy: A Retrospect of India's Fifty Years of Independence.

Singh, M.P., 24 July 1999. 'The Status of a Caretaker Government', *The Hindu* (New Delhi).

Singh, M.P. and Rekha Saxena, February 1999. *Denouement*, Special No. on Party and Electoral and Constitutional Reforms.

Singh, M.P. and Rekha Saxena, July 1999. 'India Independent: The First Half Century of Political Development and Decay', *Indian Historical Review* (New Delhi: ICHR-Motilal Banarsidass), vol. XXVI.

Sridharan, E., 1999. 'Towards State Funding of Elections in India? A Comparative Perspective on Possible Options', *Policy Reform*, vol. 3.

Swain, Ashok, 1997. 'Democratic Consolidation?: Environmental Movements in India', *Asian Survey*.

Varshney, Ashutosh, February 2000. 'Is India Becoming More Democratic?' *The Journal of Asian Studies*, vol. 59, no. 1.

Venkatesh, V., 31 July–13 August 1999. 'Cover Story: Chequered Relations: Big Business and Elections', *Frontline*, vol. 16, no. 16.

Wood, John, 1975. 'Extra-Parliamentary Opposition in India: An Analysis of Populist Agitations in Gujarat and Bihar', *Pacific Affairs*, vol. 48, no. 3.

Yadav, Yogendra, 21–28 August 1999. 'Electoral Politics in the Times of Change: India's Third Electoral System, 1989–99', *Economic and Political Weekly*.

Yanai, Nathan, 1999. 'Why Do Political Parties Survive? An Analytical Discussion', *Party Politics*, vol. 5, no. 1.

Yells, Tom, 1999. 'Two Cheers for Party', *Political Quarterly*.

Books and Chapters

Althusser, Louis, 1984. *Essays on Ideology* (London and New York: Verso).

Arora, B. and Douglas Verney (eds.), 1955. *Multiple Identities in a Single State: Indian Federalism in Comparative Perspective* (Delhi: Konark).

Bakvis, Herman (ed.), 1990. *Canadian Political Parties, Leaders, Candidates and Organization*, vol. 13 of Research Studies for Royal Commission on Electoral Reform and Party Financing (Toronto: Dundurn).

Beteille, Andre, 1997. *Society and Politics in India: Essays in a Comparative Perspective* (Delhi: Oxford University Press).

Bidwai, Praful, Harbans Mukhia, and Achin Vanaik (eds.), 1996. *Religion, Religiosity and Communalism* (New Delhi: Manohar).

Blackburn, Robert, 1990. *The Meeting of Parliament* (Aldershot, Hants: Dartmouth).

Bolingbroke, 1997. *Political Writings,* Edited by David Armitage (Cambridge: Cambridge University Press).

Brass, Paul R., 1991. *Ethnicity and Nationalism: Theory and Comparison* (New Delhi: Sage Publications).

Butler, David, Ashok Lahiri, Prannoy Roy, 1991. *India Decides: Elections 1952–1991* (New Delhi: Living Media, 2nd edition).

Chandra, Satish, 1979. *Parties and Politics at the Mughal Court 1701–1740* (New Delhi: People's Publishing House, 3rd ed.).

Chibber, P.K., 1999. *Democracy Without Associations: Transformation of the Party System and Social Cleavages in India* (Delhi: Vistar).

Datta, P.S., 1995. *Ethinic Peace Accords in India* (New Delhi: Vikas).

Duverger, Maurice 1963. *Political Parties,* 'Foreword' by D.W. Brogan, Trans. by Barbara and Robert North, (New York: John Willey and Sons,; first published 1951 in the French).

Eldersveld, Samuel J., 1971. *Political Parties: A Behavioral Analysis* (Bombay: Vora and Company; first published 1964 in the USA).

Gandhi, M.K., 1970. *Gandhi: Essential Writings,* Selected and edited by V.V. Ramana Murti (New Delhi: Gandhi Peace Foundation).

Gould, Harold A., 1994. *Grassroots Politics in India: A Century of Political Evolution in Faizabad District* (New Delhi: Oxford and IBH).

Habermas, Jurgen, 1987. *The Theory of Communicative Action, Volume 2, Lifeworld and System: A Critique of Functionalist Reason.* Trans. by Thomas McCarthy. (Cambridge, U.K.: Polity Press. First published in German in 1981).

Hofstadter, Richard, William Miller and David Aaron, 1959. *The American Republic, Vol. One: To 1965* (Engelwood Cliffs, New Jersey: Prentice-Hall).

Jaffrelot, Christophe, 1996. *The Hindu Nationalist Movement in India* (New Delhi: Viking: Penguin; First published in French 1993).

Jayal, Niraja Gopal, 1999. *Democracy and the State: Welfare, Secularism and Development in Contemporary India* (Delhi: Oxford University Press).

Kaviraj, Sudipta (ed.), 1997. *Politics in India* (Oxford in India Readings, General Editor T.N. Madan) (Delhi: Oxford University Press)

Kochanek, Stanley A., 1968. *The Congress Party of India* (Princeton: Princeton University Press).

Kothari, Rajni, 1970. *Politics in India* (New Delhi: Orient Longman).

Kothari, Rajni, 1973. 'India: Oppositions in a Consensual Politics' in

Robert A. Dahl (ed.). *Regimes and Oppositions* (New Haven: Yale University Press).

Kothari, Rajni, 1976. *Democratic Polity and Social Change in India: Crisis and Opportunities* (New Delhi: Allied).

Kothari, Rajni, 1988. *State Against Democracy* (Delhi: Ajanta).

Kothari, Rajni, 1990. *Politics and the People: In Search of a Humane Governance* (Delhi: Ajanta Publications, 2nd ed., first published 1989), 2 vols.

Lapalombara, Joseph and Myron Weiner (eds.), 1966. *Political Parties and Political Development* (Princeton: Princeton University Press).

Lipset, S.M., 1963. *Political Man: The Social Bases of Politics* (New York: Double Day, first published 1960).

Lipset, Seymour Martin and Stein Rokkan (eds.), 1967. *Party System and Voter Alignments: Cross-National Perspectives* (New York: The Free Press).

Malik, Yogendra K. and V.B. Singh, 1995. *Hindu Nationalists in India: The Rise of Bharatiya Janata Party* (New Delhi: Vistar/Sage).

Mallick, Ross, 1994. *Indian Communism: Opposition, Collaboration and Institutionalization* (Delhi: Oxford University Press).

Mitra, Chandan, 1998. *The Corrupt Society: The Criminalization of India from Independence to the 1990s* (New Delhi: Penguin).

Mitra, S.K. and V.B. Singh, 1999. *Democracy and Social Change in India: A Cross-Sectional Analysis of the National Electorate* (New Delhi: Sage).

Manor, James, 1995. 'The Political Sustainability of Economic Liberalization in India' in Robert Cassen and Vijay Joshi (eds.). *India: The Future of Economic Reform* (Delhi: Oxford University Press): 339–363.

Michels, Robert, 1962. *Political Parties,* 'Introduction' by S.M. Lipset,Trans. by Eden and Cedar Paul (New York: Collier; first published 1911).

Molyneux, John, 1978. *Marixism and the Party* (London: Bookmarks; 3rd reprinting 1986).

Moore, Barrington, Jr., 1966. *Social Origins of Dictatorship and Democracy: Lord and Peasant in the Making of the Modern World* (Boston: Beacon Press).

Morris-Jones, W.H., 1968. 'Candidate Selection: The Ordeal of the Indian National Congress, 1966–1967', in M.S. Rajan (ed.). *Politics: National and International* (New Delhi: Vikas): 33–54.

Nandy, A. *et al.* (eds.), 1995. *Creating a Nationality: The Ramjanmabhumi Movement and Fear of the Self* (Delhi: Oxford University Press).

Narain, Iqbal (ed.), 1967 and 1971. *State Politics in India* (Meerut: Meenakshi Prakashan).

Nehru, Jawaharlal, 1982. *The Discovery of India* (Delhi: Nehru Memorial Fund/Oxford University Press; Ist published 1946).

Ostrogorski, M., 1902. *Democracy and the Organization of Political Parties*, 'Preface' by the Right Hon. James Bryce, M.P., Trans. from the French by Frederick Clarke (London: Macmillan, 2 vols.).

Panebianco, Angelo, 1988. *Political Parties: Organization and Power*, Trans. by Marx Silver (Cambridge: Cambridge University Press; first published 1982 in the Italian).

Prakash, A. Surya, 1995. *What Ails Indian Parliament? An Exhaustive Diagnosis* (New Delhi: Indus, Harper Collins).

Qureshi, I.H., n.d. *The Administration of the Mughal Empire*, (Patna: Janaki Prakashan).

Roy, Ramashray, 1987. 'Selection of Congress Candidates' in his *Perspectives on Indian Politics* (Delhi: Discovery): chap. 4.

Roy, Ramashray and Paul Wallace (eds.), 1999. *Indian Politics and the 1998 Election: Regionalism, Hindutva and State Politics* (New Delhi: Sage Publications).

Roy, Prannoy and Dorab Sopariwala, 15 April 1996. 'Cover Story: Political Alliances', *India Today.*

Rudolph, Lloyd and Susanne H. Rudolph, 1987. *In Pursuit of Lakshmi: The Political Economy of the Indian State* (New Delhi: Orient Longman).

Sartori, Giovanni, 1976. *Parties and Party System: A Framework for Analysis*, vol. I (Cambridge: Cambridge University Press).

Saxena, Rekha, 1994. *Indian Politics in Transition: From Dominance to Chaos* (Delhi: Deep and Deep).

Saxena, Rekha, 1998. 'Federalization of Predominantly Parliamentary Regimes: Role of Inter-governmental Agencies in India and Canada', in Subrata Mukherjee and Sushila Ramaswamy (eds.), and M.P. Singh and Rekha Saxena (guest-eds.), *Political Science Annual 1997*, Special Volume on India at 50 (New Delhi: Deep and Deep).

Saxena, Rekha, 1998c. 'Democracy-Development Interface: Divergent Concerns', *Ideologies and Institutions in Indian Politics* (eds.) M.P. Singh and Rekha Saxena (New Delhi: Deep and Deep).

Saxena, Rekha, forthcoming 1998. 'Party System Transition and Electoral Turning Points', *Trends in Social Science Research*, Delhi.

Sheth, D.L. and Ashish Nandy (eds.), 1996. *The Multiverse of Democracy: Essays in Honour of Rajni Kothari* (New Delhi: Sage).

Singh, M.P., 1981. *Split in a Predominant Party: The Indian National Congress in 1969* (New Delhi: Abhinav).

Singh, M.P., 1990. 'The Congress in the 1980s and Beyond: Patterns of Recruitment, Strategies of Mobilization and Inter-Party Alignments', in Richard Sission and Ramashray Roy (eds.). *Diversity and Dominance in Indian Politics*, vol. I, *Changing Bases of Congress Support* (New Delhi: Sage).

Singh, M.P. and Rajesh Kumar, 1992. 'Three Models of Electoral Politics and Landmarks of Premiership and Party System Evolution', M.P. Singh (ed.), *Lok Sabha Elections 1989: Indian Politics in 1990s* (Delhi: Kalinga).

Singh, M.P. (ed.), 1992. *Lok Sabha Elections 1989: Indian Politics in 1990s* (Delhi: Kalinga).

Singh, M.P., 1994. 'India: The Constitution and Consensus' in J.S. Grewal and Hugh Johnston (eds.). *The India-Canada Relationship: Exploring the Political, Economic and Cultural Dimensions* (New Delhi: Sage).

Singh, M.P., 1995. 'Accommodating Regionalism: Federal Constitutional Discourses in Canada and India' in Chandra Mohan (ed.). *Regionalism in Canada: A Multi-disciplinary Approach* (New Delhi: Allied).

Singh, M.P., 8–9 December 2000. 'The Impact of Global and Regional Integration on Federal Political Systems: A Case Study of India', paper presented to an *International Seminar on Comparative Federalism* organised by Institute of Intergovernmental Relations, Queen's University, held in Crowne Plaza Hotel, Ottawa.

Singh, M.P. and Rekha Saxena (eds.), 1996. *India's Political Agenda: Perspectives on the Party System* (Delhi: Kalinga).

Singh, M.P. and Rekha Saxena (eds.), 1998. *Ideologies and Institutions in Indian Politics* (New Delhi: Deep and Deep).

Singh, M.P. and Rekha Saxena (eds.), 1998. *Political Science Annual 1997* (New Delhi: Deep and Deep).

Singh, M.P., 1999. 'Electoral and Party Politics and Determinants of Voting Behaviour in India: An Essay in Interpretation and Reforms' in S.K. Chaube and Susheela Kaushik (eds.). *Indian Democracy at the Turn of Century* (New Delhi: Kanishka): ch. 12.

Singh, M.P. and Himanshu Roy (eds.), 2000. *Indian Political Thought*, (Delhi: Madhyam).

Singh, M.P., 2000. *Towards A More Federalized Parliamentary System in India: Explaining Functional Change and Exploring Perceptions of Members of Parliament* (Typescript).

Stanbury, W.T., 2000. 'Regulating Federal Party and Candidate Finances in a Dynamic Environment', Thorburn and Whitehorn, (eds.). *Party Politics in Canada* (Toronto: Pearson, 8th ed.).

Thapar, Romila, 1997. *Ashoka and the Decline of the Mauryas* (Delhi: Oxford University Press, 3rd ed., first published 1961).

Weiner, Myron, 1967. *Party-Building in a New Nation: Indian National Congress*, Chicago: University of Chicago Press.

Weiner, Myron (ed.), 1968. *State Politics in India* (New Jersey: Princeton University Press).

Weiner, Myron, 1987. 'Empirical Democratic Theory', 'Introduction' in Weiner and Ozbuden (eds.). *Competitive Elections in Developing Countries* (An American Enterprise Institute Book published by Duke University Press).

Weiner, Myron and Ergun Ozbuden (eds.), 1987. *Competitive Elections in Developing Countries* (An American Enterprise Institute Book published by Duke University Press).

Wood, John (ed.), 1984. *State Politics in Contemporary India: Crisis or Continuity?* (Boulder: Westview).

Popular Journals

Denouement (Delhi).

Economic and Political Weekly (Mumbai).

IIPA Newsletter (New Delhi).

Panchayati Raj Update (New Delhi).

Seminar (New Delhi).

Newspapers/Magazines/Files

Asian Recorder (New Delhi).

Frontline (Chennai).

Indian Recorder (New Delhi).

India Today (New Delhi).

Outlook (New Delhi).

Parliament of India Library. Laardis newspapers clippings, file No. 324.3B, 1996.

The Economic Times (New Delhi).

The Hindu (New Delhi).

The Hindustan Times (New Delhi).
The Indian Express (New Delhi).
The Pioneer (New Delhi).
The Times of India (New Delhi).
UGC Research Project on Federalism and Political Parties in India, newspapers clippings files, Department of Political Science, University of Delhi (1996–99).

The Hindustan Times, New Delhi.
The Indian Express, New Delhi.
The Pioneer, New Delhi.
The Times of India, New Delhi.
UGC Research Project on *Television and Political Parties in India*, newspapers clippings files, Department of Political Science, University of Delhi (1996–98).

Index